ROUTLEDGE LIBRARY EDITIONS: WW2

Volume 32

SPECIAL INTERESTS, THE STATE AND THE ANGLO-AMERICAN ALLIANCE, 1939–1945

SPECIAL INTERESTS, THE STATE AND THE ANGLO-AMERICAN ALLIANCE, 1939–1945

INDERJEET PARMAR

LONDON AND NEW YORK

First published in 1995 by Frank Cass & Co. Ltd.

This edition first published in 2022
by Routledge
2 Park Square, Milton Park, Abingdon, Oxon OX14 4RN

and by Routledge
605 Third Avenue, New York, NY 10158

Routledge is an imprint of the Taylor & Francis Group, an informa business

© 1995 Inderjeet Parmar

All rights reserved. No part of this book may be reprinted or reproduced or utilised in any form or by any electronic, mechanical, or other means, now known or hereafter invented, including photocopying and recording, or in any information storage or retrieval system, without permission in writing from the publishers.

Trademark notice: Product or corporate names may be trademarks or registered trademarks, and are used only for identification and explanation without intent to infringe.

British Library Cataloguing in Publication Data
A catalogue record for this book is available from the British Library

ISBN: 978-1-03-201217-9 (Set)
ISBN: 978-1-00-319367-8 (Set) (ebk)
ISBN: 978-1-03-210946-6 (Volume 32) (hbk)
ISBN: 978-1-03-210963-3 (Volume 32) (pbk)
ISBN: 978-1-00-321793-0 (Volume 32) (ebk)

DOI: 10.4324/9781003217930

Publisher's Note
The publisher has gone to great lengths to ensure the quality of this reprint but points out that some imperfections in the original copies may be apparent.

Disclaimer
The publisher has made every effort to trace copyright holders and would welcome correspondence from those they have been unable to trace.

SPECIAL INTERESTS, THE STATE AND THE
ANGLO-AMERICAN ALLIANCE, 1939–1945

SPECIAL INTERESTS, THE STATE AND THE ANGLO-AMERICAN ALLIANCE, 1939–1945

Inderjeet Parmar
University of Manchester

LONDON AND NEW YORK

First published in 1995 in Great Britain and in the United States of America by
FRANK CASS & CO. LTD

Published 2013 by Routledge
2 Park Square, Milton Park, Abingdon, Oxon OX14 4RN
711 Third Avenue, New York, NY 10017 USA

Routledge is an imprint of the Taylor & Francis Group, an informa business

Copyright © 1995 Inderjeet Parmar

British Library Cataloguing in Publication Data

Parmar, Inderjeet
  Special Interests, the State and the
  Anglo-American Alliance, 1939–45
  I. Title
  327.41073

  ISBN 978-0-7146-4569-8 (cloth)
  ISBN 978-0-7146-4226-0 (paper)
  ISBN 978-1-315-03737-0 (eISBN)

Library of Congress Cataloging in Publication Data
Parmar, Inderjeet.
  Special interests, the state and the Anglo-American alliance
  1939–1945 / Inderjeet Parmar.
    p.   cm.
  Includes index.
  ISBN 978-0-7146-4569-8 (cloth)
  ISBN 978-0-7146-4226-0 (paper)
  ISBN 978-1-315-03737-0 (eISBN)
  1. United States – Foreign relations – Great Britain. 2. Great
Britain – Foreign relations – United States. 3. Pressure groups–
Great Britain – History – 20th century. 4. Power (Social sciences) –
Great Britain – History – 20th century. 5. World War, 1939–1945–
Diplomatic history. 6. Great Britain – Foreign
relations – 1936–1945.   I. Title.
E183.8.G7P28   1995
940.53'2241 – dc20   95-14432
                                                                 CIP

All rights reserved. No part of this publication may be reproduced in any form or by any means, electronic, mechanical, photocopying, recording or otherwise, without the prior written permission of the publisher.

Typeset in 11/13 Berling
by Vitaset, Paddock Wood, Kent

Contents

	Preface	vii
1.	The Context and the Questions	1
2.	Special Interests and Political Parties I	22
3.	Special Interests and Political Parties II	62
4.	The State and the National Interest	106
5.	The Role and Influence of Special Interests, Political Parties and the State in the Formation of the Anglo-American Alliance	141
6.	Conclusion	179
	Index	195

Preface

The idea for the postgraduate thesis that has become this book was grounded in some of the key political concerns of the 1980s, especially with reference to Britain's relationship with the United States. As the anti-nuclear and anti-war movements swelled during that period, a number of questions were raised about the American political, and especially military, presence in Britain. Charges that Britain had become a satellite or client state of the USA were made quite widely at the time.

To me, as a student of British society and as an individual concerned about its present and future, the question was: how did we get here? What does the process by which we got here mean? What does it tell us about who holds the reins of power in British society? This book tries, in a modest way, to address these big questions. In the process of researching and writing this book, I learned a lot more than I thought I would! Apart from the fact that the British state proved to be far more powerful than I had imagined when I began research, I also learned something of more enduring value to me as a full-time academic: that the theoretical models with which I began my research should not have been as rigid and fact-resistant as they were; rather they should have been used as mere guides, not mental cages. I am not sure that I have overcome the problem; maybe it is one that needs to be confronted permanently to prevent complacency.

Another thing that struck me as I wrote the book was the total absence of references to slaughter in my study of the Second World War. This was brought home to me most forcefully by a belated reading of Paul Fussell's *Wartime*, in which death, and the cheapness of life, are everywhere. I realised that the 'war-is-hell' refrain had become such a cliché that my own thinking about the Second World War had become sanitised and cleansed of the death and destruction of people's lives and homes that war inevitably brings.

I may have been helped to see war in this sanitised way by the documents left behind by the foreign policy élites whose words, ideas and actions are examined in this book. In the Foreign Office and other official records, and in the boardrooms of various elite organisations, the talk was of the 'new world order' that was to be built by the old, wise and experienced Imperial Britain and the new, gangly, uncertain but incredibly powerful United States.

The book has been several years in the making and I have accumulated more debts of gratitude than I could possibly acknowledge here. I should, however, thank my family for creating the space in which a jobless, grantless sociology graduate could begin advanced study. To my parents-in-law, whose hospitality and assistance have been so freely forthcoming throughout, and without which the completion of this book would have been delayed by several years, many thanks. Thanks to Dr. Leslie Sklair of the LSE Sociology Department, who has been a source of great encouragement to me since October 1980, when I first nervously walked into his office as his personal student. It was Leslie who suggested that I pursue postgraduate work, agreeing to supervise it and doing so with tact and care. Thanks also to Mike Burrage who was always generous with his time and full of challenging ideas (which irritated me no end at the time, and which I have only recently begun to appreciate). Thanks to all those archivists and librarians at the Public Record Office (Kew), Modern Research Centre (Warwick University), the TUC, the BLPES' rare books and manuscripts collection, the British Library Newspaper Library at Colindale, and at Chatham House.

I should like to single out three people for their unique contributions to the completion of this book: my late father, a former schoolmaster, who encouraged me to embrace learning; my wife, Meera, who so lovingly allowed me time and space to research and write this book; and to my eldest son, Rohan, who not only proved to be the most wonderful of distractions, but also allowed me time to reflect on the book as he played and sang during the summer of 1993. It is to them that I dedicate this book.

Inderjeet Parmar
December 1994

1
The Context and the Questions

The relationship that has existed between Britain and the United States since the Second World War has been the single most important alliance that Britain has constructed and maintained in modern times. This relationship has formed the basis of British defence policy, with the vast majority of Britain's defence efforts being concentrated on the North Atlantic Treaty Organisation. NATO has always been led by American generals and admirals,[1] by American military and industrial power. As even the conservative *Daily Telegraph* pointed out in 1956: 'NATO is concentrating the power to take life and death decisions more and more in the hands of the major powers, in particular, of the United States.'[2] Military information has been freely exchanged, nuclear co-operation has taken place, and American military aid to the United Kingdom totalled over £700 million in the 1950s alone.[3] The US armed forces have around 100 military and other bases in Britain, with over 400 fighter aircraft, and tens of thousands of fighting men.[4]

In the late 1940s and early 1950s, in the early stages of the Anglo-American alliance, quite a debate raged about the desirability of the American military presence, both on the left and the right of British politics.[5] This issue became a live one again in the 1980s. The level of interest in the character of the Anglo-American relationship varied in the 1980s, but many political storms centred on this question: for example, the decision to allow the stationing of American cruise missiles in Britain and the related question of their control; the dispute concerning the extraterritorial power of the US over its European allies on the matter of trade restriction with the eastern bloc; the American bombing of Libya with British-based F-111 jets; the Westland affair, and so on. Even a cursory examination of these issues shows that certain fundamental issues have been raised about the close relations between Britain and the United States and about the influence that the US has over British affairs.

The decision to site 96 Ground-Launched Cruise Missiles at RAF

Greenham Common (in practice a US Air Force base) was taken on 12 December 1979. There was no public or parliamentary debate.[6] The Conservative government's decision to accept the missiles provoked much unease and opposition, especially when it was realised that Britain would have, at best, only a tenuous say on their launching in an emergency. Opinion polls showed large majorities against the siting of these US-controlled missiles,[7] with one poll indicating that 73 per cent of the British electorate did not trust the United States on the question of joint US–British control. These fears appear to have been solidly grounded if the words of senior American leaders are to be believed: they have asserted that, in a crisis, the Americans alone would decide whether or not to launch the missiles.

The aim of the still unsigned *modus vivendi* between Britain and the US of 1948, before the first two American bomber bases were established in Britain, according to the official Foreign Relations of the United States documents, was 'to terminate the provision concerning United Kingdom consent' on the use of those bases.[8] It was often said that there would be consultation of Britain before any decision was made to use the bases for war, but the 'US News and World Report' gave its interpretation of 'consultation' as: 'Consultation would be a matter of a telephone call as United States planes with atom bombs took off for targets.'[9] Even the 'understanding' of 1952, between Churchill and President Truman meant very little as far as the USAF representative at the talks was concerned: 'Certainly the 1952 agreement does not give Great Britain joint control over American nuclear weapons,' he noted.[10] Robert McNamara, Defence Secretary under Presidents Kennedy and Johnson, gave his view of joint control: 'I don't conceive of it as a veto . . . I think "consultation" means a discussion . . with the party having the authority – in this case the US – making the final decision.'[11]

These very open admissions of total control of US weapons by US interests have been played down by more generous interpretations of 'consultation' by British leaders, despite the fact that Churchill admitted in the House of Commons that he did not know exactly how joint US–British control was supposed to work.[12] Nevertheless, Prime Minister Harold Macmillan told the House of

The Context and the Questions

Commons in 1960 that he trusted the Americans: 'I am perfectly satisfied that no decision to use these missiles will ever be taken without the fullest possible consultation . . . Like the agreement on the bomber bases . . . it will serve and strengthen the whole NATO alliance.'[13] Every British government of the post-war period has ratified the Truman–Churchill communique, but much disquiet occurred even in Conservative circles, with Alan Clark MP calling for 'a mechanism for sovereign physical control'.[14]

The issue of British 'control' over UK-based American weaponry again came to a head in April 1986, when American F-111 fighters bombed Tripoli and Benghazi from bases in Britain. The then Prime Minister, Margaret Thatcher, told the House of Commons that it would have been 'inconceivable' to refuse the Americans permission to use the bases, even though opinion polls showed two-thirds of Britons were opposed to such permission. (More recently, John Major has voiced support for further air attacks on Libya by British-based American bombers, over the Lockerbie air disaster.)[15]

The furore caused by the American attack centred upon the fact that America appeared to use the British bases only to involve another ally in the missions; upon how much 'consultation' had actually occurred; and upon what this attack had to do with defending NATO countries, since that is the role that US forces in Europe are supposed to play. What made the US attacks even more unpalatable, of course, was the fact that the publicly cited cause for the attack, a bomb in a Berlin night club frequented by US servicemen, was later traced to the Syrian regime.[16]

The question of control was central in many of the crisis points in the Anglo-American alliance during the 1980s, and resurfaced during the Westland affair in 1985–86, over the issue of the US–Italian rescue plan for the ailing British helicopter company. Anti-Americanism increased sharply as the Opposition Defence spokesman claimed that most of the technology and production would be transferred out of Britain, leaving Westland as 'tin-bashers for the Americans'.[17] Edward Heath, the former Prime Minister, explained the anti-American sentiments as based on the desire to prevent 'our country and our industries [being] handed over more and more to the American firms'.[18]

A related controversy that has only occasionally raised some interest since the late 1940s is the question of American powers to prevent allied nations from exporting 'sensitive' or 'strategic' materials to the Soviet bloc and China. In 1948, the *Daily Herald* reported that the American chief of Marshall Aid to Europe, Paul Hoffman, had told the allies not to export certain goods to the communists. A list appeared in the United Kingdom as 'Board of Trade Order Number 652' in March 1949, and in December of that same year as 'Export of Goods Control Order Number 2466', prohibiting 200 goods considered to enhance Soviet military capability.[19] According to *The Observer* of 26 November 1950 another 300 goods had been added by the end of 1950, and *The Economist* stated that some 100,000 items had been prohibited by the 1951 Battle Act and Kem amendment.[20]

In the 1980s, more tension occurred as Britain accused the Americans of using the 'red' threat argument as a pretext for winning the eastern bloc markets from which the allies were being forced out. The British Trade and Industry minister, Norman Tebbitt, also criticised the American laws requiring US-owned IBM (International Business Machines) to ensure that its British customers obtain American licences before selling IBM hardware even to other UK firms. The extraterritorial application of American laws was condemned by many as a gross violation of British sovereignty. Two Britons were even imprisoned for illegally exporting US-made computers to Bulgaria.[21]

One of the most recent controversies in Anglo-American relations was the 'friendly fire' incident during the US-led war against Iraq, in which nine British servicemen were killed in error by American Air Force pilots. The issue is raised here because it demonstrates certain important characteristics of the Anglo-American relationship that have endured since the Second World War.

The main issue, as far as the parents of the nine British soldiers were concerned, was to gain factual information as to how the incident occurred. To that end, several of them wanted the two unnamed American pilots concerned to appear at the coroner's inquest in Oxford in 1992. So frustrated was one parent at the lack of co-operation and credibility of the British Ministry of Defence (MoD) and the negative American response that she called for an 'enquiry into the MoD's board of enquiry'.[22] Another parent literally 'chased the US government's observer, Colonel Robert Bridge, down the street and demanded to know why the pilots were not present [at the inquest]'. Bridge replied that the pilots had chosen not to attend, although later he admitted that the said pilots, 'may not even be aware of this inquest'.[23]

The parents also wanted to know why six other USAF pilots on the same mission had correctly identified the British tanks by using sophisticated equipment but the final two pilots had not. There were suggestions of a cover-up.[24] Ultimately, the two US pilots were found guilty of unlawful killing by the inquest jury, and the families' lawyer called on the Director of Public Prosecutions to consider the case for trying the pilots for manslaughter.[25]

The attitude and actions of the British government during the entire period, however, were almost entirely deferential towards the Pentagon and President George Bush. Under pressure, Prime Minister John Major said that the matter had been raised 'at the highest level' but Defence Secretary Malcolm Rifkind said that it was a 'matter for the US administration' which he believed to be 'handling the affair in a sensitive manner'.[26]

A week later, after the verdict from the coroner's court, even *The Times*, normally a rather deferential newspaper, noted that 'The reluctance of Ministers to press the US for further action was evident in the Commons, as Malcolm Rifkind, the Defence Secretary, spoke of the need to learn the lessons of the incident and John Major paid tribute to the achievements of the American pilots in the war.'[27]

The subordinate position of Britain could hardly be more clearly demonstrated. Nine British soldiers were killed; an unlawful killing verdict was given; yet the pilots could not even be brought to court to provide information, let alone for prosecution. And the British government's final word was to praise the US Air Force in general. The Crown Prosecution Service at one point argued that nothing could be done because the incident involved foreign nationals acting on foreign soil. Observers of Anglo-American relations need no reminding of the 1983 admission in *The Times* that an American serviceman in Britain who commits an offence while on duty is not subject to British law, only to US military rules, under the 1952 Visiting Forces Act.²⁸ It seems that certain US laws may be applied extraterritorially while certain British laws do not even apply on British territory.

These issues and others (such as the US invasion of Grenada) brought the Anglo-American relationship to the forefront of British politics and made it one of the most enduring questions of the 1980s and 1990s. The questions that lie at the heart of the matter are these: has this relationship significantly diminished British sovereignty? If so, and many people believe that it has, how did such a situation come about? For Duncan Campbell, the Conservative governments of the 1980s, and, by implication, all post-war governments have 'regarded [sovereignty] both as negotiable and almost irrelevant'. They have kept little record of American military activities in Britain, thereby implicitly acknowledging that there is no cause for concern. But concern there has been, and opinion polls showed a major decline in British support for the United States, both as an ally and as a world power.

After the Westland affair and the attack on Libya, an ITN/Harris poll showed that 49 per cent of the British population believed the 'special relationship' to be harmful; surveys by Gallup in March 1981 and 1984, and April 1986, showed that the percentage of people who thought that Britain was too close to the United States rose from 22 per cent to 34 per cent to 47 per cent. Between 1981 and 1986, the percentage which thought that Britain and the US were not close enough fell from 15 per cent to seven per cent. According to a Mori poll, only six per cent believed that Britain's future lay with the United States, while 32 per cent supported Europe, and 29 per cent the Commonwealth.

Despite the fact that 70 per cent of the British public favoured nuclear defence in general, 51 per cent opposed the American nuclear presence in Britain. Dean Godson concludes from these poll findings that: 'There can be no doubt that scepticism of – indeed, hostility toward – the closeness of the "special relationship" has been heightened during the Reagan years.'[29]

The British electorate has less faith in the United States' ability to deal wisely with world problems than they had during the Watergate scandal and the Iran hostage crisis. In 1985, only 21 per cent believed the US to be a capable force in world affairs, as opposed to

72 per cent who had little or no confidence in them at all. In the same year, the British public split almost evenly on the question of whether the US or the USSR posed the greater threat to peace in Europe (32 per cent and 33 per cent respectively); while 28 per cent regarded both powers as equally dangerous.[30]

The Westland affair also highlighted one other feature of the close relations between America and Britain: how dependent the British economy had become on American investments over the past 40 years or more.

J.P. Koszul writes that between 1936 and 1966, US direct investment to Britain increased from $474 million to $5,657 million.[31] By the 1960s, 39 per cent of all US foreign direct investment came to Europe, with Britain as the biggest single receiver.[32] M.R. Hodges showed that in the 1964–70 period, American investments accounted for 6.2 per cent of British GNP; 7.1 per cent of net capital stock; and 10.7 per cent of net profit;[33] while another survey added that US companies accounted for ten per cent of all manufacturing sales and 17 per cent of all manufactured exports. Glyn and Sutcliffe also added that by 1964, American firms accounted for over 40 per cent of the turnover in computers, petroleum products and agricultural machinery, and 50 per cent of all cars, razor blades and refrigerators.[34]

By the 1970s, John Dunning has shown that American economic influence was still continuing; 12 per cent of all UK manufacturing production (that is, sales of £8 billion); 16 per cent of all manufacturing exports; and US corporations employed nine per cent of all British workers. He concluded that: 'Certainly in no other country do US manufacturing investments assume such a proportionately important role.'[35]

The late 1970s saw a boom in US bank lending to British manufacturers (£3 billion in three years) and US control over 43 per cent of the flow of North Sea oil. By 1981 the book value of all foreign investments in Britain equalled £25 billion, with the larger part being of American origin. Fifty per cent of all new foreign investment up to 1983 was by US firms.[36] It can be seen, therefore, that American economic influence in the United Kingdom appeared to equal in importance, to some degree, its military influence.

Politically, the Anglo-American alliance has been paramount in maintaining a world position for Britain. The post-war belief that Britain should play a world role was predicated on a 'special relationship' with the US, with the idea that some equitable division of labour between the two powers could be arranged. This assumption has characterised the debate in British political life for decades, with the questions of the Commonwealth and Europe being considered of far less importance. Until the 1980s, the defence debate had assumed a strong alliance with the Americans, but this decade saw the gradual decline in support of US world policies and its economic and military position in Britain. While the Conservative Party remained a firm ally of the US, the Liberal/SDP voted to cancel Trident, Britain's US-dependent 'independent' deterrent; the Liberal Assembly voted to remove American missiles from Britain in 1984. But it was the Labour Party that most vociferously opposed the American military presence: the then leader, Neil Kinnock, admitted to an American audience that he felt that Britain had become the 'fifty-first state' of the US, while Michael Meacher attacked the encroachment of British national rights. Denis Healey, a previously pro-US Labour figure, also declared about the nuclear presence in Britain: 'they are going, the whole bloody lot'. Accordingly, Labour Party policy became the expulsion of American nuclear forces from Britain.[37]

The Anglo-American alliance raises many questions about the nature of the British political system, especially about sovereignty, but also much broader questions about the distribution of power. In whose interests was or is the Anglo-American alliance? Which groups, classes, or élites were served by a policy that allowed Britain to become an advanced base for anti-Soviet attacks and at the same time a target of massive nuclear retaliation? Equally, how is it that the most vociferous defence of sovereignty has been in relation to the relatively recent growth of the European Community, while so many 'patriots' have remained silent or acquiesced or actively sought to increase American economic, political and military penetration of British political life? In short, who are 'the powers that be' that have provided the dynamic underlying the unequal alliance, around which a 'special relationship' mythology has been constructed?

This book aims to help answer some of these questions by

The Context and the Questions

examining the Anglo-American alliance during the Second World War. An analysis of the alliance in its cradle provides us with clues as to the motives behind it, and the interests that sought satisfaction from its creation. But this study of power attempts to do more than this. At its broadest, the study aims to examine the meaning and limits of British democracy itself. Policy is never made in a social or economic vacuum, and the creators of the Anglo-American alliance had to tread very carefully because, at the time, such a policy constituted a repudiation of numerous established canons about the basis of British foreign policy, especially about the future of the Empire. At the same time, British policy-makers had to mobilise all the forces at their disposal to ensure that, whatever else happened, America was bound to Britain and vice-versa, and that such a departure would be acceptable to the most powerful groups and interests in British society. Finally, policy-makers had to isolate and marginalise any political forces that suggested any fundamental alternatives to the alliance.

The argument is that by studying the formation of the Anglo-American alliance, through analysis of the role of the state and special interest groups, we may come to understand the nature of the power process in general. A crisis such as the Second World War should not be seen as unrepresentative or atypical as a period for study, and from which no generalisable conclusions can be drawn. The essence of the exercise is to understand the relationship between state and society, and the working of the political system, and it is only reasonable to explore that relationship under a variety of different conditions. Merely examining a political system during periods of 'stability' and 'order' offers only a partial understanding. It is essential to examine politics and the state during 'crises' and 'wars' to gain greater understanding. Neil Stammers, in his study of civil liberties during the Second World War, shows the utility of such an approach. He uses an analogy from the car industry to emphasise his point that a car's strengths and weaknesses cannot be determined by testing under temperatures that are equable and on roads that are smooth. Indeed, cars can only be judged after testing under extreme circumstances, in conditions of stress. In relation to politics, wartime studies may be 'expected to tell as much, if not more, about a political system than similar studies during periods of peace and stability.'[38] Stammers' conclusion, after considering the evidence of declining liberties, is that in large part such decline resulted not from specifically wartime legislation but from laws made during peacetime.

That conclusion is instructive: it suggests that the relationship between 'war' and 'peace' is neither simple nor straightforward. Indeed, students of war go to great lengths to demonstrate the degree of commonality between war and peace, the degree to which wars accelerate, destroy or create trends of pre- and post-war eras.[39]

The historical evidence reveals a record that is at variance with the interpretation of the alliance advanced by many 'mainstream' historians and political leaders of the post-war era. This is a reference to the 'special relationship' view of Anglo-American relations which this study thoroughly rejects. The 'special relationship' view is like a drug – long after its lack of explanatory power has been recognised it continues to form part of the title of key studies of Anglo-American relations.[40] At its heart lie two notions about Britain's foreign policy and system of domestic power: the first suggests that strategic or economic interests are of secondary importance in Anglo-American relations, because of the power of a common Anglo-Saxon heritage, shared language and belief in liberty; the second suggests that the British state is primarily animated by a democratic impulse to exercise power to promote the 'national interest'.

This study takes such notions as hypotheses for testing rather than timeless truths. From the first moment, it has to be seen that such an hypothesis is only one among many, however widely accepted such a view may have been in the past. There are several competing theories as to the nature of British democracy and foreign policies that have been fostered and developed. The notions underlying the 'special relationship' hypothesis fall broadly within a pluralist theoretical framework, which will be discussed briefly below. Until recently, the most tenacious challenge to the pluralist framework has been Marxism, in its various forms. The next section of this chapter will outline these theories, criticise them and advance what is considered a more adequate explanation of political power in modern British society – statism. It is the intention to test these rival themes against the historical evidence and come to some conclusions about the nature of British policy-making, the state, and democracy.

PLURALISM

As this is not a book about theory, only a brief outline of pluralism will be provided here, although references to the broader literature will be made. At the centre of pluralism lies the notion of competing groups which represent the whole variety of interests that proliferate in modern societies. The writings of Bentley, Truman, Robert Dahl and Nelson Polsby[41], all attest to the centrality of the special interest group in a democratic political order. It is such groups that compete for influence with one another, that bargain, negotiate and compromise with each other and with the official holders of powers of decision who constitute the life-blood of the political system. Through this process democracy is maintained and strengthened because of the opportunities it affords for the populace to influence political decisions, especially between elections, and hold accountable the actions of the goverment.

In this schema, there is no oligarchic power élite or ruling class that can effectively subvert the democratic process: according to William Kelso pluralism represents 'a competitive market-place in which any entrepreneur can gain entry . . . politics is seen as an open, fluid process'.[42]

The role of the state (pluralists prefer to use the term 'government') is to moderate group conflict and act as mediator between competing interests. But the state is not independent: it usually, according to Bentley, acts on behalf of powerful unofficial interests.[43] Ultimately, the policy that emerges is one which will serve a very broad range of interests, which may be termed the 'national interest'.

MARXISM

At the heart of Marxism is the notion of social classes in conflict over the ownership and control of the means of production and the distribution of the fruits of the productive process. Politics in capitalist societies is founded upon an unequal pattern of economic power and reflect that inequality, because of the Marxist belief in the primacy of material factors in determining social, political and intellectual life. The state is the reflection of a society that is class-divided and stands as the moderator of class conflicts; but it is not neutral. It is, in fact, in the 'grip' of the dominant economic class and acts on its behalf. There are a variety of Marxist views of the state but they all ultimately agree that the state acts in defence of capitalist interest.[44]

Kees van der Pijl and Peter Burnham[45] provide two varieties of Marxist analysis of Anglo-American relations, illustrating some points raised above. Pijl focuses on transatlantic fractions of capital that compete with one another to forge 'concepts of control' or hegemonic projects that have led to the domination of international finance capital. The Anglo-American alliance is living proof of overall economic and political power, over the state, of international capital and the broad coalitions they lead. Pijl's analysis is (rightly) criticised by Burnham as merely another version of pluralism due to its 'fractional' focus, while Burnham contends that the origins of state policy are to be found in its role as the guardian of the general interests of capital.

The outlines have been necessarily brief, and perhaps crude, but the main elements of each theory have been presented. While there are fundamental differences between pluralism and Marxism, particularly concerning the question of democracy in capitalist societies, there are also a number of commonalities. Of these common features, one is of direct relevance here: both theories underemphasise the increasing power of the state because of their interest in groups or classes. Both theories suggest that the state is essentially a vehicle for either organised interests or social classes to use as they deem necessary, and that the state has no independent power or interests of its own. Yet, if the course of events of the twentieth century reveals anything, it reveals the increasing concentration of power in the hands of the state: coercive and police powers, taxation, education, over the economy and employment, health and social welfare, among others. Any theory that seeks to explain state policy formation must allow room for the concept of independent state power. One theory that has gone in this direction is 'statism', which allows for greater levels of autonomy for state leaders. Statists maintain that the state is autonomous, and has its own needs and objectives. Stephen Krasner argues that his study of official US foreign economic policy in raw materials demonstrates that, despite the power of petroleum companies, the state has generally prevailed in achieving its objectives. Krasner also suggests that the actual and potential powers of the state are so great that not only can they overcome organised group/class resistance, but can also 'transform potential opposition into passive acceptance or even active support'.[46]

Statists such as Theda Skocpol *et al*[47] point out the importance of the fact that the state stands at the interface of domestic society and transnational relations, and must therefore manoeuvre for advantage in both spheres. Given that the state is legally empowered to defend the 'national' interest, it has a high degree of political 'space' or autonomy from societal interests. State leaders attempt to maintain or enhance 'their' state's position in the interstate system, which may imply the reorganisation of domestic social/economic relations from above. The state, in this perspective, is not an instrument of class or group power, but an autonomous institution in its own right.

These three theories are to be tested in the course of this study by examining the historical data on a wide range of interest groups and on their interaction with the state which, in this study, refers primarily to the foreign policy related institutions such as the Cabinet, Foreign Office, Treasury and the Board of Trade. The aim is to isolate the 'key decisions' taken during the course of the war that constituted the basis of the Anglo-American alliance, and then to examine the relative roles and influence of the state and interest groups in taking such decisions. There are, of course, objections to the use of such a method but given the vast range of historical material available, it should yield some interesting insights into the activities of the powerful in British society.

Methodological problems

The study of power is a methodological minefield. Power is so abstract a notion that it almost defies definition, let alone measurement. Kaufman and Jones were surely right when they argued that

> There is an elusiveness about power that endows it with an almost ghostly quality. It seems to be all around us, yet this is 'sensed' with some sixth means of reception . . . We 'know' what it is, yet we encounter endless difficulties in trying to define it. We can 'tell' whether one person or group is more powerful than another, yet we cannot 'measure' power. It is as abstract as time, yet as real as a firing squad.[48]

Consequently, a variety of definitions and approaches to the study of power have developed. Ultimately, however, all definitions involve, as Westergaard and Resler note, some 'notion of a capacity to determine events and conditions',[49] which is a development of Max Weber's classic formulation of power as 'that opportunity existing within a social relationship which permits one to carry out one's own will even against resistance'.[50]

Pluralist political scientists have operationalised Weber's definition by developing the 'decision-making' technique just mentioned. In spite of the problems with this approach, as pointed out by Bachrach and Baratz and Stephen Lukes,[51] for example, its central thrust is admirable: it demands that all conclusions about power and influence be based on concrete evidence, not purely on *a priori* conceptions and theories.

The spirit of this technique is actually very scientific; it is about rigorously and systematically considering the material evidence before drawing any conclusions. It is in that spirit that the decision-making method is used below. One qualification should, however, be made at this point: that the interpretation of the decision-making method used here is broader than many pluralists would comfortably support. In this study, decision-making by policy-makers is seen in a broader social and economic context for two reasons: first, because it allows us to appreciate that decisions are not made in a vacuum but in the context of international, economic, military, class and other conflicts; and second, because such a broad interpretation of decision-making allows for a fairer context within which to test the Marxist theory of power. That qualification made, this study is founded on the sort of question posed by Nelson Polsby in the 1960s, when he asked 'How can one tell . . . whether an actor [that is, a special interest group or ruling class] is powerful unless some sequence of events, competently observed, attests to this power? If these events take place, then the power of the actor is not "potential" but actual. If these events do not occur, then what grounds have we to suppose that the actor is powerful?'[52]

In order to operationalise such a technique in this case study of the formation of the Anglo-American alliance, five 'key' decisions have been selected. These five decisions were made during the course of the Second World War and constituted the *de facto* basis of the Anglo-American alliance. The decisions were part of an overall orientation towards a definite objective that appears to have become firmly entrenched after the fall of France in June 1940. That occurrence put Britain in a most vulnerable position not only in relation to the immediate problem of German aggression, but also with reference to the post-war world situation. In retrospect, the fall of France proved to be a turning point in Britain's orientation to the post-war world. Sir Stafford Cripps, Britain's ambassador to Moscow, summed up the situation in a telegram to the Foreign Office at the time. He wrote that long-term planning was necessary in order that Britain could take her rightful place in the post-war world, which would be dominated by large national groupings led by the big powers. As Britain could not really dominate Europe, she should become 'associated with the United States in an Anglo-Saxon group' in which Britain 'would constitute . . . the European outpost of that group and its link with [the European] group'. Cripps believed that: 'It may well be that before long such a policy will be the only practical and permanent method of saving Anglo-Saxon civilisation'.[53]

Cripps' telegram led to a flurry of minutes by members of the Foreign Office and the Government, with Lord Halifax, the Foreign Secretary, scrapping plans for post-war Anglo-French union, in favour of 'some sort of special association with the USA'.[54] In a sense, this change of orientation represents the backdrop to the positive decisions taken, the sum of which constituted an Anglo-American alliance in the post-war period.

The first of the five key decisions taken during the war which had a decisive impact on the creation of the alliance was the 'Destroyers-for-Bases' Agreement of August 1940, which led to the exchange of 50–60 rather old American naval warships in return for the leases to a number of military facilities in the Caribbean. The Agreement was designed to draw the USA closer to an alliance with Britain.[55]

The second major decision was the joint declaration of war aims by Britain and America in August 1941, that is, the Atlantic Charter, the aim of which, according to the official history of the war, was to prevent the USA from drifting into isolationism after the war by 'Bringing the United States into close collaboration over economic reconstruction . . . to get some kind of international organisation which would put into effect the terms of the charter'.[56]

A vital step that advanced the British movement towards an alliance was the decision to sign the Mutual Aid Agreement (Lend-Lease) in February 1942. By the terms of this agreement, especially Article 7, the United States agreed to supply Britain's wartime material requirements in return for a British commitment 'to the eventual abolition of Imperial Preference'.[57]

The fourth major decision was the British agreement to the establishment of a new economic and financial world order, at Bretton Woods in 1944. These talks were the result of the commitment given by Britain under Article 7 concerning Imperial Preference/Empire bloc policy, and led to the creation of new multilateral trading agreements through the International Monetary Fund.

The final decision of note was the agreement surrounding the negotiations for the American and (Canadian) loan of $5 billion to Britain in 1945. The acceptance by Britain of the conditions imposed on the loan – effectively the break-up of the Sterling Area – was a major step towards the alliance between the two countries.

These five key decisions constitute the important decisions that helped build an alliance beween Britain and the United States in the post-war period, which has lasted in important respects to the present day.

Five British interest groups and three political parties have been selected on the basis of their national significance in the area of foreign policy, or their relevance as representatives of a major section of the population. The aim of the study is to consider the role and influence of these forces during the making of the decisions that created the Anglo-American alliance.

One key group under analysis is the Royal Institute of International Affairs (RIIA), also sometimes called Chatham House, which is really much more a 'think-tank' than a pressure group. It specialises, as its name suggests, in all aspects of Britain's foreign relations, and has established itself as a highly respected organisation of top civil servants, diplomats, international affairs experts, journalists and so on. Its very close relations with the Foreign Office in general, and especially during the Second World War, suggest something of its importance.

The Federation of British Industries (FBI), one of the forerunner organisations of the Confederation of British Industry, was a vital organisation of industrial and other interests, and constitutes the second group under analysis. Because of its size and the scope of its activities, it inevitably entered into close relations with the government and departments of state (including the Foreign Office) during the war.

The Bank of England is usually considered to be the voice of finance in Britain, because of its close Treasury and 'City' links. As the voice of finance, and as one key institution involved in government economic policy, the Bank can be reasonably expected to have a role in the formation of at least the financial aspects of the Anglo-American alliance. Analysis of its role and influence is important in examining the impact of finance capital over foreign policy.

The Empire Industries Association (EIA), as its name implies, was a pro-British Empire campaigning organisation, with its roots in the Tariff Reform League. Its importance lies in the fact that it successfully campaigned for Imperial Preference in the 1930s, and had at least two members in the cabinet during the war, arguing for the continuation of a strong, independent Empire policy for Britain.

The final group to be examined is the Trades Union Congress (TUC) which, as the voice of organised labour, represented a major force in British society.

This selection of organised interests provides us with some degree of variety – a 'think-tank', the voices of industry, finance and labour. It provides the basis for some potentially conflicting interests which may be reflected in the decision-making process.

Selecting the political parties for analysis was a far simpler task since Labour and Conservative dominated the political scene by the Second World War. A brief examination of their rival philosophies and programmes for post-war British foreign policy will be conducted.

The Communist Party of Great Britain (CPGB), though relatively small, did constitute an important force in working-class politics and in certain sections of the middle class. Its policies in all areas generally conflicted with that of the state and that constitutes the chief reason for its inclusion in this analysis. The nature and parameters of power in society are understood not purely by restricting analysis to those forces that gained entry into the corridors of power; they are also illuminated by analysing those forces considered 'beyond the pale'.

These groups and parties do not, of course, exhaust all the possible attitudes that existed during the Second World War as to the nature of the post-war world and Britain's orientation to it. Therefore, whenever relevant or possible, the views of the less organised sections of the population, such as working-class opinion, are provided in order to highlight the breadth and depth of public opinion. This should prove useful especially in relation to the response of the British state to such currents of opinion.

This chapter has attempted to highlight the importance of the Anglo-American alliance today and to suggest that answers to questions about its nature, origins and formation will provide important insights into the distribution of power in British society. The next two chapters begin by trying to place the formation of the alliance into its historical, international and domestic contexts of the changing distribution of world power. They then provide an introduction to the special interest groups and political parties selected for analysis, by outlining their aims, origins, and world views. Chapter 4 analyses the British state's version of the 'national interest', as it provided the focus of special interest group activity and the official centre of decision-making. A brief examination of the underlying principles of British foreign policy during the twentieth century is undertaken. Chapter 5 examines the roles and influence of special interests and political parties *vis-à-vis* the state, and Chapter 6 concludes the study by analysing the results of the survey of historical data undertaken with special reference to the nature of the state, the foreign policy process and British democracy.

The Context and the Questions

NOTES

1. NATO pamphlet: 'Britain and NATO: Over 30 Years of Collective Defence' (prepared by the Ministry of Defence Public Relations and the Central Office of Information, 1982), pp. 2–14.
2. Sancho Panza, *Labour Monthly* (April 1956), p. 187.
3. John Bayliss, 'The Anglo-American Relationship in Defence', in J. Bayliss (ed.), *British Defence Policy in a Changing World* (London: Croom Helm, 1977). At today's prices, £700m is worth in excess of £7 billion.
4. Duncan Campbell, *The Unsinkable Aircraft Carrier: American Military Power in Britain* (London: Michael Joseph, 1984).
5. See Debate on Anglo-US Relations: R. Adams, 496 HC Debates, 567–79 (22 Feb. 1952); L.S. Amery, 'Non-discrimination and Convertibility', in *World Affairs*, II (Jan. 1948); *The Times* (1 Jan. 1947), p. 5; Michael Foot, 494 HC Debates, 155 (19 Nov. 1951).
6. Owen Greene, *Europe's Folly: The Facts and Arguments about Cruise* (London: CND Publications, 1983).
7. Opinion Polls published in *The Times* (21 Jan. 1983) and *Sunday Times* (30 Oct. 1983).
8. Campbell, op. cit., p. 97.
9. R.P. Dutt, *The Crisis of Britain and the British Empire* (London: Lawrence & Wishart, 1954), p. 337.
10. Campbell, op. cit., p. 309.
11. Campbell, op. cit., p. 310. See also the statements of J.F. Dulles, Secretary of State, in 1958: 'There could be no question of a veto on the use of nuclear weapons being exercised by other countries . . . No Government could legally cast a veto against a decision of another government taken for its own defence' (p. 310). See also, Paul Warnke, Assistant Defence Secretary under McNamara: 'No piece of paper, no matter how well intentioned, is going to make any real difference at a time of crisis. The person . . . the country that physically controls the weapon is going to make the decision' (p. 310).
12. R.P. Dutt, 'Whose Finger on the Trigger?', in *Labour Monthly* (March 1955).
13. HC Debates, Vol. 629, Col. 37–8.
14. *The Times* (14 April 1983), p. 32.
15. Keesing's Contemporary Archives, (London: Longman, June 1986), p. 34458; John Pilger, *Distant Voices* (London: Vintage, 1992), pp. 146–7.
16. Pilger, op. cit., (1992), p. 148.
17. *The Times* (14 Dec., 1985), p. 2.
18. Dean Godson, 'British Attitudes Towards the United States', in M. Holmes et al (eds), *British Security Policy and the Atlantic Alliance* (Washington: Pergamon, 1987), p. 108.
19. R.P. Dutt, op. cit.
20. 'Congressional Battle Axe', in *The Economist* (25 Aug. 1951).
21. May 1985, in Keesing's Contemporary Archives, p. 33627.
22. 'Gulf War "Friendly Fire" victims unlawfully killed, jury rules', in *The Times* (19 May 1992).
23. 'American pilots "boycott friendly fire inquest"', in *The Times* (8 May 1992).
24. 'Gulf War inquest hears US evidence', in *The Times* (9 May 1992). Former US Colonel Tom McNaugher made the allegation; he had fought in the Gulf War.

25. 'Lawyer wants American pilots called to count', in *The Times* (19 May 1992).
26. 'Friendly Fire Pressure' and 'US rejects demands for pilots to go to inquest', in *The Times* (13 May 1992).
27. 'Congress takes friendly fire case', in *The Times* (20 May 1992).
28. *The Times* (11 Nov. 1983).
29. Godson, op. cit.
30. Ibid.
31. J.P. Koszul, 'American Banks in Europe', in C. Kindleburger (ed.) *The International Corporation* (Boston, MA: MIT Press, 1970).
32. L. Turner, *Politics and the Multinational Company* (Fabian Research Series, 279).
33. M.R. Hodges, *Multinational Corporations and National Government* (Hants: D.C. Heath, 1974).
34. A. Glyn and B. Sutcliffe, *British Capitalism* (Harmondsworth: Penguin, 1972).
35. J.H. Dunning, *US Industry in Britain* (London: Wilton House Publications, 1976).
36. *The Economist* (19 Aug. 1978); *The Economist* (24 Sept. 1977); *The Economist* (18 June 1983).
37. Holmes *et al*, op. cit.
38. Neil Stammers, *Civil Liberties in Britain during the Second World War* (New York: St Martin's Press, 1983), p. 2.
39. Martin Shaw, *Dialectics of War* (London: Pluto Press, 1988); Anthony Giddens, *The Nation-State and Violence* (Cambridge: Polity Press, 1985).
40. W.R. Louis and H. Bull (eds), *The 'Special Relationship'* (Oxford: Clarendon Press, 1986); Alan P. Dobson, *The Politics of the Anglo-American Economic Special Relationship* (Brighton, Sussex, Wheatsheaf Books, 1988); C.J. Bartlett, *The Special Relationship: A Political History of Anglo-American Relations since 1945* (London and New York: Longman, 1992).
41. A.F. Bentley, *The Process of Government* (Bloomington, IN: Principia Press, 1935); David Truman, *the Governmental Process* (New York: Alfred A. Knopf, 1967); Dahl, *Who Governs?* (New Haven, CT: Yale University Press, 1961); Polsby, *Community Power and Political Theory* (New Haven, CT: Yale University Press, 1963).
42. William Kelso, *American Democratic Theory* (Westport, CT: Greenwood Press, 1978), pp. 13–17.
43. Bentley, op. cit., p. 235.
44. Patrick Dunleavy and Brendan O'Leary, *Theories of the State* (London: Macmillan, 1987); Bob Jessop, *The Capitalist State* (Oxford: Martin Robertson, 1982).
45. K. Pijl, *The Making of an Atlantic Ruling Class* (London: Verso, 1984); P. Burnham, *The Political Economy of Postwar Reconstruction* (London: Macmillan, 1990).
46. S. Krasner, *Defending the National Interest* (Princeton, NJ: Princeton University Press, 1978), p. 19.
47. T. Skocpol *et al*, *Bringing The State Back In* (New York: Cambridge University Press, 1985).
48. Thomas R. Dye, *Who's Running America? The Carter Years* (Englewood Cliffs, NJ: Prentice-Hall, 1979), p. 11.

49. John Westergaard and Henrietta Resler, *Class in a Capitalist Society* (Harmondsworth: Penguin, 1978), p. 142
50. Max Weber, *Basic Concepts in Sociology* (London: Peter Owen, 1962), p. 117.
51. Peter Bachrach and Morton S. Baratz, 'Two Faces of Power', in *American Political Science Review* (Dec. 1962); S. Lukes, *Power: A Radical View* (London and Basingstoke: Macmillan, 1980).
52. Polsby, op. cit., p. 60.
53. Telegram from Cripps to Foreign Office, 27 June 1940 (Public Record Office: FO 371/25206).
54. Lord Halifax to Hankey, 15 July 1940, in FO 371/25206.
55. Aide-mémoire by the Chiefs of Staff Committee to the War Cabinet, in War Cabinet Papers – CAB Series 66 – WP (40) 174, 27 May 1940, 'Construction of Aerodromes and Naval Bases by the United States in British Colonies and Dominions'.
56. Sir Llewellyn Woodward, *British Foreign Policy in the Second World War* (London: HMSO, 1962), p. 430.
57. Arthur Greenwood reporting to the Cabinet on Article 7 in War Cabinet Minutes – CAB Series 65 – WM (42) first meeting, 1 Jan. 1942.

2

Special Interests and Political Parties I

The next two chapters aim to consider the activities and world views of key special interest groups and political parties in the foreign policy process during the Second World War period. This chapter considers the role of the Federation of British Industries (FBI), the 'city' (through the activities of the Bank of England), and the Empire Industries Association (EIA). Chapter three will consider the role of the Royal Institute of International Affairs (RIIA), Trade Union Congress (TUC), the Labour Party, and the Communist Party of Great Britain (CPGB). The groups and parties selected for analysis are interesting because they were directly engaged in the foreign policy process or were relevant as representatives of a major section of the British population. Before introducing the interest groups, however, it is important to consider the international context within which the British political system was situated and its foreign policy constructed.

THE INTERNATIONAL CONTEXT

The making of a nation's foreign policy, while having its own internal dynamics and influences, must be understood in the international context of a system of nation states. The international system is not only the backdrop to the making of national foreign policy; it may often be the source of the most profound alterations of perception at the state level.

The making of the Anglo-American alliance as a project of the British foreign policy establishment has to be considered in light of the profound alterations in the pattern of world power in the late nineteenth and early twentieth centuries. It was that period which witnessed the relative decline of Europe and the emergence of the United States and Tsarist Russia/Soviet Union. No country better exemplified this relative decline than Britain, even if its nineteenth-century hegemony had depended less on its own resources than the weaknesses of its rivals.[1] With the greatest naval force in the world, a Pax Britannica was maintained and global empire constructed, albeit haltingly and without grand designs. At its height, the British Empire spanned 13 million square miles and contained a population of around 500 million, covering one-quarter of the earth's surface.[2] Between 1870 and 1914, the United Kingdom exported capital of £2.4 billion and received interest to the tune of £4.1 billion in return.[3] Even in the middle of the depression-hit 1930s, Britain received earnings of over £155 million from her overseas investments.[4]

Wars, however, have been the undoing of British power in the twentieth century. The Boer War (1899–1902) highlighted Britain's weaknesses, first by forcing Britain to mobilise huge resources to defeat a rather ramshackle Boer military that skilfully utilised guerilla warfare for two years; and second, by forcing Britain to borrow from the United States to pay for its military effort.[5] The Great War of 1914–18 severely damaged Britain's position, with her foreign investments losing 15 per cent of their value,[6] while the Americans and Japanese won British markets in Latin America, India and East Asia. In the China market for instance, Britain's share fell from 16.5 per cent to 9.5 per cent.[7] By the 1930s, Britain again lost markets, even in Empire countries like Canada, Australia and South Africa, to the United States.[8]

Forebodings of decline were heard most frequently in the early part of the twentieth century, and publication in 1902 of books entitled *The American Invaders* and *The Americanization of the World* provide something of the flavour of the times.[9] Indeed, with hindsight, such foreboding seems rather accurate. If wars were the unravelling of British power, they appear to have been the foundations of American power. From the Civil War (1861–85) to the Spanish–American War (1898), the United States transformed itself into an economic power of global proportions. With a highly productive agricultural sector, excellent communications, and world-leading corporations in all spheres, the United States emerged by 1900 as increasingly self-confident and assertive. With its Monroe Doctrine in Latin America, its 'Manifest Destiny' for the Pacific region, the US engaged in a navy building programme that, by 1914, had given it the world's third largest naval force.[10]

The United States was almost a rival continent as far as Europe was concerned – not just a competitor nation. In 1901, for example, Andrew Carnegie's mills were producing more steel than the whole of England.[11] Its huge internal market had no rival anywhere in the world.

Before 1914, the US had been a debtor nation; after 1918, it emerged as a creditor nation, being owed over £1,200 million by the rest of the world, excluding government loans.[12] Even in 1913, the US had accounted for 14 per cent of all world exports[13] and shipping;[14] by 1937, she exported 20 per cent of the world's manufactured goods, and owned overseas capital of $12.5 billion by 1939, outstripping British capital abroad by £9.6 billion by 1949.[15] Financially, New York was replacing London, and it was the Wall Street crash that brought about the Great Depression of the 1930s.

If Britons and Europeans in general feared America's growing economic power, there were as many Americans who welcomed such a development. They looked forward to the day when their country would occupy the dominant position in world affairs that Britain appeared to enjoy in the initial decades of the twentieth century. The American ambassador in London, for example, wrote to President Woodrow Wilson in 1913: 'The future of the world belongs to us. The English are using their capital . . . Now, what are we going to do with the leadership of the world presently when it clearly falls into our hands? And how can we use the British for the highest uses of democracy?' In 1930, another American, Ludwell Denny, in his book *America Conquers Britain*, wrote that Britain was destined to become America's colony because of US technological, industrial and financial supremacy. In 1940, Virgil Jordan of the National Industrial Conference Board told investment bankers that

> Whatever the outcome of the war, America has embarked on a career of imperialism in world affairs and in every other aspect of her life . . . At best, England will become a junior partner in a new Anglo-Saxon imperialism, in which the economic resources and military and naval strength of the

United States will be the centre of gravity . . . The sceptre passes to the United States.[16]

If America was Britain's economic challenger, then others had emerged who constituted a major military threat to the Empire: Germany and Japan. These powers envied Britain's imperial possessions and captive markets, and saw their own development as squarely conflicting with British interests. A major source of their discontent was the position of Britain in the world as explained by the first Sea Lord, Admiral Chatfield, in 1934. He said that 'we have got most of the world already, or the best part of it, and we only want to keep what we have got and prevent others from taking it away from us'. The Germans and Japanese knew that Britain's overseas empire had, as Winston Churchill put it, been 'mainly acquired by violence, [and was] largely maintained by force . . .',[17] and their belief was that they would also have to resort to arms in their struggle for 'living space' or a 'co-prosperity sphere'.

Being at the heart of Europe, Germany could not but raise fears in its neighbours about the new power in their midst. Unified by 1871, by 1913 it had become the most powerful industrial and military force in the world. Its population exploded from 49 million to 66 million, while social welfare and state education had generated a literate, well-trained and highly skilled workforce for service in civilian and military spheres alike.[18] In coal and steel production, in electrical goods and chemicals, Germany was equal to or more powerful than Britain. It tripled its exports between 1890 and 1913; its merchant marine was second only to Britain in 1913; and its share of world manufacturing output, at 14.8 per cent, exceeded that of Britain, at 13.6 per cent and was more than double that of France, at 6.1 per cent.

The great demand, in those days of Social Darwinism, in Germany was for colonies. For Chancellor Bulow, colonialism was not a choice; it was objectively necessary. But, as already mentioned, German calls to build her navy and expand her army were seen as grave threats by most other powers. Yet, Germany's colonial expansion could only come through a 'redivision of the globe'.[19] The first attempt was defeated on the battlefields of Europe, and the subsequent Treaty of Versailles further punished Germany. But despite losing a significant part of her population, minerals, industrial stock and foreign concessions as a result of the Great War, Germany returned to become a great industrial power by the end of the 1920s, producing over 12 per cent of the total manufacturing output of the seven biggest powers.[20] This spectacular revival was halted by the collapse of the world economy in the 1930s and the emergence of rival trading blocs. Adolf Hitler, the new Chancellor of Germany, was 'committed to altering the international order as soon as possible', with devastating consequences.[21]

The rise of Japanese power was even more spectacular than Germany's. In the 1890s, Japan was not even a candidate member of the Great Power 'club'. But ever since 1868, Japan had decided that, in order to survive as a free and independent nation, it must come into the modern world in all respects. Scrapping its feudal structures, the Japanese élite constructed a new constitutional and legal order, an educational system, a reformed banking system, built heavy industries, railways, and armaments.[22] Despite heavy reliance on imported raw materials, foodstuffs, crude oil, coal and iron ore, Japanese economic development was extremely rapid.[23] Japan's rise, as that of the United States, was linked to war – with China in 1894–95; Russia in 1904–5; the First World War; and the invasion of Manchuria in 1931.[24]

The inter-war period saw further spectacular economic growth, this time second only to that of the revolutionary Soviet Union. By 1938, Japan had overtaken France in industrial manufacturing. But the faster it grew, the more conscious Japan was of her dependence on imported raw materials and the keener her sense of economic insecurity became. Like the Germans, Japan saw the future in military terms, backed by a nation with a belief in its cultural uniqueness and superiority. Government spending on arms burgeoned in the 1930s: from 31 per cent of the total to almost 50 per cent. By 1938, the armed forces received 70 per cent of the government's budget, which meant that Japan spent more in absoute terms on armaments than any other power in the world.[25] Under the slogan of 'Asia for the Asiatics', Japan sought to carve out an empire for herself in East Asia and beyond.

In such a context, Britain's position was seen as increasingly precarious and US-dependent, especially in the Far East. British leaders of the inter-war years, however, having witnessed the 'isolationism' of US diplomacy, were highly dubious of the public pronouncements of President Franklin Roosevelt and others. In 1932, Prime Minister Stanley Baldwin summed up Britain's view of the US: 'You will get nothing from Americans but words, big words but only words.' In July 1934, Neville Chamberlain reiterated the same belief when he declared that

> We ought to know by now that the USA will give us no undertaking to resist by force any action by Japan short of an attack on Hawaii or Honolulu. She will give us plenty of assurances of goodwill especially if we will promise to do all the fighting, but the moment she is asked to contribute something she will invariably take refuge behind Congress.[26]

But Britain's policy, as Foreign Secretary Anthony Eden stated in 1937, was 'in peacetime to increase as far as possible the likelihood of the US giving us armed support in case of war.'[27] When war came, the Chief of Staff wrote in May 1940 that, if France collapsed before the German onslaughts and no American aid were forthcoming, 'we do not think we could continue the war with any chance of success'.[28]

The decisive changes in the world situation centred on the excessive demands made by too many powers on finite colonies and resources. These demands, and their expression in German and Japanese militarism, led ultimately to the Second World War. It was during that war that plans were made in Britain as to the nature of the post-war world and her place within it. British policy-makers were operating with full realisation of the alterations in world power, and tried to develop proposals and strategies to maximise Britain's position and influence. It was because of the desire to maintain and promote Britain's world role that an alliance with the United States was constructed. It must be stressed, however, that the decision to ally with the United States was not inevitable: it constituted a choice by policy-makers. They could, therefore, have chosen another policy – as France, in fact, did. Why did Britain decide to ally with the United States? What were the alternatives for Britain's post-war plans? There is no one clear-cut answer to these questions: no one theory exists in political sociology or science that yields the 'truth'. What we have are competing interpretations and explanations that advance fundamentally differing conceptions of the bases of the British state and system of political power, that underpin differing conclusions about the nature of its foreign policy.

Foreign policy was also constructed in a domestic context, within a society that was deeply divided on class lines. Capitalist societies are generally profoundly unequal in relation to the distribution of income, wealth and power. While this view is usually associated with Marxists, it is actually conceded, in one way or another, by most liberal commentators too. It is on the causes and consequences of inequality that debate is fiercest, not on the fact itself.

Britain was thoroughly class-divided in the 1930s and 1940s with large-scale corporations controlling the economy, and thereby the livelihoods and living standards of the nation. According to Varga and Mendelsohn, by the 1930s a handful of companies controlled the iron and steel, cement, cotton, soap and other key industries. They paint a similar picture of the banking sector, where the number of joint-stock bands decreased from 98 in 1900 to only 26 by 1936. In the same period, the deposits held by the five biggest banks increased from 27 per cent to 74.6 per cent of the total; the smaller banks' deposits declined from 31.8 per cent to just 1.9 per cent.[29]

S.J. Prais has also demonstrated the growing power of the corporation, showing that the small producer has largely been marginalised in the productive process. The top 100 manufacturing companies, he argues, increased their share of national output from 16 per cent in 1909 to 24 per cent by 1935. He estimates that by 1935, the largest 800 companies produced 50 per cent of all British manufactured goods.[30]

Share ownership was largely concentrated in the hands of a minority in British society. Even in 1951, Kathleen Langley of the Institute of Statistics at Oxford University calculated that the vast majority of stocks and shares were in the hands of a mere ten per cent of the population.[31]

In income terms, Britain was also sharply divided, with 73.5 per cent of all families receiving below £4 weekly in 1937, while five per cent earned over £10. Wealth was even more unequally distributed, with five per cent of the population owning 79 per cent of all private wealth; the richest one per cent owned 56 per cent. Of the 12 million British families in the 1930s, eight million were calculated to own less than £100 of total assets.[32]

Such inequalities of income and wealth had very serious consequences for the living conditions, health and education of the people. G.D.H. and M.I. Cole showed in their 1937 survey, 'The Condition of Britain', that only 141,000 children out of the total 5.7 million of school age attended public schools; and that only 2–3 per cent progressed to university.[33] The dire consequences of poverty were indicated by the Medical Officer of Health in Newcastle: 55 per cent of the working-class population were below normal weight and 47 per cent were below normal height. These figures compared unfavourably with those for the middle classes which showed 12 per cent and 4.8 per cent as underweight and underheight respectively.[34] The eminent social scientist Richard Titmuss condemned the fact that the levels of poverty 'resolved into [the] unnecessary and untimely deaths of 150 men, women and children every day in the North and Wales throughout at least the last ten years, culminating in the total social waste of over 500,000 human beings'.[35]

Evidently, social class was a key factor in the life of British society. It was a critical factor in building and sustaining the context within which British politics operated. It could not but have an impact, in a myriad of ways, on the making of British foreign policy.

Fundamental to many theories of the British state is the role of organised special interest groups that attempt to influence policy outcomes, and a consideration of a selection of such groups is given below. It is recognised that any selection procedure is problematic, but an attempt has been made to be as non-arbitrary as possible.

THE FEDERATION OF BRITISH INDUSTRIES (FBI)

The Federation of British Industries (FBI) was founded by Frank Dudley Docker, a Midlands industrialist, who persuaded 124 companies to part with £1,000 each in 1916 'to launch a new representative organisation for industry'.[36] Docker's scheme was to establish corporate structures in Britain that included workers, in order, he claimed, to halt Britain's industrial decline.[37] At the time of its founding, the FBI consisted of firms representing around £500 million in capital, a figure set to expand over the following decade. Earlier attempts at industrial organisation had not succeeded, according to Brady, because industry had not become so concentrated locally, nationally and imperially. Only the impetus of the First World War created the conditions for a successful representative organisation of big industry.[38]

From the very beginning, the FBI had support from some official quarters. The Foreign Office seconded Roland Nugent and Guy Locock to join the FBI staff, in the belief 'that they could help in expanding Britain's foreign trade during and after the war'.[39] Locock and Nugent had worked in the newly formed Commercial Section of the Foreign Office, and relations between that section and the FBI always remained close.

By 1925, FBI membership included 195 trade associations and 2,150 individual firms. This meant that, indirectly, the Federation was connected with over 20,000 British industrial and other companies, with a combined capital of around £6 billion, employing about 5 million workers.[40] It also expanded into trade, banking and insurance.

The aims of the FBI, which received a Royal Charter in 1925, were to be the voice of British industry in relation to the government; to safeguard and advance industrial interests; and to provide information and advice to its members. Politically, its Royal Charter precluded its intervention in party politics, but 'Matters within the political sphere which react upon industrial questions are, however, considered'.[41]

The biggest industrial companies in Britain joined the FBI, and it became their central organisation.[42] Companies such as ICI, Vickers, Lever Brothers, and many others, were to provide the key leaders of the FBI over the years – men such as Lord Hirst of the General Electric Company; George Nelson of English Electric; Sir Arthur Guinness of Guinness, Mahon and Company, and Clive Baillieu of Dunlop and Midland Bank. The leaders of the FBI came from the biggest concerns because, as Finer has commented, 'Such men, the directors of very large firms, have to take broad views. In addition their activities bring them into contact with other sections of industry.'[43]

We have seen that from the very beginning, the FBI had a very close relationship with the Foreign Office Commercial Section. The main links, however, were with domestic departments dealing with the day-to-day problems of industry, upon which most members required information and advice.[44] Inevitably though, given Britain's international trading and financial interests, the FBI did have a voice and view concerning Britain's foreign relations. The Federation's governing body, the Grand Council, discussed the international issues as they affected their constituents, and assigned various tasks to the President and the Executive Committee, and other committees set up from time to time. In implementing the decisions of the FBI, its leaders and functionaries had to deal with various representatives of the state. On international issues, this meant fairly regular contact with the departments that handled various aspects of Britain's foreign relations – the Board of Trade, the Treasury, and, of course, the Foreign Office.

Before discussing the role and influence of the FBI it is important to gain some understanding of the world view it held, that is, its version of what constituted British 'national interests'.

The FBI view of national interests

At the heart of the FBI's view of the national interest lay a belief in private enterprise capitalism (more or less regulated by the state) and international trade. The protection of Britain's overseas markets and the securing of her sources of food and raw materials were also central. These goals largely conditioned the discussions in FBI committees, and the consultations with, and recommendations to, ministers and civil servants. The state was expected to assist the FBI in its trade drives and analysis of FBI archives appears to demonstrate these points clearly.

The belief that the state was bound to assist industrialists in their foreign ventures was expressed on numerous occasions. Sir George Macdonogh, the Chairman of the FBI China Committee, reported to the Grand Council in 1937 that the Chinese market was very important to British industry, and the appointment of W.M. Kirkpatrick as the representative of the Export Credits Guarantee Department by the government was a boost to the FBI. Kirkpatrick was in touch with the FBI mission in China and, because of the unfair German and Japanese competition, British markets were being threatened. If British trade were to expand, he argued, it would require

> the granting of medium or long term credits [as] an indispensable condition of obtaining contracts . . . In that connection it was thought that the Export Credits Guarantee Department could be of great assistance, and it was urged [by the China Committee] that the Department should extend its facilities to cover local construction costs in China.

The government had already agreed that the ECGD should extend credits to British merchants in China. Macdonogh further reported that British companies in China, in order to maintain their interests, should pool their resources for training and maintaining exports in that country, as well as share their knowledge of contracts.[45]

The importance of exports was also stressed by an FBI delegation to the Board of Trade in 1939, which led to 'a distinct advance in Government policy', that is, the issue of directives that certain supplies were to be used only for the production of exports.[46] The FBI belief that the United States was using Britain's weakened position to grab export markets was made known to the authorities on several occasions. The Board of Trade and Department of Overseas Trade received these complaints often with sympathy and promised some remedial action – for example, increased advertising of British goods, more foreign trade missions and visits.[47]

The benefits to Britain, and sometimes to the whole world, of an increased British trade were a major principle of the FBI. Sir Guy Locock stated that a certain level of imports were a matter of 'life and death' for Britain, and 'the means whereby these imports could be paid for could not be left to chance' or the government alone.[48]

When the issue of reforming the Foreign Service emerged in 1941, the Executive Committee was reminded that the FBI's founder, Dudley Docker, had been instrumental in the founding of the Department of Overseas Trade and the commercial diplomatic service, at the end of the Great War. Locock told the Executive Committee that he had met Sir Malcolm Robertson, the government-appointed retired diplomat who was examining the question of further reform, and had agreed with Robertson that the consular and diplomatic services be amalgamated. Later in 1941, Locock added that 'it must be brought home to the Foreign Office that the commercial interests of the country, would, after the war, be their prime concern', and that they should develop 'skill in that type of work'.[49]

Finally, Dr W.H. Coates of ICI, in a report on monetary policy in 1944, welcomed the Bretton Woods' proposal for international monetary institutions because of 'the conviction that the long-term interests of Great Britain rested on a prosperous and abundant international trade without which the country's standard of living would be endangered'.[50]

It can be seen that the references to international trade and its importance are peppered throughout the period of interest, and do in fact occupy a vital place in the FBI's definition of national interests. The necessity of obtaining foodstuffs and raw materials from abroad, and the manufacture and export of goods and services, were considered vital to Britain's continuing prosperity and to the fullest possible employment of her resources. The FBI considered that the government, of whichever party, should assist the industrialists to achieve these goals, through the provision of credits, information, advice, consultation with industry, diplomatic representation and even military intervention. The powerful industrial interest in trade led to the development of some sympathy with the plight of the primary producing countries, with Sir Peter Rylands noting that the purchasing power of the primary producers had to be increased, so that they could absorb more adequately the manfactures of the industrial nations.[51] The FBI's Reconstruction Report of May 1942 stressed the need to develop the backward colonial areas, to make them prosperous, in order to restore equilibrium between the producers of raw materials and the producers of manufactured goods.[52] Sir Kenneth Lee informed the FBI, in his private capacity, that the purchasing power of the backward parts of the world would need to be boosted in the post-war period, and that the United States concurred with this view.[53] Evidently, the 'sympathy' with commodity-producing nations was motivated by the desire to secure raw materials and sell finished products as the basis of a prosperous Britain and world. It was the means to an end.

Another vital means to this end, according to the FBI, was the necessity for international institutions that would aid the growth and development of international trade on a stable, secure and expanding basis. The institutions would ultimately have to be agreed upon by the United Nations as a whole, but in the meantime the United Kingdom and the United States were the major powers between which early agreement was desirable. The belief in the Anglo-American basis of future prosperity began to develop alongside the negotiations between the two nations on a trade agreement in 1937–38. The economic and political effects of the Anglo-American Trade Agreement were spelt out to the Grand Council by G.E. Toulmin, who stated that not only would the Agreement affect the whole export trade but 'would also have a wider justification in so far as it might lead to closer co-operation between this country and the USA in world affairs in general'.[54]

Personal contacts between British industrialists and Americans were also generally encouraged by the FBI as a means of ironing out Anglo-American differences. Locock, for example, revealed that he had met Winthrop Aldrich of the Chase National Bank of the United States to discuss possible Anglo-American business co-operation in the Far East, and had been informed that the US government were generally pro-Chinese and anti-Japan. Lord Barnby told the Grand Council 'That collaboration with the USA would be the keystone of the future. There should be close contact not only between Governments but also between industrialists so that industrialists could guide their respective Governments'.[55] The Grand Council felt that the detrimental effect of Lend-Lease aid on British exports could be resolved through meetings of British and American businessmen to arrange 'some compromise ... with regard to the sharing of markets'.[56]

Lord Dudley Gordon had early in 1941 urged the Board of Trade to 'negotiate for a proper share of the market and to point out to the Americans that the two countries' interests were most clearly connected and that a proper spirit of co-operation, not only for immediate purposes, but also for the post-war period was essential.[57] With government approval, the FBI accepted an invitation from the American-based National Foreign Trade Council 'to co-operate in a study of post-war problems'. The government, however, only approved on the basis that the FBI entered no commitments.[58] The necessity of Anglo-American commercial, industrial and financial co-operation in international institutions was considered of paramount importance. A. McKinstry 'felt that some basis of international finance was required, for without this exports would never recover. A special Commission should be established to study this matter in co-operation with the USA'.[59] The FBI Reconstruction Report also argued that the future lay in international collaboration, especially with America, because

> at the end of the War the USA will be the most economic unit in the world, and that success in reconstruction will depend largely upon the part which America is prepared to play in it ... the immediate objective after the War would seem to be the formation of a British Empire–American group, designed to get trade moving over what is a vastly important area of the earth.[60]

In 1944, the chairman of the International Trade Policy Committee again reported that if international trade were to be expanded, there had to be

> a world trading system . . Some conscious direction would be necessary to stimulate a world trading system, and the Committee recommended the creation of an International Economic Council, the nucleus of which might be found in the existing economic collaboration between the United Nations.[61]

The need for co-operation between the US and Britain was considered important because, 'Many decisions on the future commercial and industrial policy would have to be made by the United Kingdom and the USA', and, in relation to this, various British business organisations – the FBI, the Association of British Chambers of Commerce, et cetera – attended the International

Business Conference in America. Having developed a common outlook and attitude to the Conference on the boat trip there, the businessmen had proceeded to defend British policy

> in face of US attacks on imperial preference, and had made it plain that this country would work for freer trade but was not prepared to surrender any present advantages until the transitional period was over, and until it could be clearly seen what counter advantages could be obtained from their surrender.[62]

Outside the Conference, the delegates had met many important people, including Lord Keynes, Britain's financial negotiator with the Americans.

The FBI's view of Britain's international trading interests also conditioned its view of Britain's security interests. His Majesty's armed forces were considered to be the source of protection, especially in the post-war world. The FBI's Reconstruction Report suggested the need for some kind of international peace-keeping machinery as the most solid basis for a post-war economic structure because 'Otherwise any post-war economic structure will be founded on quick sand'. The report envisaged the rise of larger national groupings or economic blocs after the war – for example, an American group, a European group, an East Asiatic, 'and a British Empire group with, it may be hoped, the co-operation of the USA'.[63] The need for Anglo-American co-operation to try to ensure international peace and security seemed to have become a firm principle amongst the British industrial community, and was summed up by Sir Clive Baillieu, the FBI President, in a speech to the American Chamber of Commerce in London in 1945. He stated that the problems of the world could only be solved 'within the framework of an ordered system of international security and of domestic policies'. He recommended that some of the war-time machinery built by Britain and the USA 'must continue into the peace, if we are to establish an effective system of International Security'. He urged any and every sacrifice by the peoples of Britain and America in their attempts to build a peace structure: 'Great power and great responsibility are ours', he stated.[64]

Overall, the FBI had concluded that Britain's international economic and military position depended upon the co-operation of the United States. The need for Anglo-American co-operation became a vital part of the FBI's conception of the national interest and of its foreign policy. As this realisation grew over the years, the FBI's efforts to secure co-operation did not cease. Yet, that is only one side of the story. In fact, the process of building an enduring Anglo-American co-operation was neither so smooth nor so simple. There were always frictions, doubts and fears within the FBI about the exact content and nature of the co-operation.

'American aggression' over foreign markets
The FBI complained on numerous occasions of the American aggression against Britain's international trading interests, feared the shift in the world balance of power towards the US, and regretted the negative effects on the military and economic sovereignty of Britain that would result from Anglo-American co-operation.

The rules concerning Lend-Lease aid to Britain prohibited the use of that material in the production of export goods, which British industry saw as an American way of grabbing her export markets. Sir Patrick Hannon MP informed the Grand Council that nearly all of Central and South America had already been 'lost', and the area 'would inevitably become the province of US manufacturers'. Hannon urged that the Americans be told that this would cause great problems after the war.[65] The point had been previously made by Lord Gordon to the Executive Committee, and D.A. Bremner had declared that Britain 'had a right to maintain the position in the world for which it had been fighting for centuries and markets it had developed at enormous expense in money and human effort'.[66]

As the war progressed, the tone of the FBI leaders' complaints became increasingly alarmed when the growing economic power of the United States became clear. Leslie C. Gamage of the FBI Empire Executive Committee noted that 'British Industry, deprived of its power to export, was in a perilous condition. British industrialists were powerless to protect their overseas markets against American aggression.'[67] Lord Riverdale of Sheffield elaborated on the American aggression by pointing out that Britain was not being permitted to export steel, tools and other products to South America and Mexico; Canada had been closed to any goods that could be produced there, and Britain was still importing large quantities of high-speed steel and tools under Lend-Lease. He complained that 'attempts to cancel outstanding orders for tools (of which there was now an enormous supply in the country) were met with a demand for an indemnity from the US. Failing the payment of an indemnity or an acceptance of the goods, America insisted upon being allowed to export to Britain's export markets.' In the case of Australia, Riverdale continued, 'American penetration . . . was . . . annexing . . . the services of British agents and their staffs . . . the Lend-Lease arrangement . . . was inducing the Australians to buy goods from America regardless of prices much in excess of those charged by British firms'. Sir Clive Baillieu underlined the need to modify the Lend-Lease situation since 'otherwise there will be such an epxlosion here that it will disappear'.[68]

Anglo-American trade rivalry, therefore, was no minor issue. The whole question of imperial preference and the Ottawa Agreements was aired in FBI circles, with the need for a deferential attitude to the Americans being uppermost in their minds. The powerful world position of the US ensured that the FBI Reconstruction Report clearly recognised that the Americans were firmly opposed to trade restrictions and imperial preference, and that the American attitude would adversely affect Britain's post-war policy.[69] In October 1942, an FBI committee was informed of the same basic problem by Sir Kenneth Lee, a government representative, that the post-war position of the export trades would be difficult 'not only due to the implications of the Atlantic Charter and the Mutual Aid Agreement, but on account of the likely tendencies of the Dominions to be drawn more closely to the USA after the War'. On the issue of the Ottawa Agreements, Lee told the committee that they 'would have to face up to an American demand for their reconsideration'.[70] Again in 1944, the FBI International Trade Policy Committee was told that despite the importance to Britain of the Empire trade, Britain could not denounce the US 'Most-Favoured Nation' clause for fear of retaliation.[71]

Britain's weakened position ensured that the US was the most powerful party in the various negotiations on war-time and post-war trading policies. With the Empire disintegrating – India's future uncertain, Australia, New Zealand, Canada and South Africa increasingly more dependent on the US – Britain's immediate and future options were limited. The deferential attitude among businessmen is evidence of a growing imbalance in the power of British and American business, demonstrating the degree of hard bargaining and deference that alliance with the United States meant in practice.

A similar pattern of dependence, deference and fears emerges from an analysis of the FBI's views concerning the development of international monetary institutions by Anglo-American governmental negotiation. The Grand Council set up a Monetary Policy Panel in 1944, which included Arthur Guinness of Guinness, Mahon and Co., merchant bankers, and Dr W.H. Coates of Imperial Chemical Industries (ICI) among its membership. Although the panel welcomed the Bretton Woods proposals, there was full realisation of the damaging effects on Britain that the new Anglo-American relationship could have. The negative effect of the International Monetary Fund (IMF) on the Sterling Area was indicated by W.F. Crick, who pointed out that before the establishment of the IMF:

> If a member of the Sterling Area had a deficit on its current balance, this was settled through London, and any alteration in the exchange rate between London and the other member was a matter between that member and London. Under the new scheme the final settlement of balances ... would be made through the [International Monetary] Fund ... there would therefore be a natural shifting of the centre of the system from London to the United States.[72]

The panel had certain 'misgivings ... regarding the preponderant position of the USA in relation to the Fund', and warned of the problems of 'carrying on the sterling area arrangements in the face of any opposition from the USA, if the Bretton Woods Agreement were rejected'.[73] Given the greater economic and financial power of the US, J. Shepherd believed that in post-war conditions the sterling area would be severely weakened:

> The strength of the Sterling Area depended upon the fact that Britain could always supply foreign exchange to the members of the area on request. After the War this country would be in difficulties itself in securing the foreign exchange needed for its own requirements, in addition to which, the American system would act as a powerful counter attraction.

In such a situation, Shepherd believed, it would be better to have US co-operation in an international plan 'than for this country to reject the plan and leave the USA to take its own line'.[74]

Britain had become heavily dependent on the United States in several key respects and, despite the protesting voices in the FBI, there was not a great deal that industry could do about it. Given the level of dependence, it almost inevitably follows that there would be negative implications for national sovereignty, of which some of the FBI members were fully aware. Indeed, the Reconstruction Report of 1942 had admitted that the need for closer association between key world powers, such as Britain and the United States, would, 'in defence matters, entail an alteration in our past conception of national sovereignty'.[75] In other words, Britain would have to defer militarily on important questions to the US.

The reduction in British independence was not confined to military affairs – economic and monetary sovereignty would also be diminished. While W.F. Crick noted that international monetary plans would reduce British independence, A.H. Kilner was deeply concerned and saw the plans as 'probably the thin end of the wedge, and it was necessary to see that it was not driven too far'. Crick replied, however, that the diminution of sovereignty was not entirely negative. Each country, he stated, had to make some sacrifices in order to stabilise the world economy. In fact, he continued, 'every trade agreement and every form of international undertaking limited a country's national sovereignty. Certain portions of national sovereignty were bargained away in exchange for what was believed to be the Universal good'.[76] The tone of the discussion was pessimistic, and FBI leaders became aware that the reduction of British independence was the logical corollary to the agreements between Britain and America. Given the powerful attraction of post-war Anglo-American co-operation, despite the misgivings, it becomes quite clear that the British Empire's place in the world, and in the eyes of the FBI leadership, had also changed.

The declining significance of Empire

Analysis of the FBI's records shows that the British Empire as constituted, over the years, declined in its significance to industry. The evolution of attitudes favourable to co-operation with the US weakened the industrialists' attachment to Empire.

A useful start in examining the FBI's evolving attitude may be made by considering the content of a memorandum written by W.A. Lee of the Mining Association of Great Britian, entitled 'Industry and Foreign policy'. The government's policy on the Empire, the 1938 memo stated, was to 'resist with every means in our power any threat to the integrity of the Empire'. It was argued that the 'continuance of Europe's independence is of vital interest to the British Empire', and believed that Germany was not definitely on the path to European domination, so industry should support the appeasement policy. The key point, apart from the fact that industry was following the government's lead on appeasement, is the strength of commitment to the Empire, and the role of European independence in its defence. Nevertheless, the memo concluded that should Germany become a menace, Britian would have to move towards 'an exposition of . . . [its] . . . position to the United States of America'.[77]

By the time the FBI's reconstruction views were published, the war was almost three years old, and the US had become aware of Britain's predicament. The stress then was not on maintaining independence of action, but on the mutual reliance between the Atlantic powers. Nevertheless, the Empire was still considered important, and the aim was to conclude an agreement with the Americans that would not alienate the colonies and dominions. But the Reconstruction Report clearly recognised that America opposed imperial preference, and Britain could not ignore the fact. The report recommended Anglo-American mutual understanding, while machinery for intra-Empire consultation needed to be developed so that an Empire policy could be produced.[78] The FBI's hopes for a positive Empire policy, however, were dampened by the bleak message that Sir Kenneth Lee delivered on the need to eliminate trade barriers. Lee had been convinced by the American businessmen of the National Foreign Trade Council of their desire to scrap the Ottawa Agreements, and he had warned the FBI that 'it may well be that our relationship with our Dominions and also with our Colonies, will be very much changed after the war'. As stated earlier, the Dominions were also likely 'to be drawn more closely to the USA'.[79]

Fully aware of the likelihood of Indian independence after the war and of a radically altered political situation in China, the FBI Executive Committee prepared in 1942 for the need to secure their industrial and commercial interests through government-negotiated trade treaties.[80] Even as late as 1944, the International Trade Policy Committee warned of the American threat of retaliation if Britian denounced the 'Most-Favoured Nation' principle.[81]

It appears that the FBI definitely saw the need for the continuation of Empire, but could also see the even greater need to retain American goodwill and co-operation. During the war, the FBI realised that US co-operation would not be forthcoming unless there was some alteration in Britain's imperial relations. The International Business Conference attended by the FBI demonstrated this point. The Americans had attacked imperial preference, and the British delegates had defended it. The defence, however, had stressed that Britain would not give up any of her imperial advantages unless she could obtain suitable compensatory advantages. The Empire was not, perhaps, seen as an eternal institution; rather it could be negotiated over, as long as Britain's essential commercial and industrial interests could be protected. A general evolution of attitudes had occurred, accelerated by the destructive effects of the war and the growing strength of the United States. From a more independent Empire attitude that recognised American potential, the position altered to one of keeping together as much of the material substance of Empire – the financial, commercial and industrial connections – through negotiated treaties rather than political control, alongside an enduring and stable Anglo-American agreement.

The FBI's view of the national interest revolved around the retention of Britain's international commercial, financial and industrial interests, based on the system of free enterprise capitalism, with some state assistance and regulation. These two elements provided the skeleton around which the FBI made its assessments of the changing situation, and its proposals to government. The latter element – free enterprise – was really the foundation of the former, as Sir Francis Joseph reminded the Grand Council: 'private enterprise had been responsible for accumulating the profits which had permitted overseas investment, the interest on which had enabled this country to live in the past and to a great extent to finance purchases abroad at the present time.'[82] In 1944, the Grand Council heard again 'that free enterprise provided the most satisfactory basis for a prosperous economy'.[83] The FBI's view of the national interest and policies were, as S.E. Finer pointed out, 'sectional – they are the policies of manufacturing industry. The FBI seeks to make them conform to "the public interest", but, like most trade associations and indeed most humans, its views of "the public interest" itself are sectional.'[84]

The FBI appears as an organisation connected to the state in many ways and in many spheres. The issue is: did the FBI manage to influence official decisions? Or did the state influence the FBI? These questions will be analysed in Chapter 5.

THE EMPIRE INDUSTRIES ASSOCATION (EIA)

The Empire Industries Association advanced an alternative to an Anglo-American alliance that was taken seriously by officialdom. A study of the EIA also shows another very important aspect of Anglo-American relations – the degree to which the EIA and the 'pro-American group' of ministers misunderstood the nature of the US as a world power. To Winston Churchill the Anglo-American alliance would save the Empire,[85] despite his knowledge of President Roosevelt's 'opposition' to colonialism (on which more is said below). Conversely, the EIA believed that co-operation with the United States was possible even if Britain maintained, intact, its policy of imperial preference. What set the EIA apart from the pro-US group was the intensity of its attachment to Empire and its fear of US power. They were further separated from the pro-Americans by their mistaken belief that the Dominions were still interested in traditional imperial arrangements. The EIA failed to take into account the effect of the increased dependence of the Dominions on the US which had been brought about by the War.

A few words should be devoted to the still widely held belief about the 'idealistic' nature of American 'anti-colonialism'. In several studies, President Roosevelt emerges as a consistent anti-imperialist, an internationalist, as a leader 'of original sweeping vision, born of the highest idealism'.[86] We learn that FDR had rejected his early pro-imperialist phase by the late 1920s, when he began to believe that subject peoples should be 'educated for self-government' and that independence was an inherent right of all nations.[87] It is also argued that anti-colonialism was an autonomous intellectual and emotional force in American political life that 'helped shape the substance of defence, economic, and foreign policy'.[88]

It is often suggested that the Atlantic Charter is one of the strongest expressions of American anti-colonialism because of its espousal of the principle of self-determination, offering further evidence of US idealism in international affairs. Yet the evidence often cited, but understated, by the very same authors indicates the viability of a different interpretation of American aims and objectives. William Roger Louis notes that officials in the Colonial Office were in little doubt as to American intentions. As one official, Sydney Caine, noted 'The Americans themselves are not really interested only in the welfare of colonial peoples but also in the exploitation of natural resources in colonial territories'.[89] Of course, such an attitude from the Colonial Office is not entirely surprising, but the same view is expressed by others too. Carey Fraser has argued recently that, after the Second World War, US policy towards colonial powers and decolonisation was highly complex and founded on the consideration of a combination of factors – such as domestic racial issues and its own status as a colonial power – underpinned by 'the subordination of anti-colonial sentiment to the demands of containment'. Fraser also comments that containment was a means to 'legitimise an activist foreign policy', and that decolonisation was a way of 'maintaining its leadership role in the international system' and in 'facilitating the projection of American military power abroad'.[90] In short, America practised power politics in its 'anti-colonial' campaign.

Such an interpretation is also upheld by Arthur Schlesinger's recent analysis of FDR's internationalist credentials. Schlesinger argues that FDR learned power politics from Theodore Roosevelt and the writings of Admiral Alfred T. Mahan, but he also learned how to veil such ignoble analyses and considerations from Woodrow Wilson, under whom he served as Assistant Secretary of the Navy. While FDR believed that concepts like the balance of power held the key to international affairs, he also knew that 'it was the Wilsonian dream, and not the balance of power, that moved his countrymen. His task now was to reconcile international geographical inevitabilities . . . with domestic political myths, such as the wickedness of spheres of influence. He talked idealism but played the power game'.[91]

During the Second World War, therefore, the United States fully recognised the changing patterns of world power, and aimed to maximise its own position, or at least satisfy its 'needs', inevitably at the expense of others. FDR's notion of trusteeship, Sbrega suggests, came to nothing despite 'praiseworthy objectives and good intentions'. But Louis points out that FDR's 'interest in trusteeship schemes [was] . . . a means of stabilising unsettled areas and opening the door to American commerce'.[92]

If its anti-colonialism was a veil for the United States' own expansionist ambitions, it was never consistently applied. US officials also realised that they had to be pragmatic, that is, use the threat of US opposition to colonies to gain French collaboration in North Africa and British co-operation over US bases in the Pacific. Gabriel Kolko also maintains that America did not want the British Empire to disintegrate completely because 'the continuance of the British Empire in some reasonable strength is in the strategic interests of the United States', according to a War Department memo.[93]

In sum, US 'anti-colonialism' was a complex affair but in essence it represented the attitude of an emerging world power that sought its own spheres of influence and other institutions associated with a 'forward projection' of American might. Certainly, it is far from being imbued with the idealism mentioned earlier.

The analysis reveals the complexities involved in the determination of British policy when faced with such a major force as the US, and in a crisis such as the Second World War. In effect, a debate was stimulated by the changing pattern of world power and Britain's position within it. How should Britain respond to the rise of United States' power? was the key long-range question facing British wartime policy-makers. As this study shows, the answers were not clear-cut; there appeared to be no easy choices. Within this period, the EIA made its intervention to defend and promote the 'Empire' option.

Origins and aims

The EIA was formed in 1926 as an organisation to take over 'the mission of the Tariff Reform League' by a number of prominent imperial enthusiasts such as Lord Milner, Leopold Amery, Neville Chamberlain and Sir Henry Page Croft.[94] The main aim was to promote closer imperial ties through the dissemination of 'educational matter on this [Empire and Tariff] policy'. The EIA, therefore, operated as a source of pro-imperial literature and speakers, and as an organisation holding public meetings and rallies. Not only did it seek to influence public opinion on imperial questions, it also had a very important parliamentary presence which it used to try to influence official policy.[95]

Despite its name, the EIA was not a body that attempted to form an organisation of industries, but a more political organisation supporting the cause and ideals of the Empire.

World outlook

The EIA's world outlook was founded upon a belief in the fundamental strength of the British Empire. Whether it was a question of world trade or world peace, the development of the Empire was held to be the key mechanism to further those 'noble' objectives. With this belief as their guiding principle, the EIA leaders resented the rise to world status of the United States, and were determined to ensure that Britain 'held her own'. They claimed to see, with some foresight it has to be said, in the growing tendency towards Anglo-American co-operation, before and during the War, the step-by-step dismantling and 'selling' of the Empire. What the

EIA wanted was a strong, united Empire that could equal in stature the continental-sized powers, the United States and the Soviet Union. Numerous examples drawn from the EIA's archives may be cited to demonstrate these points.

With reference to the pre-war Anglo-American Trade Agreement of 1938, Amery pointed out to the EIA's Parliamentary Committee that it was designed to weaken Empire trade, because of the Americans' insistence on the 'most-favoured-nation' principle, by which any trade concession Britain made and received from the United States had to be extended to all other countries, even to Germany and Japan. Even before the Trade Agreement, Amery believed that when it came to international trade, 'it was in . . . [the Empire] direction that the main hopes of the country are centred'.[96]

The peace-preserving importance of the Empire was stressed by the Association's Council in March 1939, in a resolution that emphasised 'the need of the closest co-operation of all parts of the British Empire in trade, counsel and defence and of a determination to maintain its integrity as the strongest insurance for the preservation of world peace'.[97]

The United States' emphasis on a policy of international free trade for all aroused much criticism in EIA circles. The Association's wartime *Monthly Bulletin* provides a fairly clear account of the EIA's view of developments on that issue. While recognising the importance of the United States, one bulletin stated that 'we should be careful not to depart from the well-tried policy which bases its hopes for the future upon the cooperation of the Empire as a whole'.[98]

The most sophisticated defence of the Empire option, however, was not to be found in the bulletins but in a confidential memorandum written by Amery at the end of 1941, which was circulated to a number of officials, including the Governor of the Bank of England, Sir Montagu Norman, who was a fairly fervent imperialist himself. L.S. Pressnell argues, for example, that it was firmly perceived to be in the Bank's interests to defend the Sterling Area, to guarantee London's international financial position and to maintain its imperial network.[99] Norman was impressed with Amery's analysis and shared the latter's alarm 'at the American attempt to convert the British Empire into a group of American dependencies'.

Special Interests, the State and the Anglo-American Alliance, 1939-45

Norman replied that 'I greatly admire and envy the foresightedness shown in this memorandum', and that he had no 'doubt . . . that Cordell Hull, like most other good Americans, looks forward to our island funeral! . . . I agree, we can't live by leave of the U.S.: we shall have to consult and compromise in places whilst firmly remaining imperially minded.'[100] As the memorandum provides a very detailed defence of the views of the pro-Empire 'lobby', it is worth quoting at length. Amery began by calling for a frank and open discussion on the American insistence on the 'most-favoured-nation' principle and the abolition of imperial preference, because these were issues of 'transcendant importance'. Amery argued that

> The advocates of compromise with this demand usually urge that unless we accept the economic views of the present [US] administration we cannot hope to induce the United States to join us after the war in establishing and maintaining a tolerable international order in policing the future peace settlement, that we shall be selfishly failing to play our part in the economic recovery of the world, and that the United States, in their disappointment will cease to regard us equal partners with them in world affairs and will tend to disregard our interests.

Amery challenged what he claimed were the four assumptions that lay behind this flawed view: first,

> that it is desirable, or possible, that we and the United States should set ourselves the task of policing the world. Second, that our responding to the economic views of the present American administration can prevent the swing back of American opinion after the war – almost certainly by then under a Republican administration – to the traditional policy of isolation; third, that the Americans' views actually correspond to real world developments; and fourth, that their [America's views] acceptance by ourselves is compatible with the vital economic interests of the British Empire, with the political principles on which it is based, or with any sort of political and economic equality in our future dealings with the United States.

United States isolationism, which sabotaged the League of Nations, Amery argued, would rise again because of the constitutional arrangements of that country. America was incapable 'of pursuing a policy of active and anticipatory intervention in issues and disputes which do not directly concern it'. America and Britain should really do as Britain had done after 1815, that is, set up 'a stable and self-balanced political and economic system in Europe, and, so far as may be, in the Far East'. Any direct intervention in Europe, Amery believed, would only 'draw [Britain] further apart' not only from America, but from the Dominions. And, in the long run, the 'unity of our Empire, coupled with Anglo-American co-operation, should be the supreme aims of British policy'.

Amery rejected the laissez-faire and 'internationalist' ideals of the American adminstration in favour of an economic future based on a nation-state, or group-of-states, basis. He further argued that the US promoted laissez-faire because of the size and quality of its own economic power:

> American industries have grown to a scale and power to which nothing else in the world affords any real parallel, and are now in a position, from the secure base of their immense home market, to go out and conquer the world. A corporation . . . like the United [States] Steel or General Motors is economically more powerful than all the comparable industries of Europe added together and, under Free Trade conditions, could hope to control the world. The American economic policy of today, like that of Cobden's day, is a curious blend of internationalist idealism and economic imperialism . . . American industry also favours the unconditional MFN Clause because it prevents the formation of economic groups that would, by the creation of sheltered markets more nearly comparable to the American home market, enable the industries of other countries to stand up to American competition.

Amery urged that the only defence Britain had against American economic domination was to maintain intra-imperial co-operation and imperial preference. The abandonment of Empire unity would mean that 'All hope of an independent policy of economic development, all hope of being able to negotiate with the United States, or other nation groups, on a footing of equality would [also] have to be abandoned'.[101] An alliance between Britain and America, without reference to the Empire, was unthinkable to Amery.

This clear, forthright and, on occasion, curiously insightful analysis of the changing distribution of world power, and the stance that Britain should adopt towards those changes, constitutes one of the most interesting and precise statements of the EIA's position. It effectively encompasses the principles of the EIA, its agenda and its chief guide to British foreign policy formation. It was at the same time a set of conclusions based on long and serious contemplation of the future of British policy and a guide to future action.

Throughout the war, the EIA's bulletin maintained and defended the positions of the Empire 'lobby'. The June 1941 edition contained a major attack on the so-called Five Peace Principles enunciated by the US Secretary of State, Cordell Hull, opposing trade restrictions which, according to the *Bulletin*, were merely 'free-trader' talk for British tariffs (which had actually increased Empire trade in the 1930s). The Hull proposal for non-discriminatory trade policies on the basis of the 'most-favoured-nation' clause was criticised as an attempt to destroy 'the whole policy of Empire cooperation initiated at Ottawa'; his suggestion that all nations should have access to necessary raw materials was dismissed as German propaganda; Hull was criticised for ignoring the plight of the primary commodity-producing nations; and the very idea of international monetary institutions was not considered seriously at all.[102]

Despite its opposition to the drift towards an Anglo-American alliance, certain sections of British society alarmed the EIA by their indifference to the Empire and its problems. For instance, while the EIA welcomed the Federation of British Industries' (FBI) report on post-war reconstruction, it was dismayed by the FBI's 'internationalist' outlook and the fact that the FBI 'is somewhat inclined to shelve the question of the Colonial Empire and of Imperial Preference . . . [T]here appears to be some diffidence about tackling the problem of Colonial administration, maintenance and development, in the light of post-war conditions.' Did the FBI defer to American views? The *Bulletin* of the EIA could not be sure.[103] In a similar vein, the July 1942 *Bulletin* bemoaned the fact that there was 'a regrettable habit in this country to ignore the existence of the British Empire'.[104]

The EIA refused to compromise on the imperial question, despite becoming increasingly isolated. Yet the Association was realistic enough to see that the United States would play a significant role in post-war affairs – economically and militarily.[105] There would, consequently, need to be a certain level of Anglo-American co-operation, but it would have to include Britain and the Empire as a single item. The tried and tested policy and institutions of the Empire had to remain firm, because what Britain stood to lose by liquidating Imperial Preference would not be equalled by any agreement with the United States.[106]

However brief the above outline, there can be little doubt concerning the central principles of the EIA. The pro-imperial idea dominated the thoughts and actions of the EIA, while the idea that co-operation between Britain and the United States should form the basis of post-war foreign policy was anathema. A number of questions arise at this stage: how did the EIA respond in practice to the gradual official movement towards Anglo-American co-operation? Did their views have any impact whatever on policy-makers? How do we account for the EIA's total defeat in policy debates? These questions will be addressed in Chapter 5.

THE BANK OF ENGLAND

If the Federation of British Industries was the 'peak' association of manufacturing industry, then the Bank of England is often considered its more powerful counterpart in the world of British finance, especially with reference to the 'city'. Frank Longstreth[107] in his important study of the City and the Bank of England considers that financial capital dominates the British state largely for its own particular 'fractional' interests. The state, in Longstreth's analysis, is 'a system penetrated and structured by particular class relations', with the city prevailing over 'industrial' interests. As the dominant 'fraction' of capital, the 'city's position . . . has been institutionalised within the state system . . . through the Bank of England and its relation to the Treasury'.[108] A little later in his analysis, Longstreth further emphasises the critical and privileged position of finance in relation to state policy: 'The Bank of England is the linchpin of this presence', he argues; 'The bank's position of authority is the locus of financial interests in the state. In its self-description it mediates between the City and the government.'[109]

Michael Mann, a Weberian sociologist, adds to the credibility of Longstreth's argument by suggesting that financial interests have historically backed the state through taxation and loans because official foreign policy focused 'on naval and commercial enterprise'.[110] As a result, he argues, the 'state and wealthy classes became closely entwined [and] . . . their co-operation centred on the nexus of City/Treasury/Bank of England'. Mann also emphasises the relatively greater influence of the City as opposed to industry.[111]

Although both Longstreth and Mann are primarily concerned with economic policy, their arguments do lend themselves to consideration in debates on foreign policy. This is especially true in the case of Mann, because he underlines the importance to Britain of foreign commerce and sterling as an international currency, both of which were concerns fundamental to the formation of the Anglo-American alliance during the Second World War.

A critical challenge to the Longstreth thesis, however, has been mounted by Geoffrey Ingham in his *Capitalism Divided?*, in which he convincingly argues that neither the Bank of England nor the Treasury were mere instruments of City power because they had their own institutional interests. In fact, Ingham assigns the state a far greater level of autonomy than either Longstreth or Mann, and suggests that the historical evidence demonstrates that it was the policies of the state itself, because of its own interests in solving its chronic debt problem and improving its war-making capabilities, that created the City of London as a major commercial and financial centre.[112] So autonomous is the state, in Ingham's view, that he suggests that in the 1820s it 'set itself against a section of the traditional dominant class', in order to 'weaken the system of aristocratic parasitism and patronage of "old corruption" and the state's dependence on the City's "money powers"'. The British state in the 1820s, he argues, believed that 'unless the state's finances were put in order Britain could not fight another war, and furthermore, most prominent members of the government at the time believed that monetary instability was in itself the major cause of social and political unrest'.[113]

This debate on the Bank of England is, in microcosm, also relevant to the broader questions addressed in this study. At its centre, the debate is about the forces that drive the policy process; that is, whether the actions of the state are driven by private political/economic forces or by the imperatives of the state itself. In this section, the intention is not to evaluate the rival hypothesis against the empirical record, but to furnish some of the historical data to make such an evaluation possible later in this study. The remainder of this chapter, therefore, will briefly outline the origin and development of the Bank of England and its view of the national interest.

The Bank of England was founded in 1694 as a 'joint-stock company operating under Royal Charter' but, although it was a private body until after the Second World War, it effectively operated as a 'public institution'.[114] The most senior committee of the Bank was its Commmittee of Treasury, which had seven members, including the Deputy Governor, who headed it.[115] The Treasury Committee nominated various individuals to a Court of Directors, who were generally 'men such as they themselves had been. In practice . . . the selection was limited to "members of merchant houses and representatives of individual interests".'[116] In general, bankers from the clearing and joint-stock banks were excluded from membership, as were non-English nationals and anyone who could not afford to own £2,000 of Bank stock. From 1932, Members of Parliament, except for the City of London's member, were also excluded from Bank directorship.[117]

Inevitably, the Bank of England became an important focus of City activity and very close to City interests, as shown by its 'War Book'. The war outlined the key institutions of the City with which the Bank had to maintain contact in case of an emergency evacuation of London, that is, the clearing bankers 'and discount house committees, the large insurers and investment trusts, etc'.[118] In its everyday life and work, the Bank could not but become fully enmeshed in the concerns of the biggest financial powers in the land, although this does not mean that it did not have an independent set of interests, outlook on the world and definition of Britain's national interests.

Central to the Bank's notion of the national interest was the maintenance of sterling as the premier world currency, and of London as an international financial centre. The Bank also wanted the British state to fight to maintain and develop those international institutions which it (the Bank) believed would achieve such objectives: the Sterling Area and the key elements of Britain's imperial connection. As G.L.F. Bolton, one of Governor Montagu Norman's key advisers, argued in 1941, Britain should 'integrate and strengthen the Sterling Area' despite the destruction caused by the war. He went on

> HMG should be prepared, if necessary, to enter into exchange guarantees with the Dominion Governments and independent countries in the Area in order to maintain a maximum of stability . . . Every endeavour should be made to permit and encourage the flow of trade and investments inside the Area, the objective being to aim at similar facilities to make payments between . . . London and Sydney, as between London and Glasgow: between Hong Kong and Pretoria, as between Cardiff and Belfast.

On such firm foundations, Bolton concluded, 'a stable and united Sterling Area could not fail to become a potent political factor'. So inspired was Bolton by imperial ideology that he declared that 'If it were possible to put the Sterling Area concept into words or to invent a slogan, it might be said that: Membership of the Sterling Area implies pooling of resources, mutual responsibility and acceptance of the principle of leadership.'[119] Other observers, however, have considered that resources were never pooled but extracted from the satellite and colonised nations, that there was nothing mutually beneficial, and that leadership meant little except imperial domination.[120]

Just before United States' entry into the Second World War, Bolton claimed that any purely Anglo-American post-war financial plans were dangerous because they ignored Europe and the Soviet Union. He argued that we should have put ourselves in the position of securing collaboration with America at the expense of the hostility of the rest of the world . . . [S]uch a scheme bears within it the seeds of a very rapid decay as the rest of the world would probably spend most of their time in political intrigues against America and the British Empire.

In place of the multilateral plans favoured by the Treasury and government, Bolton argued that nations should make regional pacts: for example, the 'USA would . . . develop her existing relations with Mexico which would probably become a part of a recognised dollar area. The UK, acting for the Sterling Area, would enter into special arrangements with Siam, the Argentine and Portugal'.[121]

Such views were shared by the Bank's Governor, Montagu Norman, who himself had been thoroughly schooled in the imperial world view, as his correspondence with Leopold Amery, the arch-imperialist Secretary of State for India cited earlier, demonstrates. Norman saw the United States as a threat in every way to British power and imperial prestige. His deputy, B.G. Catterns, entertained similar notions. In 1944, when so many of the Anglo-American financial plans had effectively been concluded, Catterns wrote to Sir Wilfred Eady of the Treasury warning him not to inform the Dominions that the post-war Sterling Area would operate only on restricted lines. This would avoid alarming the Dominions. Catterns believed that Britain should not 'tinker' with the Sterling Area because the area had historically been one of the vital bases 'for a cohering commonwealth' and the rich 'texture of Empire'.[122]

Despite the brevity of this outline of the position and attitudes of the Bank of England, it is clear that the Bank stood for the continuation of the status quo of a strong imperial network, defence of the sterling area, and therefore its own position of importance and influence in international finance. Despite its privileged institutional position, however, at the centre of the City–Treasury nexus, it clearly 'backed the wrong horse' as far as post-war British foreign policy was concerned.

The three special interests considered in this chapter all more or less supported the Empire: of the three, the FBI was most ambivalent about the Empire, and later discussion will show the powerful role played by state officials in the evolution of FBI policy. The Empire Industries Association and the Bank of England were the most imperialistic to the end and were, as history shows, defeated in policy debates. Why did the EIA's members in particular, opt for and tenaciously cling to the Empire option, given that its members were largely of the same historical generation as those state leaders who were more 'internationalist' in outlook? That question will be addressed later in this study. For now, it is more appropriate to introduce a force allied to those discussed above, the Conservative Party.

CONSERVATIVE PARTY

The Conservative Party was obviously a formidable force in foreign policy formation. It was a Conservative-led coalition which governed Britain during the period from spring 1940 to mid-1945, headed by the Prime Minister, Winston Churchill. Power within the party has always been heavily biased in favour of the leaders and their closest advisers, although consultations with the National Union of Conservative and Unionist Associations and the Parliamentary Association do occur. Given the oligarchical nature of party organisation, however, an examination of its role in the formation of the Anglo-American alliance need only seriously entail an analysis of its leaders in Cabinet positions.

The philosophy of the party during the war generally revolved around a reverence of established customs and traditions at home and abroad, although well-managed and orderly change was never out of the question. Conservatism, then as now, was taken by its adherents to be 'an expression of "common sense"', and its 'truths' were regarded as self-evident.[123] Such an attitude is not surprising since the Conservatives have held power longer than any other modern British political party. John Ross is surely correct in his assertion that 'the Conservative Party is not just "another party" in British politics. It is the dominant party of the modern political system. It is the Conservative Party which has been in office for three times as long as any other party. It is the supporters and backers of the Conservative Party who control the economy and highest positions of the state.'[124] The Conservatives' approach to politics, despite the emergence of a mass electorate, was to remain primarily preoccupied with the problems of the state. As Andrew Gamble has suggested, the party is a government party – governing is what Conservatives do. Gamble goes on to say that although Conservatives learned to become 'a movement of the nation', they remained 'primarily a party of the state, and they approached politics from that standpoint – the state's institutions, functions and requirements'. Consequently, Conservatives 'regarded the British state and its encircling civil society as their own. They supply its leaders and rulers, and its institutional labyrinth is peopled by the party's natural supporters.'[125]

Despite the strong, indeed profound, connections between the party and the wealthiest and most privileged sectors of British society, the Conservatives articulated their popular message in national rather than class terms. They were the champions of the 'national interest', they claimed, rather than the divisive class-based appeals of the Labour Party. Quintin Hogg, for example, wrote after the Second World War that Conservatism was founded on the principle of 'the underlying unity of all classes of Englishmen, their ultimate identity of interest, their profound similarity of outlook . . . The nation, not the so-called class struggle is therefore at the base of Conservative political thinking.'[126]

The Conservative preoccupation with the private enterprise system and the British Empire are too well known to require elaboration here. What is more interesting is the fact that leading Conservatives, such as Churchill, could preside over governments that could reform Conservative policies on such questions, leading to a new cross-party consensus on the welfare state and on the Anglo-American alliance. An overriding concern with the position of the British state within domestic society and the world order, it is argued here, must form the key basis of an explanation of such policy departures.

The Conservative world-view, therefore, was fundamentally constructed around the concerns and 'needs' of the state. As a political party, the Conservatives were virtually always at the heart of the state. It is not necessary to belabour this point, as the power of the party over the key decisions that constructed the Anglo-American alliance will become clear in later chapters.

NOTES

1. David Reynolds, *Britannia Overruled. British Policy and World Power in the Twentieth Century* (London and New York: Longman, 1991), p. 19,
2. R.P. Dutt, *The Crisis of Britain and the British Empire* (London: Lawrence & Wishart, 1954).
3. P. Sweezey and H. Magdoff, *The Dynamics of US Capitalism* (New York: Monthly Review Press, 1972), p. 33.
4. F.W. Paish, 'Britain's Foreign Investments: The Post-War Record', *Lloyds Bank Review* (May 1956).
5. Reynolds, op. cit., p. 74.
6. W. Ashworth, *A Short History of the International Economy since 1850* (London: Longman, 1987), pp. 228, 230.
7. Reynolds, op. cit., p. 105.
8. Dutt, op. cit., p. 155.
9. Frederick Mackenzie, *The American Invaders*; W.T. Stead, *The Americanization of the World*.
10. Paul Kennedy, *The Rise and Fall of the Great Powers* (London: Fontana, 1989), pp. 317–19.
11. Ibid., pp. 313–14.
12. Ashworth, op. cit., p. 230.
13. H.G. Aubrey, *The Dollar in World Affairs* (New York and Evanston: Harper & Row, 1964), p. 13.
14. Ashworth, op. cit.
15. Dutt, op. cit.
16. Ibid., pp. 149–51.
17. Reynolds, op. cit., p. 61.
18. Kennedy, op. cit., p. 270.
19. Ibid., pp. 271–4.
20. R. Krooth, *Arms and Empire* (Santa Barbara, CA: Harvest, 1980).
21. Kennedy, op. cit., p. 400.
22. Ibid., p. 266.
23. Ibid.
24. Ryoshin Minami, *The Economic Development of Japan* (London: Macmillan, 1986), pp. 47–8.
25. Kennedy, op. cit., pp. 386–8.
26. Reynolds, op. cit., pp. 110–28.
27. David Reynolds, *The Creation of the Anglo-American Alliance, 1937–1941* (London: Europa Publications, 1981), p. 22.
28. Ibid., p. 98.
29. E. Varga and L. Mendelsohn, *New Data for Lenin's 'Imperialism': The Highest Stage of Capitalism* (London: Lawrence & Wishart, n.d.).
30. Prais, *The Evolution of Giant Firms in Britain* (Cambridge: Press Syndicate of the University of Cambridge, 1981).

Special Interests and Political Parties I

31. Quoted by L. Frankel, *Capitalist Society and Modern Sociology* (London: Lawrence & Wishart, 1970).
32. Noreen Branson and Margot Heinemann, *Britain in the Nineteen Thirties* (St Albans: Panther Books, 1973), pp. 171–2.
33. G.D.H. Cole and M.I. Cole, *The Condition of Britain* (London: Gollancz, 1937).
34. Cited by Sir Percy Alden, *Aspects of a Changing Social Structure* (London: Allen & Unwin, 1937).
35. R. Titmuss, *Poverty and Population* (London: Macmillan, 1938).
36. Michael Wilcox, *The CBI Predecessor Archive* (University of Warwick, 1984), p. 13.
37. Stephen Blank, *Industry and Government in Britain: The Federation of British Industries in Politics, 1945–65* (Farnborough: D.C. Heath, 1977).
38. Robert A. Brady, *Business as a System of Power* (New York: Columbia University Press, 1943).
39. Blank, op. cit., p. 14.
40. 'The FBI: What it is and what it does', MSS 200/F/4/40/3, 1925, FBI Archives, Modern Records Centre, Warwick University.
41. Ibid., p. 2.
42. Brady, op. cit.
43. S.E. Finer, 'The Federation of British Industries', in *Political Studies*, Vol. 4 (1956), p. 70.
44. Ibid.
45. Minutes, Grand Council (GC), 13 Oct. 1937, MSS 200/F/1/1/4, p. 27.
46. Minutes, Executive Committee (EC), 8 Nov. 1939, MSS 200/F/1/1/17, p. 48.
47. Minutes, EC, 8 Sept. 1943, MSS 200/F/1/1/18, p. 20.
48. Minutes, GC, 10 March 1943, MSS 200/F/1/1/188, p. 6.
49. Minutes, EC, 13 Aug. 1941, MSS 200/F/1/1/17, pp. 130–1.
50. Minutes, GC, 15 Nov. 1944, MSS 200/F/1/1/188, p. 72.
51. Minutes, GC, 15 April 1942, MSS 200/F/1/1/4, p. 172.
52. *Reconstruction Report by the Federation of British Industries* (hereafter *Reconstruction*), May 1942, MSS 200/F/4/57/2.
53. 'Report on an informal discussion between Sir Kenneth Lee and Members of the FBI Committee to consider American views on reconstruction', 8 Oct. 1942, MSS/F3/S1/23/35. Lee was the representative of the Industrial and Export Council of the British Board of Trade in the United States.
54. Minutes, GC, 12 Jan. 1938, MSS 200/F/1/1/4, pp. 35–6.
55. Minutes, GC, 15 April 1942, MSS 200/F/1/1/4, p. 174.
56. Minutes, GC, 8 Oct. 1941, MSS 200/F/1/1/4, p. 155.
57. Minutes, EC, 12 Sept. 1941, MSS 200/F/1/1/17, p. 141.
58. Minutes, EC, 10 June 1942, MSS 200/F/1/1/17, p. 167.
59. Minutes, GC, 15 April 1942, MSS/F/1/1/4, p. 173.
60. *Reconstruction* p. 7.
61. Minutes, GC, 9 Feb. 1944, MSS 200/F/1/1/188, p. 35.
62. Minutes, EC, 13 Dec. 1944, MSS 200/F/1/1/18, p. 60.
63. *Reconstruction*, pp. 3, 6.
64. 'Cooperation or Chaos? Anglo-American Relations', 1 June 1945, MSS 200/F/4/60/1, pp. 4–11.

65. Minutes, GC, 8 Oct. 1941, MSS 200/F/1/1/4.
66. Minutes, EC, 12 Sept. 1941, MSS 200/F/1/1/17. Bremner was a leader of the Engineering Employers' Federation.
67. Minutes, Empire Executive Committee (EEC), 16 Feb. 1944, MSS 200/F/3/DD1/61.
68. Minutes, EEC, 16 Oct. 1944, MSS 200/F/3/DD1/61.
69. *Reconstruction*, pp. 7–9.
70. Douglas Walker Papers, 8 Oct. 1942, MSS 200/F/3/S1/23/35.
71. Minutes, GC, 9 Feb. 1944, MSS 200/F/1/1/188.
72. Minutes, Monetary Policy Panel (MPP), 14 Sept. 1944, MSS 200/F/1/1/156.
73. Minutes, GC, 13 June 1945, MSS 200/F/1/1/188.
74. Ibid.
75. *Reconstruction*, p. 3.
76. Minutes, GC, 15 Nov. 1944, MSS 200/F/1/1/188.
77. Memorandum, 'Crisis in Retrospect: Industry and Foreign Policy' contained in a letter from Lee to Locock, 1 Nov. 1938, MSS 200/F/3/S1/23/18, p. 10.
78. *Reconstruction*.
79. 8 Oct. 1942, MSS/F/3/23/35.
80. Minutes, EC, 9 Dec. 1942, MSS 200/F/1/1/17.
81. Minutes, GC, 9 Feb. 1944, MSS 200/F/1/1/188.
82. Minutes, GC, 15 April 1942, MS 200/F/1/1/4, p. 174.
83. Minutes, GC, 9 Feb. 1944, MS 200/F/1/1/188, p. 35.
84. Finer, op. cit., p. 70.
85. W.S. Churchill, *The Second World War: Vol. 3, The Grand Alliance* (London: Cassell, 1950), pp. 539–40.
86. J.J. Sbrega, 'The Anti-colonial Policies of Franklin D. Roosevelt: A Reappraisal', in *Political Science Quarterly*, Vol. 101, No. 1 (1986), p. 84.
87. Foster Rhea Dulles and Gerald E. Ridinger, 'The Anti-colonial policies of Franklin Delano Roosevelt', *Political Science Quarterly* (March 1955).
88. William Roger Louis, 'American Anti-colonialism and the Dissolution of the British Empire', in *International Affairs*, Vol. 61, No. 3 (1985).
89. W.R. Louis, *Imperialism at Bay: The United States and the Decolonization of the British Empire, 1941–1945* (New York: Oxford University Press, 1978), p. 402.
90. C. Fraser, 'Understanding American Policy Towards the Decolonization of European Empires, 1945–1964', *Diplomacy and Statecraft*, Vol. 3, No. 1 (March 1992), p. 107 and notes 9 and 26, pp. 121 and 123.
91. Arthur M. Schlesinger, Jr, 'Franklin D. Roosevelt's Internationalism', in Cornelis A. van Minnen and John F. Sears, (eds), *FDR and his Contemporaries: Foreign Perceptions of an American President* (London: Macmillan, 1992).
92. Louis, op. cit., p. 449.
93. Gabriel Kolko, *The Politics of War: The World and United States Foreign Policy, 1943–45* (New York: Random House, 1968), p. 313.
94. Commonwealth and Empire Industries Association, *History and Constitution* in MSS 221/4/3/1, Modern Records Centre, Warwick University.
95. Carl Kreider, *The Anglo-American Trade Agreement* (Princeton: Princeton University Press, 1943), pp. 37–8.
96. Minutes, Parliamentary Committee (PC), 8 June 1937, 21 July 1938 and

27 Feb. 1935, all in MSS 221/1/1/2.
97. Minutes, Council of EIA, 21 March 1939, MSS 221/1/1/2, p. 2.
98. EIA *Monthly Bulletin*, No. 4 (April 1941), MSS 221/4/2/1.
99. L.S. Pressnell, *External Economic Policy since the War*, Vol. 11 (London: HMSO, 1986), pp. 141–2.
100. Letter, Amery to Norman, 17 Jan. 1942; Norman to Amery, 27 Jan. 1942, OV31/35, location no. 873/1, Bank of England Archives, Threadneedle Street, London.
101. Memorandum, 'Anglo-American Relations', 10 Dec. 1941, OV31, location no., 873/1, Bank of England Archives.
102. *Monthly Bulletin*, No. 6 (June 1941), MSS 221/4/2/1.
103. *Monthly Bulletin*, No. 18 (June 1942), MSS 221/4/ 2/1.
104. *Monthly Bulletin*. No. 19 (1942), MSS 221/4/2/1.
105. *Monthly Bulletin*. Nos. 10, 20, 24, MSS 221/4/2/1.
106. Minutes, PC, 25 April 1945, MSS 221/1/2/2.
107. Frank Longstreth, 'The City, Industry and the State', in C. Crouch (ed.), *State and Economy in Contemporary Capitalism* (London: Croom Helm, 1979).
108. Ibid., pp. 159–61.
109. Longstreth, op. cit., p. 185.
110. Michael Mann, *States, War and Capitalism* (Oxford: Blackwell, 1988), p. 216.
111. Ibid., p. 218.
112. Geoffrey Ingham, *Capitalism Divided? The City and Industry in British Social Development* (London: Macmillan, 1984), pp. 7–9.
113. Ibid., pp. 12–13.
114. R.S. Sayers, *The Bank of England 1891–1944*, Vol. II (Cambridge: Cambridge University Press, 1976), p. 593.
115. Ibid., p. 629.
116. Sayers, op. cit., p. 596.
117. Sayers, op. cit., pp. 596–7.
118. E6/10, location no. 189/4, Bank of England Archives.
119. Memo, 'Post-War Exchange Control', 25 Sept. 1941, OV 38/1, location no. 1335/3, Bank of England Archives.
120. Dutt, op. cit.
121. Memo, 'Keynes' Amended Plan and the Bank's Proposals', 24 Nov. 1941, OV 8/1, location no. 1335/3, Bank of England Archives.
122. Letter, Catterns to Eady, 9 Feb. 1944, OV 3817, location no. 1337/3, Bank of England Archives.
123. Martin Durham, 'The Right: The Conservative Party and Conservatism', in Leonard Tivey and Anthony Wright (ed), *Party Ideology in Britain* (London and New York: Routledge, 1989), p. 50.
124. J. Ross, *Thatcher and Friends: The Anatomy of the Tory Party* (London: Pluto Press, 1983), p. 2.
125. A. Gamble, 'The Conservative Party', in H.M. Drucker (ed.), *Multi-Party Britain* (London: Macmillan, 1979), pp. 26–7.
126. Quoted by Durham, op. cit., p. 51.

3

Special Interests and Political Parties II

ROYAL INSTITUTE OF INTERNATIONAL AFFAIRS (RIIA)

The vigour with which the Foreign Office has traditionally guarded its foreign policy-making role is well known. The exigencies of total war and the need for total mobilisation in the 1939–45 period, however, meant that even the Foreign Office opened its doors a little to influential and knowledgeable outside individuals, especially to those connected with the Royal Institute of International Affairs (RIIA, known as Chatham House).

This semi-secret group, a by-product of dissension among temporary civil servants at the Paris Peace Conference of 1919, had in the inter-war years established a key position for itself in the study and discussion of foreign affairs. According to Thorne, many foreign governments have considered the group to be a quasi-governmental organisation, so close did it appear to them to be to His Majesty's Government.[1] Conversely, some critics of RIIA have been suspicious of its influence over British policy-making. Eyre Crowe and Charles Hardinge of the Foreign Office, as Dockrill points out, were extremely anxious about that particular possibility.[2] Crowe argued that as

> The avowed object is to establish direct contact between our officials and people whose aim is to influence public opinion ... [it] will be obvious that the same machinery will lend itself, in the very measure in which it is successful, also to the inverse process. Outside opinion will seek opportunities, and may find them, to influence the judgement and attitude of our officials ... there is the other danger that private interests may use the machinery to direct the policy of the Foreign Office into channels specially fertilising those interests.

Of course, the RIIA's 'Cliveden Set' connections only add fuel to the controversy.[3]

For itself, Chatham House proclaimed its objectivity, its scientific, non-ideological and non-political character. Its emphasis on objectivity was part of the Anglo-American trend in social and political circles towards the rational analysis of social and other phenomena, with a view to finding solutions to pressing problems.[4] The American foundations such as Rockefeller and Carnegie, and individuals like Thomas W. Lamont of J.P. Morgan, provided vital funding for the Institute in its international studies programme, of which more will be said later. As Chatham House grew in size and stature, it attracted some of the most influential and authoritative figures in leading academic, political and administrative circles, such as Winston Churchill and Anthony Eden. Inevitably, it came into ever closer relations with the official makers of foreign policy.

It is in the context of such close links with government that some controversial issues arise: did the RIIA influence or gain control of British foreign policy, as Crowe feared? Was Chatham House a quasi-governmental organisation, merely echoing the government line? Was it truly objective, detached and independent, having no institutional policy? It is one of the aims of this study to try to clarify these issues by considering the role played by Chatham House in the development of the Anglo-American alliance during the Second World War. This will shed light on whether the RIIA had any *de facto* institutional policy, or whether it operated as a conduit for official pronouncements.

Origins and aims of Chatham House

The founding of the British Institute of International Affairs (it gained a Royal Charter in 1926) in 1920 is inextricably linked with the names of a small number of men, among whom the most instrumental was Lional Curtis.[5] It was Curtis who set off the train of events at the Paris Peace Conference of 1919 that led to the creation of the BIIA which, initially, had been formed as the British branch of an Anglo-American institute of international affairs.[6] Curtis, a graduate of Alfred Milner's 'Kindergarten', and of the 'Round Table' movement of scholars and imperial administrators, was nicknamed 'the prophet' by his friends and associates[7] because of his image as a visionary and his espousal of new forms of international and imperial co-operation. It was this 'mystical vision'[8] combined with boundless energy and single-mindedness of purpose which probably led Curtis to say of himself that his 'task in life seems to be that of a pipe which collects the spare energies of a lot of people and concentrates them in one stream strong enough to generate electricity.'[9] Although he was a fervent supporter of Empire, believing it to be nothing less than the embodiment of the teachings of Jesus Christ, this did not imply that he was blind to the changes that were occurring within its structure, especially in relation to the growing nationalist feeling in the Dominions.[10] In that sense, Curtis was grappling with the same problem as many other men of his generation – some of whom had also been with Milner in South Africa – such as Phillip Kerr, Geoffrey Dawson and Leopold Amery.[11] The First World War led some of these men to reject the notion of nationhood and nationalism in favour of some greater form of international co-operation or federalism. As Butler states in his biography of Kerr, by 1915 Kerr was already in favour of some form of world state based on the principles of the British Empire. Within this world state, Kerr was 'red hot for a close and perfect understanding between Great Britain and the United States'.[12] Curtis had also become convinced of the importance of the future role of the United States in world affairs, especially in terms of utilising 'American skills and American resources.'[13] In an article in *Round Table* in December 1918, Curtis reiterated that conviction when he wrote: 'The future position of America in the world, not that of Germany, Austria or Turkey, is the great issue which now hangs on the Peace Conference.'[14]

It is in the context of the changing structure of the Empire (Curtis preferred the term 'Commonwealth'), the relative inability of British power after 1918 to defend the 'freedom of the seas', and the relative increase in American power that the creation of Chatham House has to be seen. It was a response to a serious and changing world situation, but with the intention of managing that change. Curtis' indefatigable activity at the Peace Conference struck a chord with those who believed that foreign affairs had been for too long the exclusive concern of a minority.[15] Harold Nicolson, who attended the meeting to found the Institute of International Affairs, wrote of Curtis' 'admirable speech'[16] in favour of 'the scientific study of international affairs' which was, according to Curtis, 'the indispensable basis for statesmanlike action'.[17] The plans for founding the Institute had been discussed with A.J. Balfour, the Secretary of State for Foreign Affairs, which Clement Jones (a co-founder of RIIA) believed had made the task a lot easier.[18] The general plan for the Institute was to function as a forum where 'experts should meet experts'; for example, 'Members of Parliament, businessmen, university professors, writers, historians, journalists and others qualified to speak on international affairs'.[19] In a memorandum he co-wrote with Whitney Shepardson,[20] Curtis argued that the new institute's structure would be determined by clearly defining its aim, which was 'to educate public opinion'.[21]

The ex-Foreign Secretary, Lord Grey, urged the fledgling Institute to beware of 'propaganda' and focus on providing not only facts, but also pointing out the interrelations between facts, and provide guidance as to the respective importance and value of the facts. This, Grey argued, would 'not interfere with policy, but provide materials from which politicians, statesmen and journalists can form sound opinions in regard to policy'.[22] He added that what was really needed was 'an organisation which will provide the material from which those who are most influential and who have the greatest amount of knowledge, comprehension and perspective in foreign affairs can form public opinion'.[23] He urged the press and politicians to use the services of the Institute and thereby 'lay the foundations for sound public opinion'.[24] The Institute would operate at the 'quality' end of the public opinion spectrum, according to Curtis, while the daily press operated at the other. 'Between the two are any number of intermediate agencies such as the weekly, monthly and quarterly reviews', he wrote. Curtis believed that 'Right public opinion was mainly produced by a small number of people in real contact with the facts who had thought out the issues involved'.[25] Such élitist conceptions of public opinion were, of course, developed in Curtis' mind over many years, as Deborah Lavin points out, especially during his period as Beit lecturer at Oxford University in 1912–13. He saw himself as the instructor of the future administrators of the Empire. So skilled was Curtis in personal and group discussion that one of his undergraduates was moved to say of him that

He was not preaching dogmatically. He was just being nice and friendly and trying to get to know what our ideas were. It was all informal. It was the most perfect kind of public relations, of spreading ideas, that I've ever seen, but it was done deliberately . . . He believed the way to spread an idea was to capture the élite and convert them and they . . . would spread the ideas.

Lavin further underlines Curtis' élitism when she observes that he wanted all of his undergraduates to conduct research, the conclusions to which Curtis believed he already knew! In a sense, the future theoretical foundations of Chatham House's mission were also developed during Curtis' time at Oxford, when he suggested that theory and practice were inextricably interlinked, that an Oxford education had to provide an adequate basis for future action. Arguing that Oxford must rigorously teach politics and government, he asked 'How can Oxford properly train men for their work in India, the Sudan, the Crown Colonies and the diplomatic services unless it is studying the facts with which they are to deal, and is drawing on the experience of those who are already dealing with them?'[26]

The qualified and experienced foreign affairs experts that the Institute hoped to attract were to be provided facilities for private meetings, as otherwise frank discussion would be jeopardised. As the BIIA Executive Committee argued in 1920: 'In any body created for the study of such delicate matters by experts there are things which ought to be said but which cannot be printed or even written.'[27] The discussions were, therefore, not only among those considered by the Institute to be 'qualified' to do so, but were also to be aimed at the '"attentive" and "opinion-forming" publics'.[28] In addition, the results of Institute studies and research had to be 'accessible to those whose business it is to form policy . . . Even the proposed year book should not be designed for direct consumption by the public at large.'[29]

This élitist attitude towards public opinion remained throughout the inter-war years. McLaine underlines this attitude when he quotes an RIIA memorandum of 1939 on wartime propaganda (requested by the government), in which the Institute aired its belief that ordinary people did not need to know the whole truth, as their support for the war-effort could be guaranteed by providing a few 'simple facts, anecdotes, descriptions and so forth'. Indeed, Ivison Macadam, the Institute Secretary, suggested the need to 'shepherd public opinion' on occasions.[30] This attitude obviously played a major role in the membership selection policy that the Institute operated. 'Quality' rather than quantity was the principle that guided the Chatham House selection panel. The Institute was not to be a place for the idle rich but for 'those who have some valuable contribution [to make] in the shape of information or thought on international problems', and on that basis a limit of 1,000 members was placed (although this was to be revised upwards later).[31] Four classes of members were to be recruited: officials from the Foreign, India and Colonial Offices and elsewhere; journalists; politicians; and 'special experts', that is, academics, and the like.[32] The proposed membership of Chatham House was, therefore, to be drawn from the active ranks of the élite – the 'doers', activists and the influential, which is symptomatic of the concerns and aspirations of the organisation.

The Chatham House 'line'

Practically all Chatham House publications carry a disclaimer to the effect that the organisation is precluded by the terms of its charter from advocating an instututional policy. This was also meant to be the spirit in which Chatham House study groups sought to operate. Stephen King-Hall of Chatham House expressed this idea to the Conference of Institutions for the Scientific Study of International Relations in 1932, when he spoke about policy-making: 'That is not our job. In our eagerness to push forward, it is not always easy to avoid straying over the shadowy borderline which exists between a discussion directed towards producing an agreed policy and one which has the function of scientifically arranging and analysing the facts so that other people may be in a better position to frame policies.' He added that 'Such an object is not unambitious and, as experience has shown elsewhere, such decisions may lead indirectly to results of first class practical importance'.[33] Elsewhere, King-Hall stated that the Institute was non-party political, being purely interested in 'objective and disinterested research'.[34]

As we have already seen, however, the research of Chatham House was always meant to have a close relationship with the policy-making process, as the Institute's desire to include civil servants and politicians clearly shows. From the statement by King-Hall, it is evident that while Chatham House did not directly make policy, it aimed to conduct the 'pure research' that was an essential basis on which policy should be made. But what does the term 'pure research' mean? Could an organisation like Chatham House really afford to ignore the major international 'problems' of its time and still remain a credible institution? Given the origins and aims of the Institute, the only realistic answer is in the negative. The real question is, how did the Institute come to determine what were the key 'problems' that needed to be researched and debated with an eye to practical applications? In this respect, one can advance towards gaining some understanding if we remember the intensely pro-British Empire convictions of the founders of Chatham House. King-Hall, despite his claims about the Institute's objectivity, believed that it existed to serve 'the whole nation';[35] that the Institute needed money urgently 'for a national and imperial service' which would contribute 'to the unity of the Empire'.[36] Chatham House, therefore, defined problems in relation to the need to defend and preserve the Empire and the 'national interest'. It is becoming increasingly apparent, however, that the Institute's definition of entities such as the 'public' and 'nation' were rather restrictive.

The issue of a Chatham House 'line' or policy may only be determined by an analysis of its various publications, the topics of its meetings, conclusions of its study groups and the stance taken by its leading members. Although Wilfrid Knapp has argued that Chatham House publications were a 'motley collection' with no real guiding thread,[37] he also points out that the Institute tradition was empirical: that is, guided by the practical concerns and requirements of policy-makers.[38] In that respect, the lists of publications provided in the Chatham House annual reports reveal that all of the key issues in international affairs of the 1920s through to the 1940s were covered: books on the problems of the British Empire; international economic crises; collective security and disarmament; the Far East; nationalities; and so on. In addition, hundreds of meetings were held on a far wider number of issues, and the study group system allowed for more detailed analysis, and usually led to the publication of the deliberations.

The tendency towards a Chatham House 'policy' favouring Anglo-American co-operation has already received mention in passing. A brief examination of the deliberations of some of the study groups and general meetings demonstrates this tendency more clearly. For example, the 'Special Group on Anglo-American Relations' of 1928–29, chaired by Phillip Kerr (later, as Lord Lothian, the British ambassador to the USA), believed it to be a 'fundamentally sound conception, that the interests of the United States and Great Britain are so nearly identical'.[39] Kerr's memorandum, which opened the Group's proceedings and set the tone for the ensuing discussion, aimed to outline the differences that divided the two countries 'with the object of seeing what can be done to remove them'.[40] He argued that the United States' policy of 'isolationism' had been based 'not on a question of principle . . . but to avoid responsibility'.[41] He believed that the fact that both countries were manufacturers and exporters of good and capital meant that they were 'therefore in a position to influence the development of the rest of the world to suit their economic requirements if there is intelligent co-operation between Wall Street and the City, Washington and London'.[42] Britain and America, in Kerr's view, had a great deal of common ground. 'They are both against political autocracy of the Napoleonic type, against revolution of the Bolshevik type, against "militarism" and conscription and the diplomacy of threat and force'.[43] There was, consequently, a basis for future and present co-operation, Kerr argued, and the rest of the Group concurred with this belief.

Dozens of meetings were also held in Chatham House on issues concerning the United States, some of which are relevant to this discussion. In most of those meetings, all except two in fact, the speakers favoured Anglo-American co-operation.[44]

In two speeches, in 1932 and 1933, Archibald Rose, a prominent member of the Chatham House Council and a former Foreign Office China expert, pointed out the importance of defending

British interests in the Far East, especially in view of the economic depression.[45] Those interests were predominantly material in nature: imports and exports, shipping, insurance, investment and industrial co-operation.[46] The defence and development of Britain's Far Eastern interests could not, however, be achieved in isolation, Rose argued. He pointed out that the United States also had vital trading interests in the region, and there was a welcome 'new spirit of co-operation between the United States and our own country'.[47] In the discussion that followed, Toynbee added that Japanese militarism threatened the interests of Britain and the Dominions. A firm supporter of Anglo-American co-operation, he was also wary of its dangers 'if Great Britain abdicated in the Pacific, the Dominions would become the United States' Dominions; because the United States had a vital common interest with Canada, Australia and New Zealand, *vis-à-vis* Japan, from which she could not and would not dissociate herself'.[48] Toynbee, therefore, was implying that because the United States had 'vital interests' in the region, US forces would operate there whatever Britain did. Consequently, there was a distinct probability of Anglo-American co-operation in the Far East, which he welcomed.

The views of Kerr (by 1934, Lord Lothian) were stated again at a meeting in which he stressed that Britain had come to an understanding with the Americans in the Pacific: 'It is suicide for us not to – so long as we make it clear to the United States that we will go wherever she goes but that we cannot go alone.'[49] During the discussion, Lothian added that a more active United States 'would solve a good many problems, for the United States was the balancing factor in the world'.[50]

Sir Stafford Cripps, British ambassador to the Soviet Union, reported to Chatham House after a five-month trip to the Far East in May 1940 that the Americans strongly distrusted British Far Eastern policy because of a feared Anglo-Japanese 'deal'. Nevertheless, despite being nervous, the Americans 'were, however, prepared at the moment for parallel action'.[51]

Another official, Frank Ashton-Gwatkin of the Foreign Office and the Chatham House Council, also insisted that the future lay in Anglo-American co-operation. In a paper to the Institute's Economic Group entitled 'The New Order', Ashton-Gwatkin emphasised that if Britain won the war she would be in a position to demand 'the bisection of Germany'[52] and to control the world's shipping, and surplus production. In this situation, he argued, if 'we have the USA beside us and in agreement with our policy, our economic control will be almost world-wide'.[53] He urged the preparation in advance for post-war Anglo-American co-operation 'as the future role of the USA will be of decisive importance'.[54] Clearly, the argument advanced by Ashton-Gwatkin was one which demonstrates the practical nature of Chatham House deliberations.

This was no call for 'pure research' or 'disinterested and detached study'; it was, in a sense, an unofficial communication from officialdom on the main lines along which they believed Britain's post-war position would develop. As the war progressed, of course, the Chatham House framework of perceptions became even more clearly oriented towards Anglo-American co-operation. Ivison Macadam, the Institute's Secretary and Director-General, reported his observations upon a North Atlantic Relations Conference he had attended, which shows once again the immediate nature of the Institute's orientation. He had attended the conference 'to find out what intelligent groups throughout the country [USA] were thinking about post-war problems'.[55] He complained that: 'In our work here at Chatham House on post-war planning we were constantly coming up against the difficulty of not knowing the views of representative American attitudes on the problems we are studying.'[56] Macadam reported that the Americans' attitudes on four key issue areas were very positive: that is, they would take part in post-war reconstruction, help build an international organisation of nations, participate in an international police force, and act as the world's creditors.[57]

Numerous other meetings and study group proceedings could be cited to demonstrate the existence of a powerful pro-Anglo-American co-operation tendency within the Institute[58] which constituted a *de facto* institutional policy. When the leaders of an organisation so clearly favour a line of action, and perceive problems within a specific framework, this cannot but influence them in their selection of research topics and the manner in which they are studied. Chatham House was not, and could not be, detached and 'independent'. On the contrary, it became completely absorbed by the practical problems in British foreign policy and, as the above section tries to show, the Institute's orientation did constitute a *de facto* policy favouring Anglo-American co-operation. Whether the Institute was powerful enough to have influenced official foreign policy, however, will be determined in Chapter 5.

TRADE UNION CONGRESS (TUC)

At first glance, it may seem a little strange that a predominantly manual working-class organisation should be included in an analysis of British foreign policy. The TUC, however, was one of the largest mass membership organisations in Britain, growing spectacularly during the period under consideration. It is as a large organisation, representing the interests and aspirations of important sections of the working class, operating in a theoretically open and fluid political system that the TUC's importance needs to be understood. If we are to understand and draw conclusions about the nature of the British system of power, we need to consider the behaviour of organisations (and the state's response to them) that represented the labour movement. The notion of the 'open society', when applied to politics, implies that in principle the system is an inclusive one – which allows previously excluded groups to enter the political arena and the right to participate in the policy-making process. It is important, therefore, to consider the role of the TUC in this study because, at the very least, we can come to understand more about the British political system and even the adequacy of the TUC as an organisation.

The TUC was founded in 1868 at a congress held amidst trade unionists' fears that a forthcoming report by the Royal Commission on Trade Unions could have devastating anti-union consequences.[59] A paltry 34 delegates representing 100,000 workers discussed issues affecting trade societies, and decided that it would be highly useful to meet annually.[60] The broad aim of the TUC, according to Lovell and Roberts, was to act in 'the general interests of the working classes.'[61] R.M. Martin adds that, 'The TUC has always been concerned with influencing, at some remove, the decisions of national government,[62] in line with working-class interests.

Although initially the union leaders were on the 'radical' wing of the Liberal Party,[63] by the end of the nineteenth century they had become so frustrated with their lack of political clout that they initiated the formation of the Labour Representation Committee, to secure a higher parliamentary profile for British labour.[64] During the period up to the Second World War, the TUC grew massively, and by 1931 it had 210 affiliated trade unions with a total membership of 3.75 million.[65] By 1945, TUC membership exceeded 6.5 million.[66] The men, writes Martin, who would have 'been dazzled by the thought of being appointed a Justice of the Peace' in 1868, were now discussing issues like rearmament and the Spanish Civil War with government ministers. TUC leaders Walter Citrine and Arthur Pugh were even knighted in 1935.

The slide to war also enhanced the governmental role of the TUC; by March 1938, Prime Minister Neville Chamberlain had approached Congress leaders to co-operate in Britain's war preparations. During the eight months of Chamberlain's wartime government, at least ten ministers had trade union representatives on various advisory and consultative bodies.[67] The tremendous wastage of manpower resources that had occurred during the 1930s was brought to an end by the outbreak of total war, which elevated the status of organised labour in a significant way, and the appointment of Ernest Bevin of the TGWU and the TUC's General Council to the Cabinet provided the icing on the cake.[68]

The TUC's main role during the war was to help mobilise the total labour resources of Britain for the war effort. The questions that they were involved with in government, therefore, concerned wages, hours, workers' holidays, food production, transport, manpower, and so on.[69] They were vital questions in terms of modern warfare which is so heavily based on modern industry and its efficient administration. The importance of labour in wartime government, therefore, must not be underestimated.

The TUC's World Outlook

The TUC's world outlook was basically 'social reformist' from its formation. Martin writes that the early trade union leaders represented an aristocracy of labour: 'Their manners and lifestyle were closer to those of the small employer than those of the unskilled labourer; and their unions were designed to protect them as much against competition from the unskilled as against oppression by employers . . . their temper was far from revolutionary.[70]

Lenin was more forthright and condemnatory of this upper stratum of the proletariat which was represented in the trade unions. In Lenin's view, Britain was an imperialist state that had conquered huge areas of the world with important consequences for the British working classes. He argued that 'Imperialism has the tendency to create privileged sections also among the workers and to detach them from the broad masses of the proletariat'. Britain's vast colonial possessions and monopolist position in world markets meant that super profits were earned by British capitalists, a portion of which were used to 'buy off' a section of the working class – the 'labour aristocracy'. Even before Lenin, Frederick Engels had argued along the same lines in a letter to Karl Kautsky, the German Marxist leader: 'You ask me what the English workers think about colonial policy? Well exactly the same as they think about politics in general. There is no workers' party here, there are only conservative and Liberal Radicals, and the workers merrily share the feast of England's monopoly of the colonies and the world market.'[71]

As already stated, the TUC leaders were for many decades allies of the Liberal Party. Their essential objection to the social and political system was that of its refusal to recognise the rightful place in society of skilled labour. It was to redress this grievance that the TUC established, with others, the forerunner committee of the gradualist Labour Party. Despite the reformism of the leadership, however, the occasional voice of radical dissent could be heard in the annual conferences. The 1925 TUC conference, for example, overwhelmingly adopted the following resolution:

> This Trades Union Congress believes that the domination of the non-British peoples by the British Government is a form of capitalist exploitation having for its object the securing for British capitalists (1) of cheap sources of raw materials; (2) the right to exploit cheap and unorganised labour and to use competition of that labour to degrade the workers' standards in Great Britain. It declares its complete opposition to imperial-

ism and resolves (1) to support the workers in all parts of the British Empire in organising trade unions and political parties in order to further their interests and (2) to support the right of all peoples in the British Empire to self-determination, including the right to choose complete separation from the Empire.[72]

The TUC leadership's interpretation of such resolutions and sentiments, however, would have dismayed many of its members had secrecy not prevailed. Walter Citrine, TUC General Secretary (1926–46), collaborated with the Colonial Office in developing 'responsible' trade unions in the colonies. As members of the Colonial Labour Advisory Committee, TUC leaders were considered vital in cultivating reformist labour movements 'that did not threaten British imperial rule'.[73] Coinciding with their own reformist convictions and desire for closer connections with the British state, the TUC eagerly seized any opportunity that came along, including heading off 'disturbances in the [colonial] political and economic structure', as William Ormsby-Gore, the Colonial Secretary in the late 1930s, put it.[74] As part of its colonial effort, Walter Citrine was appointed a member of the Royal Commission on the West Indies 1938–39 where he proceeded to 'look out for a young and reliable [trade union] man . . . [and] give . . . advice on the formation of Trade Unions'. In speaking about trade unions, however, Citrine ensured that he did not introduce 'politics', on the grounds that 'it would hamper the Trade Union movement in these places if too much stress was placed on the political aspects'.[75]

To be sure, Citrine was not unaffected by the appalling social conditions and political injustice he observed in the West Indies. He often wrote of his 'tussles with planters' and other members of the Royal Commission. At one point he condemned the white settler populations of the West Indies and the Colonial Office for lacking vision and for treating the locals as inferior. In one of his final letters from the West Indies to his secretary in London, Citrine concludes that, 'after seeing conditions in the West Indies, I am ashamed to be British. The white people treat the natives like dirt. Naturally this makes me indignant.'[76]

Despite his indignation, however, Citrine never questioned his belief in the imperial mission, or at least the imperial outlook. His conclusion was to try to suggest reforms to alleviate the worst excesses of the colonial order. Such an approach was, of course, a mirror image of Citrine's attitude towards British capitalism as a whole. To Citrine, capitalism was simply too powerful to be swept away by any workers' revolution; the abortive General Strike of 1926 had shown that. Instead, the aim of the unions had to be 'to get better conditions here and now . . . [to] concentrate more upon trying to secure changes in capitalism which will elevate working class standards'.[77] In 1928, Citrine told members of the London School of Economics Sociology Club that capitalism 'was neither tottering nor static', contrary to what militant trade unionists argued. Being in no way duped into believing that capitalism was by any means altruistic, Citrine nevertheless concluded that capitalism was 'not doing so badly all said and done'.[78] By the end of the 1930s, Citrine was in an almost celebratory mood when he praised stores like Marks and Spencer and British Home Stores for supplying goods to workers at reasonable prices. In his autobiography, Citrine wrote that this phenomenon 'helped me to refute the foolish allegations of the communists and their like, who asserted that the standard of life under capitalism must decline'.[79]

Having accepted the inevitability of capitalism, it was only a short step to developing a 'corporatist' outlook with regard to the British state. If there was one lesson that Citrine and his fellow TUC General Council member, Ernest Bevin, learnt from the events of 1926, it was to get and stay close to government. By the end of the 1930s, Bevin confidently announced that the TUC was 'virtually . . . an integral part of the state, and its views and voice upon every subject, international and domestic, heard and heeded'.[80] Citrine noted that 'I had interviews galore with ministers and their top civil servants; I almost wore out the door mats in Whitehall, and I was regarded by the staff in the entrance hall as a regular customer'.[81] If Citrine felt it vital to get close to the power centres in British society, the feeling was mutual: the powers-that-be were also interested in keeping close to organised labour. Hence the controversial knighthood offered to Citrine in 1935, and accepted by him despite considerable pressure to reject it from the labour movement. It was after this knighthood that such honours were condemned by the Labour Party and several trade unions. The National Federation of Building Trade Operatives were told at their conference that knighthoods were 'an attempt . . . to get hold of their [union] leaders and create an aristocracy inside their movement', while the Labour Party resolved that such honours were means 'by which the decaying capitalist system seeks to maintain its prestige and influence over immature minds'.[82] Such criticisms had no observable effect on Citrine, who accepted membership of the Privy Council in 1940 from Prime Minister Winston Churchill. His oath to become a Privy Counsellor read in part: ' I will to my uttermost bear faith and Allegiance unto the King's Majesty.'[83] The *Daily Mail* explained to its readers that Sir Walter Citrine was 'the number one trades union leader and one of the most conscientious public men of today'.[84]

By the Second World War, then, TUC leaders definitely displayed their support for the political institutions of capitalist Britain, and firmly pledged to 'safeguard the free institutions for which we [TUC and the British Employers Confederation] stand'.[85] In October 1940, the TUC leaders pledged to defend 'the foundations of liberty and the democratic way of life' – that the Axis powers threatened to destroy. They felt that Labour had achieved its rightful position 'in the social life and economic organisation of a community of free citizens built upon democratic foundations'.[86] Prime Minister Winston Churchill was, therefore, only echoing Labour's view of itself when he said that it had become 'the Fourth Estate of the realm'.[87]

The TUC always tended to follow the conventional political wisdom in most areas. In the nineteenth century, the TUC accepted the principal tenets of the laissez-faire orthodoxy in economics; by the 1930s and 1940s, the established thinking in most political and intellectual circles expected greater state regulation of the national and international economy, more social welfare, and so on. The TUC also accepted this orthodoxy. On questions of post-war reconstruction, the TUC's policy was to restrict itself largely to domestic matters, as opposed to international issues.[88] Consequently, its views and proposals for post-war foreign policy were rather vague and undeveloped. But, as Citrine's autobiography shows, the TUC did favour Anglo-American co-operation during (and after) the Second

World War. In October 1940, for example, Citrine embarked on a speaking tour of the US at the invitation of its counterpart, the American Federation of Labour (AFL). The semi-official nature of the tour was indicated by the support given to it by Prime Minister Churchill who assured Citrine that both the government and the British Embassy in Washington would give him 'every facility . . . [Churchill] thought it important that America should come into the war at the earliest possible moment'. Once in the US, Citrine's speeches were widely reported in the press and radio. Of his address to the AFL delegates in New Orleans, one publication suggested that Citrine had moved his listeners

> to tears . . . Citrine painted for his audience a picture of the horrors confronting his people, told of the amazing courage and resistance displayed by the British, and pointed to the vital war role of British Labor.

Dismayed that he might have created the impression that Britain was about to collapse, Citrine emphasised the 'no surrender' attitude prevailing there. The semi-official nature of Citrine's purpose in the US was also demonstrated by his meeting with President Roosevelt. Churchill had provided a letter of introduction in which he urged Roosevelt to trust Citrine because he was a Privy Counsellor. 'You can count in every way upon his responsibility and discretion,' Churchill wrote.[89]

TUC and post-war reconstruction

The government (with TUC urging) established the Reconstruction Joint Advisory Council (RJAC) in 1942, which consisted of six representatives from the TUC and three each from the Federation of British Industries and the British Employers Confederation, and various civil servants. This council considered the international aspects of reconstruction, and by analysing the views that the TUC advanced there and elsewhere, some conclusions may be drawn as to the main features of their attitudes to international questions.

In the report of the first RJAC meeting, the chairman, Sir William Jowitt, wrote that reference had been made to the desirability of early agreement with the United States of American on certain fundamental issues, and it was suggested that approaches might be made to American interests both through the management side and the labour side.⁹⁰ It was confirmed that both the FBI and the TUC had already been in touch with their American counterparts regarding post-war co-operation.

The TUC Economic Committee was also concerned with foreign policy and had met with Arthur Greenwood when he was minister for post-war reconstruction, and had been told that 'at the end of the war the USA would be the greatest economic power in the world, and consequently he was hoping and trying to get the co-operation of the USA'.⁹¹ Officialdom, therefore, was keeping in touch with Labour opinion on foreign policy. George Gibson, the TUC Vice Chairman informed a meeting of the Royal Institute of International Affairs of the need for 'international economic planning under an international and supernational authority, exercising many of the powers now vested in sovereign States, whose competition has created the present conditions of universal anarchy'.⁹² He believed that this 'presupposes that the USA will be ready after the war to take a share of the responsibility for the re-establishment of order and law'.⁹³ The basis of post-war peace and prosperity was to be Anglo-American co-operation, he concluded.

At the second RJAC meeting, the TUC agreed with the analysis of the FBI that Britain's post-war international position would be vulnerable unless export markets could be won back and a system of international monetary exchange established.⁹⁴ The basis of such an international order had to be Anglo-American co-operation, it was understood.

In November 1943, the TUC Economic Committee heard the views of Sir Edgar Jones of the World Trade Alliance Association (WTAC) on the need for the regulation of world trade by inter-governmental bodies after the war, in order to prevent glut and restrictionist policies. The committee approved these ideas in principle,⁹⁵ but were silenced by a resolution at the 1944 Conference that 'exposed' Jones as a member of the tin plate cartel, and another member of WTAC, Lord Davidson, as chairman of the Conservative Party under Stanley Baldwin's premiership.⁹⁶ Hugh Dalton, the President of the Board of Trade, further emphasised the precarious post-war position in relation to export markets.⁹⁷ All of these meetings show that the TUC leaders were considering the international environment Britain would face after the war, and were coming to favour a strong Anglo-American accord. The International Federation of Trade Unions, in which the TUC played a leading role, issued its ideas on the post-war international situation in 1944. Among other things, they called for a world security organisation to preserve peace; the removal of the economic and social causes of war; regional alliances; currency stabilisation; and the international supervision of colonies.

The TUC clearly favoured strong Anglo-American co-operation after the war. Citrine, however, was also fully aware of the importance of the USSR, especially after June 1941. At the same time, Citrine was careful to avoid the new relationship with the Soviet Union being beneficial to British communists. His anti-communism ran very deep, and his experience in fighting radicals was long. Citrine even refused to provide the Ministry of Information with a statement endorsing the new Anglo-Soviet unity against Nazi Germany, arguing that 'I honestly believe . . . Russia is not fighting for any principle we cherish'. Given popular pro-Soviet attitudes, however, Citrine switched tactics and began to espouse pro-Soviet views and founded, with Churchill's and Anthony Eden's support, the Anglo-Soviet Trade Union Committee. This did not herald any personal conversion to communism on Citrine's part, but was his manoeuvre to monopolise official workers' links with the Soviet Union in order to 'contain' Soviet influence in the British labour movement and to marginalise or de-legitimise any other (more radical) Anglo-Soviet committees.[98] In addition, the TUC leadership became more popular among the rank and file of the labour movement.

It can be seen, therefore, that the TUC did have views on international post-war questions. The problem, however, is that these views were not developed to any realistically workable degree and, in any case, did not differ from the kinds of views being put forward by numerous other organisations, such as the Labour Party, RIIA and FBI. The TUC seems to have accepted the prevailing ideas on foreign affairs, much as it accepted the conventional economic wisdom of the age.

The evidence available at the Public Record Office shows that the TUC had little or no direct influence over the formation of Britain's post-war international plans. They were not invited to participate in foreign policy debates in any significant way. They had no say over the question of leasing British Caribbean bases to the US in 1941; no say on the Mutual Aid Agreement or Bretton Woods. They were not considered important enough to be consulted on international issues, and they offered no alternative policy to the decision-makers. They listened and agreed with the ideas advanced by Arthur Greenwood, Hugh Dalton and Sir William Jowitt – all government representatives. Towards the end of the hostilities, Anthony Eden and Clement Attlee both explained to Sir Walter Citrine that it would be undesirable even to send a TUC representative to the San Francisco conference.[99] Although this made Citrine extremely angry, because the TUC had been 'squeezed out', it did suggest that the position of organised labour was always precarious. Even the United States government had allowed unions adviser status in their delegation to the UN conference.

POLITICAL PARTIES: THE LABOUR PARTY

The Labour Party was founded in 1900 as a federation of trade union and socialist societies because, as mentioned earlier, organised workers felt increasingly dissatisfied with the parliamentary Liberal Party. In fact, one of the fundamental sources of the party's 'labourism', explained a little more fully below, lies in its trade union origins. The party was originally known as the Labour Representation Committee, and it was created to strive for

> a distinct Labour group in Parliament, who shall have their own whips, and agree upon their policy, which must embrace a readiness to co-operate with any party which for the time being may be engaged in promoting legislation in the direct interest of labour, and be equally ready to associate themselves with any party in opposing measures having an opposite tendency.[100]

This heavy emphasis on a narrow range of 'labour' questions is but one component of the 'labourism' of the party. Another is to 'not question the social system by which wealth was produced', but work to reform the 'system' in order to enhance the position of the working class through constitutional means. The principal basis for this attitude was the belief that capitalists as employers were a productive force and therefore had shared with labour an interest in the wealth production system.[101]

Nevertheless, the more radical sections of the party proved victorious in their campaign to 'revolutionise' its programme in 1918. It was that year's conference which adopted the famous Clause IV of the party's Constitution, declaring it to be one of the fundamental aims of Labour

> To secure for the producers by hand or by brain the full fruits of their industry, and the most equitable distribution thereof that may be possible, upon the basis of the common ownership of the means of production and the best obtainable system of popular administration and control of each industry and service.[102]

The party became fully committed to a socialist society, free from exploitation. As the emerging union leader and Labour Party stalwart Ernest Bevin said, Labour would transform British society; it is 'destined to replace the old order and bring in a new . . . [a] life of liberty and love . . . [to replace] the master-class oppression'.[103] Such radical principles were also applied to international relations, with Labour committed to consigning 'power politics' to the historical scrapheap and developing a new and more just foreign policy for Britain.

Michael R. Gordon has analysed the Labour Party's conception of foreign affairs, and some of the reasons why it rejected so-called traditional foreign policy. Gordon describes traditional foreign policy as having become considered 'natural' by policy-makers,

> a near inviolable law embodying timeless wisdom . . . with its subtle overtones of inevitability. Briefly, the policy reduced to self-regarding promotion of national interests, defence of the far-flung imperial and commercial network, and management of a European balance as a condition of British security – all backed, whenever necessary, by the application of force.[104]

Special Interests and Political Parties II

The British Empire had grown and flourished as a result of traditional foreign policy, and was, therefore, living proof of its correctness, according to the orthodox view. Labour's view, however, was that traditional foreign policy was merely that of 'power politics', of narrow class interests, 'calculated to further, not the well-being of the entire British people ... but rather the selfish interests and privileges of the capitalist ruling classes'.[105] Socialist foreign policy would be quite different, as Clement Attlee, the leader of the party, claimed in 1937:

> There is a deep difference of opinion between the Labour Party and the capitalist parties on foreign as well as on home policy, because the two cannot be separated. The foreign policy of a Government is the reflection of its internal policy ... Particular instances of action which can be approved by Socialists do not affect the proposition that there is no agreement on foreign policy between a Labour Opposition and a capitalist government.[106].

This 'socialistic' foreign policy outlook may be further broken down into four major principles: internationalism; international working-class solidarity; anti-capitalism; and anti-militarism.

Labour rejected notions of nationalism and national sovereignty as they were major contributors to world rivalry that made war inevitable. They believed that Britain should take the lead in the world in developing internationalist institutions that would lead to world co-operation. Labour argued that international co-operation would lead to some form of socialist world community. Labour particularly supported the League of Nations because of such convictions, hoping that a lead from Britain would assist in the growth of internationalism. The party's belief in international working-class solidarity was demonstrated by the rank-and-file support and sympathy for the Soviet Union; for example, Labour endorsed the Triple Alliance of trade unions' demand in April 1919 for a withdrawal of British troops from Russia. Ernest Bevin played a key role in establishing the joint TUC–Labour Party 'Council of Action' favouring self-determination in Russia. Bevin, as the council's spokesman, informed Lloyd George, the Prime Minister, that 'We feel we cannot admit the right, in the event of a revolution in a country, of every other nation using . . . their armed forces to crush out or stem a change that is being made'.[107]

Labour's anti-capitalism at home was also reflected in its foreign policy: capitalism's foreign policy was imperialistic, and imperialism was the cause of war. The Labour Party wanted to democratise the foreign policy process, to abolish secret diplomacy, and to give power to Parliament to decide on the ratification or otherwise of international treaties. The fourth element of Labour's foreign policy, 'anti-militarism', rejected as immoral the use of force as an instrument of foreign policy. Together, these four principles, Gordon argues, constituted the 'party orthodoxy . . . Different sections, different spokesmen and leaders, might emphasise this facet or that facet . . . But always the differences between the two sides turned on tactical matters, not fundamentals.'[108]

These principles of socialist foreign policy were stated on many occasions in official party pamphlets and memoranda throughout the Second World War. For example, the Secretary of the Party, J.S. Middleton, sent a memo to members of the National Executive Committee in January 1940, stating the necessity for a co-operative world commonwealth. He also declared that in order 'to have peace we must subordinate national sovereignty to world institutions and obligations'.[109]

In 1939, the Advisory Committee on International Questions had noted that the Labour Party opposed the use of force in international relations. The problems of the world would not be solved through aggressive nationalism, it was argued, but in a new international economic order based on freer trade and equality of access to raw materials.[110]

The close relationship between Labour's anti-nationalism and its anti-capitalism was shown in a 1942 paper by the International Relationships Sub-Committee (Economic Section), which stressed the need to abolish capitalism at home, and to control international capitalism through international economic agreements and planning. The nation-state would and should yield some of its authority and economic sovereignty to international institutions.[111]

It would seem clear, therefore, that the Labour Party did, in theory, put forward a totally different foreign policy from the conservative traditionalists. The practice, however, as pointed out by so many observers, is shown to have been radically different. After having joined the wartime government in spring 1940, it seems that the Labour leaders – including Attlee, Bevin and Greenwood – all took up the theory and practice of traditional foreign policy. The general lack of socialistic thinking behind the views of the Labour War Cabinet members on post-war policy is amply demonstrated by the papers left behind by Hugh Dalton. Dalton was Minister of Economic Warfare for two years and then President of the Board of Trade in the period up to 1945. His diaries include entries on discussions within the party and the government and, taken together, do give a good idea of the political developments at the time. Dalton fully supported Anglo-American post-war co-operation, for example, for the maintenance of full employment and the financing of development schemes.[112]

Dalton along with his Labour Cabinet colleagues, supported the plan put forward by the Treasury for an International Commercial Union to be headed by the United Kingdom and the USA.[113] In an earlier discussion, Ernest Bevin, the Minister of Labour and National Service, had denounced the plan as 'an Anglo-American bankers' conspiracy against the working classes' that would cause unemployment. After an explanation, identical to the one given by the Treasury from Keynes and Hopkins, Bevin deferred.[114] The traditionalistic 'realism' of Dalton was emphasised in a Cabinet discussion on commercial policy in 1943, when he agreed with Churchill's argument that the most important task facing Britain was for her to sell as much abroad as possible for the greatest profit, and to buy her food and raw materials as cheaply as possible.[115] Again, in 1943, Dalton steered through the Cabinet the main papers for the forthcoming Anglo-American discussions in Washington, dealing with questions like the Clearing Union (which later became the International Monetary Fund), Buffer Stocks, International Investment (the future World Bank), and post-war commercial policy (dealing with the policy debate concerning Imperial Preference and Multilateralism).[116]

Dalton believed that Britain's export markets had to be vigorously defended, especially against encroachment by the Americans. He agreed with the Lord President's Committee that 'something must be done',[117] while he gave the Federation of British Industries a categorical assurance 'that there would be an improvement soon, as regards the limitations imposed on our exports by our Lend-Lease white paper'.[118]

In the clash that occurred in Cabinet between those who wanted to retain Imperial Preference and those favouring abolition, Dalton joined the latter, the majority side. He wrote in his diary that 'the plain truth is that the Dominions now no longer care much about Imperial Preference, and that here is a wonderful opportunity to sell it in return for a good multilateral arrangement. The alternative is gradually to have it whittled away with no quid pro quo.'[119] The Bank of England and Lord Beaverbrook staunchly opposed the IMF et cetera, but Dalton believed that they 'were totally unconscious of post-war realities, and in particular of our need to get very substantial assistance from the US during the transitional period'.[120]

As President of the Board of Trade, Dalton proposed that British–American unity was essential. In a paper entitled 'Post-War Commercial Policy. A Proposal for an International Clearing Union' in 1942, he stressed the need for Anglo-American co-operation in establishing 'constructive economic arrangements and new international institutions or practices which Ango-American influence could be used to encourage in the post-war world'.[121] Dalton outlined Britain's post-war commercial difficulties in a manner identical to that of the Treasury and other departments, that is, that Britain survived by importing essential foods and raw materials which were paid for by export revenues. 'As a community, we have a powerful interest in the general removal of restrictions in international commerce.'[122] Britain must trade multilaterally and avoid undue discrimination, as otherwise the Anglo-American relationship would be endangered.

The commercial and political negotiability of Imperial Preference was made abundantly clear in Dalton's statement of January 1943 in a rejoinder to Sir Hubert Henderson. Dalton pointed out that Imperial Preference had to be modified for the sake of imperial unity – Canada would go into the American orbit if there were no Anglo-American agreement; and, secondly, because of Britain's commitments under Article 7 of the Mutual Aid Agreement of 1942 to scrap Imperial Preference 'for the sake of Anglo-American political relations'.[123]

Another indication of the traditionalism of the Labour leaders as shown in the Dalton Papers are the discussion papers written by Evan Durbin, Attlee's personal assistant. Durbin wrote the papers for Attlee but sent them to Dalton for his comments. The first paper discussed three possible options for post-war foreign policy: imperial isolation; a system of alliances; and membership of a peace-loving international organisation like the United Nations. The imperial option was rejected because of the general disunity of the Empire, that is, Eire was independent, and Australia had become closer to the US. An alliance with the Americans, however,

> would enable us to keep the peace of the Pacific and of the Atlantic . . . an Anglo-American programme of economic co-operation could do an immense amount to stabilise the prosperity of the world and develop its backward areas. We share certain fundamental ideas and traditions with the Americans that would ensure a beneficent use of the extraordinary power, that acting together, we should jointly come to possess.

The UN option required the use of force, a high level of British armaments, and possibly some form of regional alliances too. Durbin suggested a strong policy, which should be supported by all political parties – a return to the nineteenth-century doctrine, 'that foreign policy must be above Party differences although within the control of Parliament'.[124]

In the second paper, Durbin pointed out that the USA would be a 'reasonable' power, that is non-isolationist, after the war. 'The cornerstone of our foreign policy must therefore remain a political alliance with the United States. For that we should be prepared . . . to subordinate our temporary and sectional commercial interests to larger agreements, and to associate American Administrations with the solutions of our colonial problems.'[125]

The conversion of even left-winger Sir Stafford Cripps seems to have been fairly rapid. While serving as the British ambassador to the Soviet Union, he had written an analytical telegram urging the Foreign Office to work out a policy of alliance with the US for the post-war period.[126] The approach of Cripps's analysis suggests that he accepted the situation and its underlying rules, and was planning the best means for Britain to secure her national interests. The socialist approach, in theory, stressed the need to alter the rules and principles involved in international affairs. Cripps's approach was that of the classical traditionalist, and in no way different from that of the established foreign policy-makers.[127]

Ernest Bevin is also said to have been transformed into a 'power politics' practitioner by the experience of wartime government. Bevin upheld the Labour view that there would have to be a modification of the concept of national sovereignty in the post-war world, and that order would have to be built through some form of world organisation.[128] He also felt, according to Bullock, that the traditional approach to foreign policy was flawed – it was 'limited to national security, the protection of overseas investments and the increase of facilities of trade, all matters for decision with men at the top of politics, finance and business'.[129] Despite this, Bevin defended every major decision made by the Churchill government in foreign affairs, including the decision to intervene in Greece in 1944. In many ways, Bevin's socialism translated into a paternalistic imperialism with regard to the wider world. Beginning with his fondness for the music hall – with all its tales and songs of heroic Britons and exotic 'natives' as John MacKenzie shows in his excellent *Propaganda and Empire*[130] – Bevin retained his effective love of Empire throughout his trade union and political career. Even when denying such sentiments, he seemed only to reiterate the opposite. As a member of the governmental Advisory Committee on Colonial Development in 1929–30, Bevin informed the TUC General Council that 'I am no imperialist, but an Empire exists [with a] tremendous fund of raw materials', which are in need of development 'for the advancement of humanity as a whole'.[131] By 1938, Bevin had begun to urge all the great powers to enter a British Imperial system, and give 'everyone' a chance to access colonial resources.[132] Peter Weiler argues convincingly that once Bevin became Foreign Secretary he firmly believed that the British Empire was 'the greatest collection of free nations'.[133] Bevin was not transformed from socialist to 'realist' by experience of government alone; such experience merely nurtured and developed attitudes that already existed. After all, it was Bevin's scathing anti-pacifism and 'realism' in the 1930s that had convinced the Labour Party to support 'collective security' and rearmament. Of course, the rhetoric of Labour leaders tended to utilise radical slogans and phrases, such as Dalton's demand for Labour to recognise that Britain was a 'Great Power' and should use such power for mankind's betterment. Once in power, however, Labour leaders tended to remember only the first half of such radical declarations.

By 1945, Bevin had informed the Labour Party Conference of the 'facts' that any Labour government would have to deal with in world affairs: Britain 'is at the centre of a great Empire and Commonwealth of Nations, which touches all parts of the world ... I would ask the conference to bear this in mind. Revolutions do not change geography, and revolutions do not change geographical need.'[134] At the same conference, Bevin explained that the welfare and livelihood of the British worker was tied to a policy of improving the lot of the peasants of the poor countries. To that end the Labour leaders supported the talks at Bretton Woods, aimed at stabilising and enhancing world trade and prosperity, an approach not dissimilar to that of the Federation of British Industries.

While Bevin had become immersed in the imperialist culture of the music hall, Clement Attlee had been socialised into it at one of Britain's foremost public schools, Haileybury. Attlee writes in *As it Happened* that, during the Boer War, Haileybury 'as a whole was strongly Imperialist. The influence of Rudyard Kipling was very strong, especially as the school had a great tradition of service in the army and the Indian Civil Service.' Indeed, so imperialistic was Attlee that he suffered corporal punishment after attending 'a patriotic [pro-Boer War] demonstration' against the wishes of the headmaster.[135] At University College, Oxford, Attlee engaged in only one debate at the Union – in favour of 'Protectionism' against 'Free Trade'. Even after Oxford, Attlee continued to believe in 'the legend of the White Man's Burden and all the rest of the common place of imperialist idealism'.[136] Such 'imperialist idealism' remained with Attlee upon becoming Prime Minister in 1945, when retaining certain vestiges of the Empire became conceived of as a basis for some level of independence from the more powerful United States.[137] By that time, however, Attlee had sharpened his 'power politics' with wartime experience of government, when he was seen by men such as Harold Laski and R.H. Tawney as Winston Churchill's shadow.[138]

Kenneth Harris cites numerous examples of Attlee's foreign policy contributions in Cabinet deliberations, which read as fine examples of *realpolitik*. For example, in July 1943, Attlee wrote a memorandum on the problems of post-war Europe – with reference to Germany and to Russian expansionism. The only way to prevent such expansionism, Attlee argued, was for Britain to involve herself in Europe as she never had before.

> If she tried to shoulder the burden on her own, [however] she would have no strength to deploy in the rest of the world and the Americans would become the power in areas now part or dependents of the British Empire . . . The solution . . . was to persuade the Americans to take over a large share of the burden of Europe: then Europe could be made secure against Russian domination, and Britain could still preserve her Empire.[139]

It is hardly surprising, then, that the US Secretary of State, James Byrnes, could write of Attlee and Bevin that when they replaced Churchill and Eden at the 'Big Three' conferences, 'Britain's stand on the issues . . . was not altered in the slightest, so far as we could discern'.[140]

When the various views and ideas put forward by the Labour leaders are compared to those of the traditionalists, it can be seen that there was no substantial disagreement at all. In fact, the views were almost identical. The Labour leaders fully accepted the state's view as to British national interests – that is, the protection of trade routes, investments, raw material and markets. From the documents available at the Public Record Office, it has been impossible to distinguish an individual's party political affiliation (apart, perhaps, from Bevin's). The policies that the Labour leaders proposed were contributions to a general discussion between men who shared assumptions about national interests. The only issue was: how are national interests to be realised? And even on that question there was little or no disagreement.

Analysis of the archive material of the Labour Party also reveals that there occurred a gradual evolution in the thinking on and approach to foreign policy within the leadership. It is interesting to note, however, that Bevin had already urged an Anglo-American alliance at the party conference in 1939 as being the most effective form of collective security, despite its limiting effects on British sovereignty.[141]

Indeed, this line of thinking – alliance with the US and acceptance of a decline in British sovereignty – became the Labour government's foreign policy after the war. As Bevin stated in a 1947 Foreign Office paper, 'Effect of Our External Position on our Foreign Policy':

> Our financial weakness has necessarily increased the need to co-ordinate our foreign policy with that of the only country which is able effectively to wield extensive economic influence – namely, the United States . . . If the corollary of the United States intervention and strength is that we find ourselves at times irked at the role of junior partner, we must recognise, nevertheless, that the partnership is worth the price . . . Only if we were to find ourselves alone with our political objectives widely divergent from those of the United States would our financial nakedness be fully apparent to the world.[142]

Indeed, so important was the American connection that Bevin was prepared to reduce British living standards in order to maintain a world role. Speaking to the American Legion in September 1947, Bevin declared, 'My dear Americans, we may be short of dollars, but we are not short of will . . . We won't let you down.'[143]

Bevin, Attlee and Dalton were also involved in the work, at various times, of the National Executive Committee and its organs, and their influence generally worked in the direction of making Labour's foreign policy a 'realistic' one. That is, they acted as channels for the growth of support for official foreign policy within the policy-initiating levels of the party.[144]

Arthur Greenwood, Minister without Portfolio and Deputy Leader of the Labour Party, told the 1941 Conference that the post-war period would see a continuation of the wartime Anglo-American alliance, encompassing the colonies and Dominions.[145] A major part of Greenwood's work in the Government was to initiate and co-ordinate studies into the probable situation facing Britain after the war, and possible options that Britain could pursue.[146] The role of the USA in the post-war world was considered vital by

Greenwood's official committee, as he had, indeed, also informed the TUC.

In June, 1941, however, many sections of the party supported post-war Anglo-American co-operation. Konni Zilliacus of the left-wing 'Tribune' faction spoke in favour of Greenwood's motion, arguing that

> The enormous importance of the United States is a thing to which I think sufficient attention has not yet been directed. The United States of the New Deal is not only the friend of this country; it is more specifically the friend of the causes for which this Movement stands . . . I therefore hope that . . . the [National] Executive . . . will . . . establish the closest possible connections with Democracy in the United States.[147]

The only major pronouncement made by the leaders about the post-war position was by Dalton in 1943, which was recommended to, and passed by, the party conference in 1944. It provided only a very general sketch of the post-war problems of international trade, the Commonwealth, and Big Power co-operation. It stressed the need for peace-preserving machinery, but in a form vague enough to appeal to most people. It differed in no essential way from the kind of plan envisaged by the Cabinet and the Foreign Office.[148] Thus, it contained nominal references to Anglo-Soviet co-operation too, as most Labour and TUC pronouncements did after June 1941. This had the effect of promoting a substantial rise in pro-Soviet feeling in Britain generally and in the Labour rank-and-file in particular. As Francis Williams observed, when Bevin became Foreign Secretary, Labour loyalists thought that it would 'assure good relations with Russia'. The fact was, however, that 'the extent of British influence depended upon her strength and ability as a World power' (and the plan for that did not include co-operation with the Soviet Union).[149] The 'power political' nature of the Labour leaders' thinking was not conveyed to the rank-and-file during the war. On the contrary, as David Howell argues, 'The Party's official pronouncements continued to suggest through their rhetoric that its leaders were committed to a coherent socialist approach to international problems.'[150] Certainly, Clement Attlee never confided (understandably) to the Labour movement as he did to Churchill that he supported continuity in foreign policy along 'the main lines which we have discussed together so often'.[151] The issue of Labour's influence over foreign policy and the reasons for the 'dramatic' failure of 'socialist' ideas will be examined later in this study.

THE COMMUNIST PARTY OF GREAT BRITAIN (CPGB)

The Communist Party was a key political force in British politics during the Second World War. Although always relatively small in membership, its influence in the nation was significant enough to bring it official 'attention'. The party also had a well-organised press – with daily and monthly newspapers and periodicals – to carry its message far and wide. Finally, the party gave a great deal of thought to international affairs, being firmly committed to one policy in particular – Anglo-Soviet co-operation. It is for such reasons that the activities and ideas of the CPGB are analysed below. There were also, of course, thousands of individual communists inside the Labour Party, greatly extending its influence.

The Communist Party was formed in 1921 after the merging of the British Socialist Party, the Socialist Labour Party and Sylvia Pankhurst's communist group.[152] Although the party is considered here as a political party, it could as easily be viewed as a special interest group. It was relatively small and it did act as a 'ginger' group within the Labour Party and the TUC, much as other groups also did at the time. It was distinguished from special interest groups, of course, by its broad range of policy interest and, most importantly, by its desire to overthrow the 'capitalist state' and to establish the 'dictatorship of the proletariat'.[153]

From the communist perspective, the British state was an instrument of class power – specifically of finance capitalist power. As the party's programme argued in 1935, 'Britain to-day is in the hands of millionaires – owners of the biggest trusts, the biggest banks, the biggest steamship companies ... [T]hese monopoly capitalists not only own or control the chief means whereby we work and live but, in fact, control the whole governing machine. They pull the strings.'[154] Despite being a tiny minority of the population, the party argued, the capitalist class was able to control the key institutions in Britain to advance their own selfish class interests. Socially strengthened by an élite education at Eton, Harrow and other top public schools, at 'Oxbridge' and thereafter in their exclusive West End clubs, the capitalist class ensured their self-perpetuation. The masses were largely 'controlled' or manipulated by the 'millionaires' press' – owned by the Astors (bankers and financiers, owners of *The Times* and *Sunday Observer*); the Berry Brothers (industrialists, owners of the *Daily Telegraph, Sunday Times, Daily Sketch, Western Mail*); the Rothermeres (*Daily Mail, Evening News, Sunday Dispatch*); Beaverbrook (*Daily Express, Sunday Express, Evening Standard*); and the Cadbury family (*News Chronicle, Star*).[155] In the communist view, such a powerful class had to be violently overthrown, it would 'never allow itself to be gradually expropriated by successive Acts of Parliament'.[156]

If capitalism meant domination of the masses at home, it also meant ruthless exploitation, rivalry and colonialism abroad. The British Empire was seen not as part of a 'civilising mission', but as attempts to advance and defend imperialist interests around the globe. The party stood in complete opposition to imperialism which, it argued, made war inevitable as the inter-imperialist competition for colonies, raw materials and markets intensified. Condemning all of the mainstream political parties as 'in favour of the tyrannical rule of British imperialism', the communists pledged 'to work for the complete freedom of these [colonial] masses from foreign domination and from all forms of capitalist exploitation'.[157]

The Second World War was declared (shortly after its outbreak at least), an 'imperialist war' by the CPGB. According to Ben Francis, the industrial correspondent of the communist *Daily Worker*, the war was 'between two imperialist powers each trying to get domination over the other for expansion and spheres of influence'. It had nothing to do with anti-fascism, he claimed, because the war was 'being used by the National Government and by the French Government itself to introduce repressive measures and to take away the democracy of the industrial workers'.[158] The communists, therefore, following the line of Lenin during the First World War, called for 'a mighty alliance of opposition to the war government and all warmongers'.[159]

For the post-war world, the CPGB urged Britain not only to

maintain the victorious unity between the (after June 1941) anti-fascist coalition, but also to retain and strengthen its alliance with the Soviet Union. As socialism was a force for peace and freedom, Anglo-Soviet co-operation would strengthen the forces against aggression and militarism, help reconstruct trade in Europe, and free the colonies.[160] Pro-Soviet feeling in Britain had increased dramatically during the course of the war, and the communists were not alone in urging Anglo-Soviet co-operation. Even the anti-CPGB 'Tribune' group argued that one key reason for Churchill's defeat in the 1945 general election was the fact that he represented 'the wrong influences in society to establish relations of permanent friendship with the Soviet Union. And the people of Britain believe that friendship with the Soviet Union is the keystone of world peace.'[161] The proposed Anglo-Soviet alliance, however, was to be within a new world organisation, not a bilateral or other arrangement to exclude the United States. The communists urged the building of an effective United Nations organisation, the destruction of German and Japanese fascism, and international economic co-operation.[162]

Communist Party attitudes to the United States were consistent; the US was generally condemned as imperialist and self-seeking. As early as October 1940, the communist *Labour Monthly* declared that the gradual and growing US involvement in the war was for purposes of expansion into the Empire. The communists noted the increasing levels of British dependence on the US, and criticised the emerging 'Anglo-American bloc' as imperialist.[163] Rajani Palme Dutt, editor of *Labour Monthly*, further warned in February 1941 of the negative impact of 'world domination' by 'Anglo-American reaction . . . for workers of the world'.[164] He later added that the nascent Anglo-American bloc would seek to impose 'the social and political conditions which they regard as representative of civilisation and order' on the rest of mankind.[165] Experience of wartime unity, however, did have an effect on communist attitudes to the United States. By 1944, Harry Pollitt even asked, 'Who really believes the scare stories of the coming domination of the rest of Europe by Anglo-American imperialism?' He also praised 'the democratic and progressive forces [in America, which were] working to ensure the full participation of their country and all its great resources in every field of international co-operation'. Even then, however, Pollitt warned Britons not to 'be blind to the campaign' to wreck the United Nations: 'There are those', he argued, 'who still oppose firm and lasting co-operation between Britain and America, and the Soviet Union, and put forward instead the aim of exclusive Anglo-American co-operation in isolation from the rest of the world. Such a policy', he suggested with some foresight, 'would lead to a most dangerous division, repeating the evils of the situation which preceded the present war and giving an easy opportunity for the revival of German reaction and military power.'[166] Any alliance between Britain and the United States, he argued, would be a 'deal' between capitalist competitors, whose old rivalries were reasserting themselves as military hostilities ceased. The immediate cessation of American Lend-Lease aid to Britain was a blow struck against a trade rival in order that the US 'may be in a better position to secure . . . [its] own domination in world markets and sweep aside the political restrictions imposed . . . by British imperialism'.[167]

These were the political ideas and attitudes which the CPGB offered to the British people during the war, and which did, in fact, command a fair amount of popular support. One indicator of the growth of communist support was the increasing membership of the party: from around 16,000 in 1938, the CPGB grew to 56,000 by 1942.[168] The party's critique of the war as imperialist found broad sympathy, especially among members of the Labour Party, a quarter of whom, after June 1941, were communists.[169] One Labour Party member declared that while he was prepared to fight Hitlerism, he could not 'help feeling that . . . I shall be fighting a defensive battle for capitalism'.[170] Further evidence of the widespread belief in the capitalist nature of the war is provided by a reporter for the 'Mass-Observation' project. In a report on 'Conscripts' Attitudes to War Politics', the *Observer* suggests of a group of Royal Air Force personnel that while they support democracy they 'know damn well that all we are fighting for is British capital. Patriotism, the Flag and the Empire are a lot of tripe – only they don't say tripe.'[171]

The communists tried to harness and mobilise anti-war sentiment during this period by organising meetings, rallies and conferences. The first of two major conferences occurred in February 1940, under the auspices of *Labour Monthly*. The conferences attracted, according to the organisers, a broad range of delegates from trade and Labour councils, trade unions, local Labour parties, co-operative societies, and from the Left Book Club. In all, 878 delegates attended, representing 379 working-class organisations with 340,000 members.[172] The second such conference – the People's Convention which was even larger – worried the authorities and even Labour's left wing. Over 2,000 delegates attended, according to *Labour Monthly*, representing 1.2 million workers. The convention declared that 'the present Government represents the interests of the rich', condemned its anti-Soviet attitude, and demanded the restoration of full trade union rights, strong bomb shelters, decent housing, independence for India, and friendship with the USSR.[173] Even the anti-communist and pro-war *Tribune* admitted that the People's Convention

> was a great success as a conference. The hall and the overflow meetings were packed. The speakers were able. The audiences were enthusiastic, and mostly composed of good, honest-to-God workers whose attachment to socialism, democracy and a decent peace and whose loathing of Fascism could not be questioned. Much of what was said was the authentic voice of large and growing bodies of opinion.[174]

The *Daily Mirror* reported that the convention reflected 'Legitimate popular grievances' and argued that 'Labour Ministers behave like pale imitations of Tory ministers. So the people feel themselves leaderless. They are beginning to turn to the Communist Party.'[175]

Communist Party publications also increased in popularity as the war progressed. While its left-wing rival, *Tribune*, declined, *Labour Monthly* sales increased more than fourfold from 7,000 to 30,000 between September 1939 and April 1941.[176] So worrying was this growing popularity of communism to certain sections of the business community that the National Association of Wholesale Newagents (NAWN), representing companies such as W.H. Smiths, refused to distribute *Labour Monthly* after June 1941.[177] The highly undemocratic move was widely condemned at the time. The *Daily Worker* had also increased its circulation by 1939 to around 40,000 for weekdays and between 75,000 and 80,000 at weekends despite NAWN's refusal to distribute it. In January 1941, it was banned by the government, under Defence Regulation 2D,[178] for allegedly obstructing the war effort. The financial impact of the ban was ironic: the monthly donations from sympathisers to the 'People's Press Fighting Fund', which had averaged £1,500 per month from September 1939, increased to £4,200 per month by April 1941.[179] The ban also galvanised into action non-communists in the trade unions who wanted to legalise the *Daily Worker* because of widespread support for the principle of free speech. The communists mobilised over two million trade union votes, numerous shops stewards' committees and over 100 trade councils to oppose the government ban.[180]

The increasing support for communist organisations and causes contrasted with declining support for the Labour Party. Between July 1940 and July 1941, Labour Party membership slumped by 25 per cent; the Party's annual income dropped by £20,000; and revenues from literature sales fell from £9,000 in 1939 to below £4,400 in 1940.[181]

The government's attitude to such developments, of course, was not neutral. According to Morgan, the government wished to ban the CPGB altogether and to intern its leaders but 'rejected [the option] on grounds of expediency'. Nevertheless, an official campaign against the party was waged, and many communists (such as John Mason) were arrested without charge, or on flimsy pretexts (such as using 'insulting words'); the police informed businesses about communists in their employ in attempts to encourage their dismissal. In the case of Wal Hannington, a *Daily Worker* correspondent who worked in an engineering firm in north London, the government having failed to secure his dismissal, 'contained' him by isolating him in a brick hut in the middle of the shop floor!derecha[182]

The Communist Party was, overall, an important and significant force in British working-class politics during the Second World War. Its popularity was growing even before the German attack on the Soviet Union and the CPGB's declaration of a war to end fascism in June 1941. After that date, their support increased even more. Since they represented an important section of working-class opinion, it would have been just and democratic for the authorities to consult with the organisation on questions of foreign policy. That they did not consult with the party is highly instructive as to the boundaries of official assumptions on the nature of the 'national interest'. It is to a more systematic assessment of such assumptions and beliefs that attention must now be turned, as the state operated at the focal point of the activities of the special interests and political parties introduced in Chapters 2 and 3.

NOTES

1. Christopher Thorne, 'Chatham House, Whitehall and Far Eastern Issues: 1941–45', in *International Affairs*, Vol. 54, No. 1 (Jan. 1978).
2. M.L. Dockrill, Historical Note: 'The Foreign Office and the Proposed Institute of International Affairs 1919', in *International Affairs*, Vol. 54, No. 4 (Autumn 1980), p. 669.
3. Although controversial in the late 1930s because of the associations of the 'Cliveden Set' with the disastrous appeasement policy, there is little evidence of any substance to indicate that the 'set' actually made British foreign policy. See, for example, Anthony Masters, *Nancy Astor: A Biography* (London: McGraw-Hill, 1981); Christopher Sykes, *Nancy: The Life of Lady Astor* (London: Collins, 1972); and Maurice Collins, *Nancy Astor: An Informal Biography* (London: Faber & Faber, 1960).
4. Donald Fisher, 'The Role of Philanthropic Foundations in the Reproduction and Production of Hegemony: Rockefeller Foundations and the Social Sciences', in *Sociology*, Vol. 17, No. 2 (May 1983), p. 207.
5. Clement Jones was Secretary to the British Empire delegation at the Paris Peace Conference, 1919; Robert Cecil was Assistant Secretary for Foreign Affairs, 1918, Lord Privy Seal, 1923–24, and President of the League of Nations Union, 1923–45. Of the role of Curtis, Jones wrote: 'There was only one founder of Chatham House – his name was Lionel Curtis' (Chatham House Archives (CHA) 2/1/2a. p. 7). Curtis represented the Colonial Office in the League of Nations section of the Paris Peace Conference.
6. Miss Cleeve's Papers, CHA 2/1/2a.
7. Arnold J. Toynbee, *Acquaintances* (London: Oxford University Press, 1967), p. 132.
8. Frederick Madden, 'The Commonwealth, Commonwealth History, and Oxford, 1905–71', in F. Madden and D.K. Fieldhouse (eds), *Oxford and the Idea of Commonwealth* (London: Croom Helm, 1982), p. 24.
9. Deborah Lavin, 'Lionel Curtis and the Idea of Commonwealth' in ibid., p. 101.
10. Lavin, op. cit., p. 99.
11. W. Nimocks, *Milner's Young Men* (Durham, NC: Duke University Press, 1968); J.E. Kendle, *Round Table Movement and Imperial Union* (Toronto: Toronto University Press, 1975); H.V. Hodson, 'The Round Table 1910–81', in *Round Table*, No. 284 (Oct. 1981).
12. J.R.M. Butler, *Lord Lothian (Phillip Kerr), 1882–1940* (London: Macmillan, 1960), p. 59.
13. Lavin, op. cit., p. 113.

14. Lionel Curtis, 'Windows of Freedom', in *Round Table* (Dec. 1918), p. 1.
15. A.J. Toynbee, *Experiences* (London: Oxford University Press, 1969), p. 61.
16. Harold Nicolson, *Peacemaking 1919* (London: Constable, 1933), pp. 352–3.
17. Toynbee, *Experiences*, p. 62.
18. Jones, in Cleeve Papers, CHA 2/1/2a, p. 6.
19. Jones, op. cit., p. 2.
20. Shepardson was a lawyer by profession, linked closely with the State Department. He was a director of the Council on Foreign Relations, 1921–66.
21. Memorandum, CHA 2/1/2, p. 1.
22. *The British Institute of International Affairs* (London: BIIA, 1920), p. 12.
23. Ibid., p. 13.
24. Ibid., p. 14.
25. M.L. Dockrill, op. cit., p. 665.
26. Lavin, op. cit., pp. 107–16.
27. 'Report of the Executive Committee of BIIA, August 1920', in *The British Institute of International Affairs*, op. cit., p. 3.
28. Thorne, op. cit., p. 1. For a fuller discussion of these concepts see Leonard A. Kusnitz, *Public Opinion and Foreign Policy* (Westport, CT: Greenwood Press, 1984); and, of course, the classic study by J.N. Rosenau, also entitled *Public Opinion and Foreign Policy* (New York: Random House, 1961).
29. Memorandum by Curtis and Shepardson, CHA 2/1/2. p. 2.
30. Ian McLaine, *Ministry of Morale: Home Front Morale and the Ministry of Information in World War II* (London: Allen & Unwin, 1979), p. 22.
31. BIIA Executive Committee Report, op. cit., p. 7.
32. Ibid., p. 24.
33. 'Fifth Session of the Conference of Institutions for the Scientific Study of International Relations' (Milan, 23–27 May 1932), in CHA, Study Groups Committee, Lord Trenchard's Private File, Vol. 2 (1931–32), p. 2.
34. King-Hall, op. cit., p. 2.
35. Ibid., p. x.
36. Ibid., pp. 114–15.
37. Wilfrid Knapp, 'Fifty Years of Chatham House Books', in *International Affairs* (Nov. 1970), Special Issue, p. 138.
38. Ibid., p. 139.
39. Admiral Richmond's note on Kerr's memorandum, in Study Group on Anglo-American Relations, Special Group, CHA 9/1.4.
40. Ibid., p. 1.
41. Ibid., p. 3.
42. Ibid., p. 5.
43. Ibid., p. 9.
44. Those two meetings heard pro-Japanese sentiments being expressed. The first speech, given by Captain M.D. Kennedy, was 'Russo-Japanese Tension in the Far East', 25 Oct. 1934, CHA 8/351; and the second, by Admiral Sir Barry Domvile, was 'The Strategic Aspects to the Situation in the Far East', 1 Feb. 1938, CHA 8/516.
45. Archibald Rose, 'The Crisis in the Far East', 13 Feb. 1933, CHA 8/183, p. 5.
46. Rose, 'The Present Situation in the Far East', 13 Feb. 1933, CHA 8/257, p. 16.
47. Ibid., p. 8.

48. Toynbee, op. cit., p. 27.
49. Lothian, 'The Crisis in the Pacific', 12 Dec. 1934, CHA 8/362, p. 14.
50. Ibid., p. 24.
51. Sir Stafford Cripps, 'The Situation in the Far East', 21 May 1940, CHA 8/633, p. 345.
52. Frank Ashton-Gwatkin, 'The New Order', 18 Dec. 1941, Economic Group Paper 3, in CHA 9/22b Group Papers.
53. Ibid., p. 7.
54. Ibid., p. 11.
55. Ivison S. Macadam, 'America Enters the War', 8 Jan. 1942, CHA 8/787. Macadam was Assistant Director-General and Principal Assistant Secretary in the Ministry of Information, 1939–41; and Secretary and Director-General of RIIA, 1929–55.
56. Ibid., p. 27.
57. Ibid., p. 39.
58. See for example, T. Tallents, 'The Relations Between Australia, New Zealand and the United States', 17 March 1942, CHA 8/865; G.E. Hubbard, 'A Far Eastern Pacific Programme', 26 June 1945, CHA 8/1130; John Keswick, 'Britain in the Far East', 1 Jan. 1946, CHA 8/1189; and the Anglo-American Pacific Group 1943, in CHA 9/30a.
59. Professor R.M. Martin, *TUC: The Growth of a Pressure Group* (Oxford: Clarendon Press, 1980).
60. Henry Pelling, *A History of British Trade Unionism* (London: Macmillan, 1963).
61. John Lovell and B.C. Roberts, *A Short History of the TUC* (London: Macmillan, 1968).
62. Martin, op. cit.
63. Ibid.
64. Ibid.
65. Walter M. Citrine, *The Trades Union Congress at Work* (London: TUC, 1931).
66. Pelling, op. cit.
67. Lovell and Roberts, op. cit.
68. Ibid.
69. Minutes, General Council (GC) of TUC, 26 Feb. 1941, Congress House, London.
70. Martin, op. cit., pp. 20–1.
71. V.I. Lenin, *Imperialism, The Highest Stage of Capitalism* (Peking: Foreign Languages Press, 1970), pp. 128–9.
72. R.P. Dutt, *The Crisis of Britain and the British Empire* (London: Lawrence & Wishart, 1954), p. 323.
73. Peter Weiler, *British Labour and the Cold War* (Stanford, CA: Stanford University Press, 1988), p. 3.
74. Ibid., p. 34.
75. Letter, Citrine to Miss Macdonald (Jan. 1939), in Section 4/6, Walter Citrine Papers, Manuscripts Collection, British Library of Political and Economic Science.
76. Letter, 19 Feb. 1939, Section 4/6, Citrine Papers.
77. Memorandum, 'The Implications of Industrial Peace', 18 Feb. 1927, Section

1/6, Citrine Papers.
78. 'The Future of Trade Unionism', 29 Feb. 1928, Section 4/1, Citrine Papers.
79. *Two Careers*, Vol. II of the autobiography of Citrine (London: Hutchinson, 1967), p. 38.
80. Weiler, op. cit., p. 18.
81. Citrine, op. cit., p. 42.
82. Press Cuttings and Memorandum, Section 6/1, Citrine Papers.
83. Ibid.
84. Cited in Citrine, op. cit., p. 54.
85. 'TUC Draft Proposal for Joint Statement with BEC', 23 April 1940, in GC Minutes file, p. 84.
86. GC Minutes, 5 Oct. 1940.
87. Lovell and Roberts, op. cit., p. 162.
88. Minutes, TUC Economic Committee, 9 April 1941.
89. Citrine, op. cit., pp. 64–78.
90. Minutes, RJAC, R J (42) 1, 18 Dec. 1942, in CAB 87/95, Public Record Office, London.
91. 'Brief Report of Mr Greenwood's Remarks to the Economic Committee', TUC Economic Committee Minutes, 14 May 1941, p. 23.
92. CHA 8/793, 29 Jan. 1942, p. 129.
93. Ibid., p. 132.
94. R J (43) 2, 3 Feb. 1943.
95. Minutes, Economic Committee, 9 Nov. 1943.
96. TUC Annual Report, 1944.
97. Minutes, TUC Economic Committee, 8 March 1944.
98. Weller, op. cit., pp. 55–7.
99. WM (45) 33rd Conclusions, 19 March 1945, CAB Series 66.
100. Geoffrey Foote, *The Labour Party's Political Thought: A History* (London: Croom Helm, 1985), p. 7.
101. Ibid., p. 10.
102. Tony Cliff and Donny Gluckstein, *The Labour Party: A Marxist History* (London: Bookmarks, 1988), p. 54.
103. Peter Weiler, *Ernest Bevin* (Manchester and New York: Manchester University Press, 1993), p. 9.
104. Michael Gordon, *Conflict and Consensus in Labour's Foreign Policy 1914–1965* (Stanford, CA: Stanford University Press, 1969), p. 1.
105. Ibid., p. 5.
106. Ibid., p. 6.
107. Weiler, *Bevin*, op. cit., pp. 20–1.
108. Gordon, op. cit., pp. 43–4.
109. Memo on minutes of the National Executive Committee's International Sub-committee (19 Jan. 1940); memo dated 25 Jan. 1940, in British Library of Political and Economic Science.
110. Memo 502A, March 1939, 'The Labour Party's International Policy', by the Advisory Committee on International Questions, in minutes of the International Sub-Committee, 1939.
111. Memo, 'A Long-Term International Economic Policy', 16 March 1942.
112. Hugh Dalton (HD) papers, Vol. 25, 3 and 6 Oct. 1941, at BLPES.
113. HD papers, Vol. 25, 1 May 1942.

114. Ibid., 31 March 1942.
115. Ibid., 25 March 1942.
116. HD Papers, Vol. 29, 27 July 1943.
117. Ibid., 7 May 1943.
118. Ibid., 5 Aug. 1943.
119. HD Papers, Vol. 30, 11 Feb. 1944.
120. Ibid., 14–17 Feb. 1944.
121. HD Papers, part 2B, section 7/4, 24 Aug. 1942.
122. Ibid.
123. HD Papers part 2B, section 7/5, 26 Jan. 1943.
124. Durbin, 'British Foreign Policy after the War', 1 April 1943, in a letter to Dalton, 20 April 1943.
125. Durbin, 'Balance of Power', 7 April 1943.
126. Telegram, Cripps to the Foreign Office, 27 June 1940, in FO 371/25206, Public Record Office, London.
127. See minutes by Foreign Office officials on Cripps' telegram in ibid.
128. Alan Bullock, *The Life and Times of Ernest Bevin*, Vol. 1 (London: Heinemann, 1967).
129. Bullock, Vol. II.
130. J. Mackenzie, *Propaganda and Empire: The Manipulation of British Public Opinion 1880–1960* (Manchester: Manchester University Press, 1984).
131. Weiler, *Bevin*, op. cit., p. 72.
132. Ibid., p. 97.
133. Ibid., p. 146.
134. Report of the 44th Annual Labour Party Conference, 1945, p. 115.
135. Clement R. Attlee, *As It Happened* (London: Heinemann, 1954), p. 11.
136. Trevor Burridge, *Clement Attlee: A Political Biography* (London: Jonathan Cape, 1985), p. 14.
137. Weiler, *Bevin*, op. cit., pp. 174–6.
138. Kenneth Harris, *Attlee* (London: Weidenfeld & Nicolson, 1982), pp. 205–6. Tawney said that 'the Labour party has temporarily ceased not only to count but to believe in itself', while Laski moaned that Attlee *et al* were content 'to maintain their happy subordination to Winston. That, Bevin always partly excepted, seems to be the only role they really enjoy. The real tragedy is that they are satisfied with their position.'
139. Ibid., p. 211.
140. Byrnes, *Speaking Frankly* (London and Toronto: Heinemann, 1947), p. 79. An English foreign affairs specialist remarked on Bevin's address at the United Nations 'that he was making a good speech, but he seems to have gotten a little stout'. (Bevin was unhealthy and overweight.)
141. Bullock, op. cit., Vol. 1, p. 633.
142. FO371/62420, cited in Weiler, *British Labour and the Cold War*, op. cit., p. 194.
143. Dutt, op. cit., p. 337.
144. Official party channels for 'educating' its members about Labour's policies included a provision of 'study circle leaders', literature on peace aims, and a Labour Book Service, providing books such as E. Durbin's *The Politics of Democratic Socialism* with additional discussion notes. See for example Party General-Secretary J.S. Middleton's letter to *Tribune*, a left Labour weekly,

for 'analysing' the causes of war without ever mentioning nationalism, capitalism or imperialism.
145. *The Labour Party Annual Report*, 1941, p. 165.
146. See Reconstruction Problems Committee, RP(41) 1, 6 March 1941, CAB 87/1 at PRO.
147. *Labour Party Annual Report*, 1941, p. 164.
148. HD Papers, part 2B, section 7/10.
149. F. Williams, *Ernest Bevin, Portrait of a Great Englishman* (London: Hutchinson, 1952), p. 252.
150. D. Howell, *British Social Democracy: A Study in Development and Decay* (London: Croom Helm, 1976), pp. 119–20.
151. Ritchie Ovendale (ed.), *The Foreign Policy of the British Labour Governments 1945–51* (Leicester: Leicester University Press, 1984), p. 5.
152. Henry Pelling, *The British Communist Party. A Historical Profile* (London: Adam and Charles Black, 1975).
153. Draft Constitution of the Communist Party of Great Britain (London: CPGB, 1932), p. 2.
154. 'For Soviet Britain. The Programme of the Communist Party adopted at the XIII Congress, 2 Feb. 1935' (London: Communist Party of Great Britain (CPGB), 1935), p. 16.
155. Harry Pollitt, *How To Win The Peace* (London: The Communist Party, 1944), p. 32. Pollitt was Party General-Secretary.
156. Draft Constitution, op. cit., p. 19.
157. H. Pollitt, *Henry Pollitt Speaks . . . A Call to all Workers* (London: CPGB, 1935), p. 76.
158. *Daily Worker*, 'Action Was Brought to Injure This Paper', 3 May 1940.
159. 'Labour and the War', in *Labour Monthly* (March 1940), p. 132.
160. H. Pollitt, *Communist Policy for Britain, Political Report* (London: CPGB, 1945), p. 3.
161. 'Reflections on a Revolution', 3 Aug. 1945.
162. Pollitt, *How To Win The Peace*, op. cit., p. 57.
163. *Labour Monthly*, 'Python and Tiger' (Oct. 1940), p. 534.
164. *Labour Monthly*, 'Notes of the Month' (Feb. 1941), pp. 53–4.
165. *Labour Monthly*, 'Notes of the Month' (Aug. 1941), p. 355.
166. Pollitt, *How To Win The Peace*, op. cit., pp. 57–8.
167. Pollitt, *Communist Policy for Britain*, op. cit., p. 3.
168. Noreen Branson, *History of the Communist Party of Great Britain, 1927–41* (London: Lawrence & Wishart, 1985), pp. 271, 275, 335; Pelling, op. cit.
169. Peter Weiler, *British Labour and the Cold War*, op. cit., pp. 7–8.
170. Letter from 'A Yorkshire man', in *Tribune* (5 April 1940).
171. Cited in Angus Calder and Dorothy Sheriden (eds), *Speak For Yourself: A Mass-Observation Anthology, 1937–49* (London: Jonathan Cape, 1984), p. 114. The observer added that there was little enthusiasm for the war and that so sceptical were airmen of the BBC's reporting of British casualties that they would tune in to Lord Haw-Haw for 'balance'.
172. *Labour Monthly* (March 1940), pp. 132–41.
173. *Labour Monthly* (Feb. 1941), p. 93.
174. *Tribune*, 17 Jan.1 1941.
175. Cited in *Labour Monthly* (Feb. 1941), p. 52.

176. *Labour Monthly* (March 1940, April 1941).
177. *Labour Monthly* (June 1941), p. 290.
178. Kevin Morgan, *Against Fascism and War: Ruptures and Continuities in British Communist Politics, 1935–41* (Manchester: Manchester University Press, 1989), p. 239.
179. *Labour Monthly* (April 1941), p. 158.
180. W. Rust, 'The Twelfth Anniversary of the Daily Worker', *Labour Monthly* (Jan. 1942).
181. *Labour Monthly* (July 1941), p. 333.
182. Morgan, op. cit., pp. 237–41.

4

The State and the National Interest

The 'state' formed the focus of activity for the competing notions of national interest that have been outlined above. While it may seem rather obvious that the state played a key role in the taking of the major decisions concerning British foreign policy, that is not the direct or indirect implication of dominant thinking in political science and sociology. Most pluralists and neo-Marxists undermine the importance of the state by considering it as a vehicle or instrument of external economic and political forces – indeed the very types of interest group described in previous chapters.

The challenge for those who suggest the notion of the 'strong state', or who support the ideas of 'statists', is to offer evidence to demonstrate that there is indeed an independently derived 'state' world view; that this has been established over time and displays a certain level of historical continuity; that there are key axes around which the state view revolved; and to show which policy it favoured during the period covered by this study. This chapter aims, in part, to establish the idea of a powerful state organisation which was certainly far more than a mere instrument of external forces. This will be further reinforced by the evidence to be cited in later chapters on the relative influence of the state and special interests in the making of the Anglo-American alliance.

This chapter will also examine the social origins of the personnel of the state, especially its civil servants, as a factor further contributing to the state's autonomy. Finally, it is also intended to outline the social origins and interconnections of all the special interest groups, the political parties and the state. Only then, it is argued here, will the full backdrop to the struggle for influence over foreign policy have been provided.

In setting out to establish the importance of the state – especially the Foreign Office and the Board of Trade – one could not hope to begin at a better place than the excellent study by D.C.M Platt, *Finance, Trade and Politics in British Foreign Policy 1815–1914*.

The State and the National Interest

Platt, whose book combines consideration of economic policy and diplomacy, establishes the notion of state autonomy. Platt's study illuminates, for the century of *Pax Britannica*, the debate between Leninist ideas about monopoly capitalist domination of the departments of state and the rather 'conservative' idea that economic forces played no role whatever in Britain's foreign economic policy. For Platt, the state itself was strengthened by the maintenance and promotion of Britain as a trading and financial power. In Platt's view

> British statesmen, however aristocratic, however inexperienced in trade and finance, could not afford to ignore Britain's dependence on overseas trade. They may have been interested in the political power which wealth brought with it, they may have believed that trade meant peace . . . The younger Pitt's remark that 'British policy is British trade' explained what lay behind so much of British diplomacy — not necessarily as the first consideration, since national security naturally took first place, but as an important element both in contributing to that security and in its own right.[1]

The British state, especially through the Board of Trade and the Foreign Office, has always had a paramount interest in the trading and manufacturing status of Britain. The literature on these departments of government demonstrates this assertion conclusively. Such interest was not, it is also shown, primarily because of the application of pressure from any 'vested interests' (although this did occur) but because the state had its own imperatives. Yet businessmen have frequently complained about official attitudes to their interest, and some of the causes of such complaints will be examined below. One businessman and politician, however, who needed no convincing of the state's positive attitude towards commerce was Joseph Chamberlain. In 1896, he declared to the Birmingham Chamber of Commerce that 'it is not too much to say that commerce is the greatest of all political interests'. He explained that

> the Foreign Office and the Colonial Office are chiefly engaged in finding new markets and defending old ones. The War Office and Admiralty are mostly occupied in preparation for

the defence of these markets, and for the protection of our commerce. The Boards of Agriculture and of Trade are entirely concerned with those two great branches of industry. Even the Education Department bases its claim upon public money on the necessity of keeping our people well to the front in commercial competition . . . and the Home Office finds the largest scope for its activity in the protection of the life and health of manual labourers who are engaged in those industries.[2]

The undeniable fact is that the state exists in a global system of states, in a highly competitive environment. One basis of a state's power in such an environment must be the level of development of its economy, the condition of its finances and, ultimately, its own war-making capacity. A state interest in trade, therefore, has a dynamic of its own, over and above any pressure group activity. In Chapter 2, in the section on the Bank of England, Geoffrey Ingham was cited to the effect that the state had instituted certain reforms in domestic finance precisely in order to pacify social unrest and to enhance the state's war-making capabilities. Indeed, it was the President of the Board of Trade, William Huskisson, who had engineered reforms in order to make Britain the Venice of the nineteenth century.[3] These reforms had been carried out against the wishes of sections of the 'dominant class'.

Hubert Smith's study of the Board of Trade also suggests that these were its main concerns. The Board's attitude towards industry, he demonstrates, depended, 'to a degree not always recognised, on critical changes in the general trend of British trade and industry in relation to foreign competition and world markets'.[4] That such an interest in trade and industry has been central to government thinking for centuries is demonstrated by Smith's quotation from the text of a forerunner committee of the Board of Trade in 1660. That earlier committee's aim, which was hardly determined by 'industrial' pressure, was to 'consider of the several manufactures of these our kingdoms how and by what occasions they are corrupted debased and disparaged. And by what probable means they may be restored and maintained in their ancient goodness and reputation'. The committee was also to ensure a vibrant level of production for 'the employment of our people and to the best advantage of the public'.⁵ From 1815 to 1914, the Board of Trade functioned to assist industry by trying to establish 'the fundamental conditions of general industrial development, rather than the direct promotion of particular branches of manufacture'.⁶

The fact that the Board refused to promote *particular* manufactures or traders may, indeed, have been one of the principal reasons for business complaints in the nineteenth century and later. Roger Pouty argues that despite heavy connections between the business world and the Board, the latter always attempted to make policy that would be in the public interest: 'they understood that their office made them responsible to the whole society, not just to one group or interest.'⁷

The Board of Trade was never the passive instrument of 'big business'; its activities are better explained as responses to the increasingly competitive world economic environment as new states emerged and threatened traditional British markets. The Board of Trade provided numerous services to enhance British traders' and producers' competitiveness: statistics, commercial intelligence, introductions to foreign agents and so on. In 1886, the British Minister in Peking stated that he had always operated on the principle that to be efficient and helpful to traders, consuls should 'also be on the look out to show British merchants and traders when and how to take advantages of commercial openings'.⁸ The Board also launched its *Journal* initially on a monthly and then on a weekly basis, with a section on 'openings for British Trade'. As world competition intensified, the Board of Trade stepped up its efforts to strengthen business: between 1900 and 1907, written enquiries to the Board increased from 938 to 4,547; personal enquiries from 299 to 2,899; and letters and circulars dispatched from 2,123 to 34,514.⁹

There were, of course, clashes and frictions between businessmen and officials, but often because of the narrowness in outlook of manufacturers. They usually wanted assistance for individual projects, while the Board of Trade, and the other official agencies, saw their role as acting for the broader interests.¹⁰ But of all the state's agencies to face charges of neglect of commercial interests and snobbishness towards traders, it was the Foreign Office that received most attention. In relation to the Foreign Office, traders may appear to be on firmer ground in their complaints because commercial work was disregarded in many ways. Platt argues that such disregard was rationalised by the laissez-faire doctrine: the aristocrats of the Foreign Office could now 'avoid . . . distasteful contact with the persons and problems of traders and financiers merely by referring, in perfect good faith to the traditions of non-intervention, free trade, and open competition'.[11]

John Tilley, an ex-Foreign Office Chief Clerk, argues, however, that those charged with British foreign affairs have always regarded trade promotion very highly. He suggests that '[Lord] Chatham founded an Empire for the benefit of British trade' and that in fact 'Excessive regard for the wishes of British traders lost us the United States, and Canning's South American policy was inspired largely by anxiety for the promotion of British trade'.[12] This tradition of Foreign Office assistance to commerce continued, Tilley demonstrates, throughout the nineteenth century and much later too. Indeed, as global competition became more intense by the 1890s, the Foreign Office created new machinery – such as the pooling of commercial information – to assist traders. Lord Salisbury informed the House of Lords in 1895 that Britain's colonial advance was inevitable because it was the state's 'business . . . to make smooth the paths for British commerce, British enterprise, the application of British capital, at a time when other paths . . . for the commercial energies of our race are being gradually closed'. Protectionism, he argued, by Germany, France and the United States excluded British trade, a situation to which the British state could not acquiesce.[13] As Platt argues, 'National security was always the prime function of foreign policy, but access to markets and fair treatment in those markets was . . . an interest only just subordinate – and closely related – to the safeguarding of our national and Imperial frontiers'.[14]

One of the best known Foreign Office documents concerning Britain's national interest – and the vital role of commerce within it – is surely Eyre Crowe's memorandum of 1907. This memorandum, according to Connell, has a revered position in British foreign policy. Crowe suggested that 'The general character of England's foreign policy is determined by the immutable conditions of her geographical situation on the ocean flank of Europe as an island state with vast overseas colonies and dependencies'. While the first priority of any nation is to maintain its national independence, the second is 'the right of free intercourse and trade in the world's markets'.[15] National security and trade were always closely connected as far as the Foreign Office was concerned, even if aristocratic social bias against 'traders' tended to undermine such a position. The influence of Crowe's memorandum dominated official thinking during and after the Second World War, as the words of Lord Strang suggest: in the making of policy, no minister could 'get away from the fact that Great Britain is a small, densely populated island with wide overseas interests, inescapably dependent upon foreign trade for the maintenance of its high standard of living'.[16] And similar sentiments were expressed by another Foreign Office member, Frank Ashton Gwatkin, in 1943. Outlining his view of British national interest, he suggested that the first parameter was national 'safety' from military attack; the second was 'security', that is 'our position in the world at large, including our commercial and economic position'.[17]

The secondary literature on the attitudes of the state to trade and industry demonstrates not only that officials had independently derived views that evolved through time, but that they also successfully resisted the pressure politics of special interests in formulating policy.[18] The brief review conducted above has dealt mainly with the nineteenth and early twentieth centuries, and has shown that economics was a key element in state policy formation; indeed, it was a key element of the 'state's' view of the national interest. The remainder of this section of Chapter 4 will focus more specifically on the conception of the national interest held by official policy-makers during the Second World War, and on their policy responses.

One of the most striking features of the state's wartime conception of national interests is the degree to which it revolves around factors very similar to those identified with the Federation of British Industries earlier. The various institutions of the British state supported an enhanced and prosperous export trade, and favoured the protection and expansion of Britain's overseas investments and economical supplies of raw materials. In order to achieve such national interest objectives, the officials of the state urged the development of international, multilateral commercial and financial institutions, at the heart of which would be a solid Anglo-American alliance.

A useful starting point in considering the elements of the state's conception of national interest is the minute by Sir J. Brenan of the Foreign Office in August 1938. In that minute, Brenan candidly admitted that Britain's 'dominant position in China [was achieved] as a result of our wars' in the nineteenth century; military means would also be required to maintain Britain's position there. In considering exactly which interests Britain should preserve in China, Brenan noted the importance of 'our numerous and valuable commercial enterprises . . . our privileges of an unusual and extra-territorial nature such as the British hold on the Customs Service, our control over the administration of the Shanghai settlement, our personnel in the railways and the maintenance of our shipping interests'.[19] Material interests were valuable enough, in Brenan's opinion, for the state to intervene militarily to protect them, if and when Britain could muster American suport for such a policy.

The protection of British foreign investments also ranked highly in the considerations of state officials. Once again, however, officials often had to defend themselves against businessmen's accusations of neglect and inefficiency. Sir Joseph Ball, a former head of the Conservative Research Department and a businessman with interests in South Africa, complained to the Treasury that Britain's overseas industrial interests were not receiving adequate governmental protection. Conversely, he claimed, Britons who held foreign bonds were protected by the Council of Foreign Bondholders (CFB), an organisation that received state support. As the threat to industrial interests was greater and their financial losses more substantial during the 1930s, Ball urged the Treasury to set up an organisation to protect them. It was after all, Ball emphasised, a fact that overseas investments meant foreign exchange earnings; in addition, 'British enterprises abroad are markets for British goods. They can be equipped with British machinery. They can use British materials. They can create an atmosphere favourable to British goods.'[20]

Ball's memorandum initiated a flurry of minutes and even a project to study his claims more thoroughly. S.D. Waley of the Treasury noted that while industrial companies could better protect themselves, the widows and children represented by the CFB could not; hence state assistance. In any case, he continued, industrialists did receive full diplomatic support. 'In fact, both the Departments at home and the Embassies and Legations abroad devote a great deal of time and energy supporting their interests.' If the results were unsatisfactory, Waley reflected, it was because officials no longer used Palmerstonian methods. Nationalist sentiment was growing all over the world, he explained, and 'the operations of foreign companies naturally awake more and more criticism'. In addition, Waley bemoaned the fact that the monetary 'lever we used to possess, in that foreign loans would not be granted to countries which did not treat our interests fairly, has ceased to be of much use to us after 1931'.[21] Sir Frederick Phillips noted that while the 'loan weapon' was obsolete, 'There is no lack of zeal on the part of Govt. Depts [sic] here' to protect foreign investments. A study of the question by the Foreign Office Research Department came to a similar conclusion. In fact, it claimed that British industrialists were probably served by their government more positively than Americans were by theirs.[22]

The importance of overseas investments to Britain was stressed in a far more apocalyptical tone by Lord Lothian, the ambassador to the United States. Towards the end of 1940, Lothian was much concerned with the gradual erosion of Britain's overseas assets and hoped that President Roosevelt would be lenient in aiding Britain. In a note that was never actually sent to FDR (though the central arguments were never challenged by officials), Lothian suggested that the post-war world would depend on Anglo-American co-operation; a Britain deprived of her foreign investments would be less able to contribute to post-war reconstruction. In addition, Lothian claimed, overseas 'investments have been essential in the past to the maintenance of those not too high standards of living which have been enjoyed by the working class. If they disappear altogether there may be a violent fall in that standard. We do not want to add a violent social revolution in England to the other problems we shall jointly have to shoulder'.[23] The only official response to this argument was that such reasoning 'would cut no ice with US Congress and public'. The idea that overseas investments were so vital in maintaining Britain's very social structure elicited no comment.

The overseas activities of British business had clearly received official support and protection. They were thought of as a vital part of the national interest. Lord Halifax, the Secretary of State for Foreign Affairs, retorted thus to the idea that academics could plan the future: 'I cannot help thinking that talks between . . . people . . . like those that the FBI [Federation of British industries] were beginning to have with the Germans last March [1939], are more likely to reconstruct the new world than a good deal of the best-devised schemes of academic planners.' The then Prime Minister, Neville Chamberlain, had been a little less subtle when he lectured that '"Economics" in practice deal with commodities; these commodities are controlled by industrialists who have invested money in them and they don't work schemes out of philanthropy but because it pays them'. It was such interests that government would and should support, he implied.[24]

While industrial interests were protected and promoted by the state, it cannot be argued that it was a result of industrialists' pressure. This line will be pursued further in later chapters; it is sufficient at this point to note that officials often rejected the opinions and advice of what were considered 'narrow-minded' interests. For example, a request from Lever Brothers in May 1939 for Britain to remain neutral in the Sino-Japanese War (and thereby allow Japan to gain the upper hand) was severely criticised by Brenan and Ashley Clarke (of the Far Eastern department of the Foreign Office) for ignoring the plight of smaller British companies in the region, and the Japanese threat to the Empire if China's resources fell into their hands. Clarke also argued that J. Hansard, the Lever Brothers' representative, had 'taken no account of the political implications' of his suggestions, especially with regard to 'American opinion'. Brenan concurred that Hansard's 'vision is limited'.[25] Contrary, then, to certain lines of thought, the personnel of the state did, and could, retain a high degree of autonomy in their outlook and policy.

The state clearly supported overseas economic interests, and it hardly requires too much documentation to show that there was also substantial official backing and promotion of British exports. The recognition by all departments of state that exports were important may be summed up by a paper written by J.R.M. Keynes, a Director of the Bank of England and a Treasury Adviser, in September 1941. Reflecting, according to members of the Bank of England, the Treasury view, Keynes argued that the failure to solve the world balance of payments problem 'has been a major cause of impoverishment and social discontent and even of wars and social revolutions'. The war, he suggested, would further undermine Britain's exporting position with respect to 'visible' and 'invisible' trade; at the same time, Britain's demand for foodstuffs and raw materials would remain large. As one part of the solution to the problem, Keynes urged use of the British home market as an inducement to food and raw material producers 'to make equivalent purchases of manufactured articles from us'.[26]

Britain needed, according to the Chancellor of the Exchequer, Sir John Anderson, to increase exports by 50 per cent over pre-1939 levels in order to get through the transitional period after war. The state's foreign currency reserves had been much depleted; and many of the Sterling Area nations who held sterling surpluses were likely to go to the US for their material requirements.[27] The Board of Trade had been doing its utmost since 1941 to promote exporting interests through the establishment of the Export Committee of the Industrial and Export Council. As an interdepartmental committee, it was to serve as a 'clearing house' for ideas and solving problems. The Committee had provided advice, advertised British goods and appointed representatives to foreign markets. Trade with the American market, it was noted, had increased as a result of such work.[28]

The importance of exports was such that it was always dealt with by the highest levels of the state, including the Cabinet. According to the Treasury, Britain could only export to a prosperous world. The key issue was how to establish world conditions that would encourage prosperity. The Treasury was convinced that only international agreements, along non-discriminatory lines, would solve the problem. The formation of an International Clearing Union was urged in order to expand trade. What the world needed was 'an organisation which will perform for participating States the functions performed for individuals by the ordinary banking system, i.e., the clearance of accounts, debit and credit, between different customers and the provision of overdrafts for those who need them'.[29]

If Britain were to protect her overseas interests and trading position in the post-war world, certain international institutions needed to be developed. One of them, the Clearing Union, has received mention above. It was assumed by the leaders of the British state that the core of such institutions would be a firm and permanent Anglo-American alliance. The Treasury paper quoted above concluded that the International Clearing Union 'would be founded by the United States and United Kingdom, who would permanently retain the management and control'.[30] The United States was the key to Britain's position in the post-war world in almost every sphere. All state agencies recognised this elementary 'fact', and the papers of the Foreign Office, Board of Trade and Treasury demonstrate this clearly. The collapse of France in the spring of 1940 increased pro-Anglo-American co-operation feelings in the Foreign Office. J. Nicholls of the North American department indicated that 'the future of the world depends on close Anglo-American co-operation, which, according to T.N. Whitehead, would only occur when Britons and Americans had become convinced 'that they are, in fact, necessary to one another'. R.A. Butler, an under-secretary at the Foreign Office, commented that Britain should be less concerned with Europe and more with a 'world . . . conception of foreign policy' based on US co-operation.[31]

One of the most interesting and insightful memoranda on Anglo-American co-operation was produced by Sir R.I. Campbell, a British Embassy official in Washington, DC. Writing in August 1941, he argued that peace and security depended on Anglo-American accord in the post-war world, and that it had to be ensured that the United States would not sink back into isolation after cessation of hostilities. What form should the relationship take? Campbell did not believe that Anglo-American co-operation could be outlined in any 'articles of association' or treaty. Instead, Britain had to try to 'educate' the Americans to accept global responsibilities in practice. At the same time, however, Campbell feared that America's greatly increased military and industrial strength, and Britain's relative weakness, might be the occasion for the US to 'desire . . . to inherit the influence and power of Great Britain and the commonwealth'. To prevent the emergence of such desire 'British experience . . . [must be used] for the proper working of the partnership'. Success in all such questions was a matter of approach, Campbell suggested. Britain 'must eschew any appearance of trying to impose a solution of any question by insistence on a superior British wisdom . . . [At the same time] we must contrive to be vigilant in driving the best bargain in particular acts of cooperation.' Campbell concluded that Britain had to secure American co-operation 'for on this almost everything would seem to depend'.[32] T.N. Whitehead suggested that if Britain failed to achieve co-operation with the US, 'then our relations might depend on considerations of "power politics" in a fairly crude form and the position of the British Empire would be in real danger'.[33]

If Campbell recognised the problems caused by America's new world position in 1941, by 1944 there were even greater fears for Britain's foreign policy independence. Sir Orme Sargent noted that Britain's power had declined to the extent that 'We could no longer rely on the weapons of the rich man such as credits, loans and subsidies, and we must get used to the position of a debtor nation'. The United States, on the other hand, could do all that and more: Sargent feared that the extension of US influence 'might even lead us into conflict'.[34] Sargent's Foreign Office colleagues all agreed that the position was serious, but were still operating in the belief that Britain had to do all it could to maintain its world role. Mr N. Butler felt that as Britain would be weaker than the US, 'our foreign policy . . . must be such as to commend itself to the US. In particular we shall need to show that we are a reliable and potentially strong partner, and one whose policies are on lines broadly acceptable to American public opinion. The US may then regard us . . . as an indispensable partner . . . and be willing to give us financial support'.[35] In the memorandum that summarised the discussion, it was noted that 'In order to preserve the good relations required, we may well find ourselves forced to follow the United States in a line of policy with which we do not fundamentally agree'.[36] Prime Minister Winston Churchill had already noted the threat to British sovereignty that the United States represented. He urged the Cabinet to 'bear in mind the risk that . . . if we accepted the financial help of the United States we might also be parting with political authority and control. Finance was interwoven with the power and the sovereignty of the State.'[37]

Special Interests, the State and the Anglo-American Alliance, 1939–45

There are certainly many similarities in the attitude of the agencies of the state and certain aspects of the attitude of the special interest groups considered earlier. In which direction 'influence' flowed is to be discussed in later chapters; it should be noted, however, that the state appeared to have a high degree of autonomy. It had ideas about the position of Britain in the world; the factors that had made such a position possible; the forces that threatened the position; and ideas about how to maintain a global role in new world conditions. In short, the state had firm ideas about the national interest, and it sought to develop policies to defend and promote that interest.

THE PERSONNEL OF THE STATE

It is clear that the personnel of the state are important in many respects. They not only execute policy; they also have control over a vast quantity of information, and are responsible for the flow and distribution of that information. As career civil servants they operate within an organisation over several decades, and inevitably develop a sense of continuity and an institutional *esprit de corps*: that is, they have some ideas about themselves as a group with their own interests, their own past and their prospects for the future. They will probably share many common ideas and develop a common moral ethos. For the maintenance of continuity of ideas and values in any organisation, recruitment must be highly regulated or controlled; the civil service, especially the Foreign Office, has remained highly élitist (and more autonomous) primarily because of such control.

Zara Steiner has demonstrated the élitism of the Foreign Office at the turn of the twentieth century: it was small and self-contained, 'its tone and ethos were created by the caste from which it recruited its staff . . . it was indeed the stronghold of the aristocracy and everything was done to preserve its class character and clannish structure'.[38] To be sure, the structural position of civil servants differentiated 'their' interests from those of their kin in the worlds of business and finance: they were responsible to department heads and ministers, for example. Yet, it would be foolish to underemphasise the role that social and economic background played in how Foreign Office personnel related to non-state individuals. Their class backgrounds influenced how they carried out their tasks. Clearly, if the class character of the Foreign Office were radically altered and members of the working class came to positions of control, its priorities and concerns would differ in many important respects. That is also the import of the numerous commissions appointed over the past century and a half on recruitment to the Foreign and Diplomatic Service. As Anthony Eden's White Paper on Foreign Service reforms summarised in 1943, 'the Diplomatic Service . . . is recruited from too small a circle, that it tends to represent the interests of certain sections of the nation rather than those of the country as a whole'.[39]

The personnel of an organisation, while they may enter an existing 'structure', exert important influence upon it and thereby change structural norms. That is why the control of recruitment is so important – it affords the possibility of change or the probability that the status quo will be maintained. The Foreign Office, as Connell argues, has had to bow to externally induced changes; but it has 'in its own subtle fashion . . . [proceeded] to absorb and moderate them'.[40]

The aristocratic nature of Foreign Office recruits inevitably increased the social distance between them and other elements of British society. They mixed with individuals who had usually been to Eton and Oxbridge, were members of the same set of London clubs, and often of the same religious background. Nine of the 16 clerks who joined the Foreign Office between 1908 and 1913 had been to Eton, and 15 of them to Oxbridge; half of the entrants between 1898 and 1907 were from aristocratic families. Steiner argues that even after the middle classes had come to dominate domestic departments, 'the Foreign ministries [of Europe] remained the strongholds of the aristocracy'.[41]

Even after the abolition of the need for private means as a qualification for entry into the Diplomatic Service in 1919, 'there was a general feeling . . . that it was not much use to apply for a nomination unless a candidate had friends at court'.[42] Despite various attempts at reform, the élitist credentials of the civil service remained almost unaffected. Giddens and Stanworth's analysis of the educational backgrounds of permanent secretaries in the whole civil service between 1920 and 1944 demonstrates this clearly. During that period, over 80 per cent of those positions were filled by public/private school-educated individuals, 79.7 per cent of them had been through the Oxbridge universities.[43]

Almost inevitably, these men had a near-innate sense of social superiority, reinforced by the level of contact with men in high position with similar backgrounds, experiences and attitudes. As Sir John Tilley, a former Chief Clerk in the Foreign Office, wrote about the attitude of permanent secretaries in his department: 'They all had great admiration for the work done under their own direction, and could hardly believe that anyone else would do it nearly as well.' He adds that they stood for tradition – for quill pens and hand copying, not machines.[44]

A detailed analysis of the civil servants involved in the making of the Anglo-American alliance has been carried out specifically for this study. Its general findings do not contradict those of other analyses of the civil service, and they are summarised below. The method of selection was to list all those who regularly attended meetings between 1939 and 1945 that were important in discussing aspects of Anglo-American co-operation. In all, there were 56 individuals from several departments, including the Foreign Office, the Treasury, the Board of Trade and the Ministry of Information. Information, however, was available on only 25 of these individuals in publications such as *Who Was Who*. The sample included such men as Sir Alexander Cadogan, Permanent Secretary at the Foreign Office, and J.R.M. Keynes, who effectively operated as a civil servant during the war. Twenty of the 25 had been educated at public/private schools (Eton, Rugby and Winchester among them); 15 had passed through Oxbridge, and five through other universities. These 25 civil servants also held at least 49 company directorships among them. (The company directorships listed under some individuals' names were too numerous to be given in full, and ended with the words 'and many others'.) The companies included multinationals such as Imperial Chemical Industries and Nobel Industries; imperially based firms such as Ashanti Goldfields and the Oriental Telephone and Electric Company; and clearing banks such as the National Provincial and the Royal Bank of Scotland. There were three who were directors of the Bank of England and one was a director of Morgan Grenfell.

The largest holders of directorships were three men connected with the Treasury: S.D. Waley held six directorships; Josiah Stamp held ten; Lord Catto held at least 13. Because of the relatively large number of directorships, there is also evidence of a certain level of interlocking, that is, civil servant directors of common companies. For example, the Permanent Secretary of the Foreign Office, Sir Alexander Cadogan, was a director of the National Provincial Bank; Sir Frederick Leith-Ross, Director-General of the Ministry of Economic Warfare was also director of the same bank. Keynes, Lord Catto and Josiah Stamp were all directors of the Suez Canal Company. The points to note about interlocking directorships are that they not only suggest awareness of the concerns of the business world which cannot but have a general effect on the work of directors as civil servants, but that they afford one more opportunity to strengthen the cohesion of a relatively small group and make more likely the development and perpetuation of a common outlook and attitude to the world. These men met each other not only as servants of the state, but as men of business too; and not only in small businesses with localised interests, but in some of the biggest companies in the world.

Their common educational experiences, common occupational career paths, and their interests in business had brought these men together in many ways. Yet, there was also the social side of their lives to be considered; there was still the West End club. According to Max Weber, membership of a club is the 'essential mark of a gentleman'; our sample of 25 civil servants reported 37 memberships. The most popular clubs were the Athenaeum with seven members, the Reform with four, and Brooks's with another four. St James's, the Travellers' and the United University clubs each reported two members from the sample. The largest number of memberships was reported by the peers Woolton and Catto (with four each, with these two having the Athenaeum club in common). While the clubs may well have lost their premier position in terms of policy-making by the 1920s and 1930s, they still retained a powerful role in terms of the social cohesion of an élite.

In combination, the world of the civil servants seems very narrow and circumscribed. Each part of an élite member's life cycle seemed to reinforce the others, creating a circle of privilege and security. One could be forgiven for thinking that despite the democratisation movements of the early twentieth century, there remained a class of people in British society who were literally 'born to rule'. They were in many ways separated from the vast majority of the population of Britain, let alone the subject peoples of an Empire of over 500 million. As Connell was cited earlier as suggesting, these men were responsive to pressure for change, but they were also striving to maintain their élitist position and their social and occupational 'differentials' from other members of society. While it was not their only source of autonomy, their social and psychological sense of superiority and 'inherited wisdom' made them highly unlikely to be the subject of any 'vulgar' pressure from 'below'.

SPECIAL INTERESTS, POLITICAL PARTIES AND THE ELITE

Certainly there were powerful factors that tended to reinforce the state's autonomy. It was the role and aim of sectional and other organised interests, however, to attempt to impose their view on policy-makers with regard to foreign policy decisions. We have already examined the policy positions taken by interests as diverse as the Federation of British Industries and the Communist Party; the aim here is to examine the nature of the membership of such organisations to get a broader picture of élite 'power' in British society. Finally, a brief outline will be provided of the important interconnections of the special interests and political parties with each other, and with the official policy élite.

The Federation of British Industries

Eighty-seven names emerged from an examination of attendance lists for meetings at the FBI, and information was available on 23 of them. Educationally, the results show that six of the FBI leaders had attended public schools – Eton, Harrow, Winchester among them – while 13 had been educated at smaller private schools. Three of the remainder reported grammar school education. Only four registrations were reported for the Oxbridge universities – one at Oxford and three at Cambridge – while eight were registered at London, Leeds, Durham, Liverpool, and elsewhere. The lower uptake of private and university education in this sample, as compared with other élites, reflects the fact that many industrialists joined the family firm or set up independent enterprises, neither of which required formal educational qualifications. Nevertheless, most FBI leaders did receive a privileged education; the vast majority had very affluent parents.

Not surprisingly, the leaders of the FBI held a large number of company directorships – 69 among the 23. The companies included some of the best known in the world at the time, such as Dunlop, ICI, Vickers and General Electric; major banks included Midland and Guinness, Mahon and Co; indeed, at one time or another, five of the FBI's leading members had been closely connected with the Midland Bank: Lord Hirst through his General Electric Company's financial connection with the Bank, and Sir Clive Baillieu, Dudley Docker, H.D. McGowan and Sir Francis Joseph as directors of the board.

The FBI leaders were industrial leaders in their respective spheres too: indeed it was as representatives of sectoral interests that they were called upon to lead the FBI itself. The sample of 23 also played leading roles in 18 other business associations representing the interests of the rubber industry, lead manufacturers, mine owners, brewers, shipbuilders and motor manufacturers; there were also three chambers of commerce leaders, representing London, British and international organisations. Coming, as they did, from some of the nation's biggest companies, these 23 men gained even greater political and economic influence through their activities as the public leaders of industrial associations. In addition, of course, their leadership roles sharpened their conception of 'business' interests, as they grappled with numerous problems and issues on behalf of their members.

Politically, the FBI leaders tended to be pro-Conservative or Liberal; the only partial exception was H.D. McGowan, the head of ICI, who had 'flirted' with Nazism during the 1930s. Dudley Docker, the FBI's founder, was president of his local Conservative Association, while solicitor H.W. Looker had been a Unionist MP.

The most 'experienced' politician among FBI leaders was J.A. Pease (Lord Gainford of Headlam) who had been Mayor of Darlington in 1889, in Asquith's Cabinet in 1910, and a Liberal MP in 1929.

The evidence available also indicates that only one of the leaders was actively involved in pro-Empire organisations. Lord Hirst was a member of four organisations: the Empire Industries Association, the United Empire Club, the Royal Colonial Institute and the British Commonwealth Union.

Twenty club memberships were also reported by 13 of the leading members. The most popular were the Reform, Carlton and Athenaeum clubs, each reporting three members.

Empire Industries Association

Analysis of the leading figures in the EIA indicates an organisation thoroughly enmeshed in a myriad of imperial networks. Information was available on 40 of the 49 leaders mentioned in the minutes of meetings.

Educational backgrounds

The table below summarises the educational data available on the 40 leaders:

SCHOOLING

Private	Public	Grammar	Other
14	15	2	3

UNIVERSITY

Oxford	Cambridge	Others
6	6	8

The figures show that, where information is available, the leaders were educationally unrepresentative of British society as a whole, with a high frequency of attendance at fee-paying and prestigious institutions such as Eton, Harrow and Rugby, and the élite universities of Oxford and Cambridge. In addition, a number had also attended schools and/or universities in the Dominions and Colonies. While unrepresentative of the population at large, the EIA's leaders were drawn from, and were thoroughly representative of, the British élite. As such, at the very least, it may be argued that they would be likely to support the social, economic and political status quo, as it so clearly implied the maintenance of their privileged positions. As yet, however, there appear to be no obvious reasons as to why these individuals should unify so solidly around defence of the Empire, while others from similar backgrounds opted for an alliance with the United States.

Company directorships
It is in the analysis of these figures that, it is argued here, one part of the explanation of the EIA leaders' attitudes emerges. Research indicates that 65 companies (at the very least, as seven directors of multiple numbers of companies do not cite all their directorships, ending their entries with 'etc', or 'and many others') were directed by 25 of the 40 leaders. Leopold Amery, the President of EIA, alone directed 14 companies. Analysis of the imperial connections of companies directed by Amery highlights firms in Australian mining, Indian rubber, south-west African trade and Canadian finance. Amery's directorships provide in microcosm some idea of the types of companies directed by the EIA leaders as a whole. There is an array of companies with imperial connections such as Tate and Lyle, ICI and Rhodesian Railways, and companies with interests in gold exploration and mining, South African diamonds, Canadian nickel and so on. In fact there are at least 25 companies that have obvious imperial locations and interests. Directorship of such companies – and, of course, the many that sell to, buy from or lend to the Empire, or have imperial branches – is likely to make the individual even more intensely aware of the needs of Empire and imperial interests. It is likely to foster a more acute desire to maintain, develop and promote imperial unity, ideals and interests. Being fairly lucrative, directorship of imperially connected companies is likely to play an important role in fostering attitudes conducive to the continuation of that source of earnings, status and prestige. Yet economics alone, while important, is only one part of the basis of pro-imperial attitudes. It may not necessarily be the cause of

pro-imperial convictions: the directorship of an imperial company may reflect the individual's support of the ideals of Empire whose source lies elsewhere. In any case, it is not the intention here to identify the key cause of pro-imperial attitudes of the EIA; it is to highlight the numerous and mutually interacting and reinforcing factors that were involved in the structure of persisting cultural and political attitudes.

Imperial business associations
The narrow economic interest in the continuation of Empire noted above was significantly strengthened by the high levels of activity of a quarter of the 40 leaders, in 15 wider business associations related to imperial production and trade. These imperial business associations included the Federation of the Chambers of Commerce of the British Empire, the British Empire Producers' Association and the Association of West Indian Chambers of Commerce. In addition, therefore, to the personal economic interests of the directors of imperially connected companies must be counted the far broader interests and concerns that membership of representative organisations implies. Necessarily, leaders of such organisations must take the broadest views since their constituents have a variety of sometimes conflicting interests which need to be harmonised. Management of such organisations requires and strengthens the imperial convictions of its leaders, and their ability to rationalise the often narrower and more short-sighted activities of its members. It also provides a source of social and political status, tying the leaders even more firmly to 'things as they are'. And the social influence of such leaders is normally great, because as leaders they tend to be among the most active of individuals.

Empire promotion organisations
Ten of the EIA's leaders were also actively involved in the operations of seven organisations that espoused the ideals of imperial unity, usually through campaigns for certain reforms (such as the Tariff Reform League) and production of educational materials (Imperial Institute), as well as providing forums for the discussion of imperial problems (Royal Empire Society). Other institutions of this type involving EIA leaders included the British Commonwealth Union

and the British Empire League. Once again, management of such bodies is likely to strengthen pro-imperial convictions.

Imperially linked political/administrative posts
Eleven EIA leaders had, at one time or another, held 29 posts connected with the administration of some aspect of empire. The posts held varied from the Cabinet ministers such as Amery who was Secretary of State for India and for Burma (1940–45), to Sir Edward Campbell who was the British vice-consul in Java (1914–20). Other posts included a trade commissioner and an ADC to the Governor of Bombay. Holding such posts adds experience to convictions, a powerful boost to pre-existing pro-imperial attitudes.

Club membership
The EIA's leaders held 59 club memberships in total, at clubs such as the Travellers', Marlborough, Athenaeum and Constitutional. The most popular, however, was the Carlton Club, which drew 23 of the EIA's leaders. The Carlton Club was (and is) one of the most élitist of such institutions, and is closely linked with the right-wing of the Conservative Party.

Overall, then, the nature of the EIA's membership conforms very closely with its pro-imperial ideals: there was a preponderance of individuals connected in a number of ways – economically, politically, socially – to the Empire and its problems and administration. There was a very powerful group of individuals with a vested interest in the maintenance of the Empire. Inevitably, some of those individuals were in a position to challenge the trend towards Anglo-American alliance, which they saw as detrimental to the imperial position.

Bank of England

The Bank, as one would expect, was also highly élitist in composition. Detailed analysis of the social and economic characteristics of 22 (upon whom information was available) of its 39 wartime directors shows that public/private education and Oxbridge featured strongly. Fifteen of the directors had been educated privately, nine of them at institutions like Eton and Rugby; only one, Sir Henry Clay, had been to a grammar school. Ten had passed through the Oxbridge universities (seven at Oxford and three at Cambridge), and two (Josiah Stamp and Josiah Wedgwood) through the London School of Economics.

The worlds of politics and the civil service appear not to have been major sources of recruitment to the Bank's leading positions: there were only three politicians – Baron Craigmyle (Liberal MP 1915–23), Sir Alan Garrett Anderson (Conservative MP 1935–40), and Sir Andrew Duncan (National MP 1940–50) – serving during wartime; and there were only three civil servants.

The largest source of supply for recruitment was the world of business. The 22 directors held 61 directorships (excluding the Bank itself) among them, in companies representing shipping, railways, armaments, cars, insurance, chemicals and other interests. The single largest holder of directorships was Lord Catto, who became the Bank's Governor in 1944, with 11; the next largest (with six) was Sir Charles Joseph Hambro, chairman of Hambros. The 22 directors were also prominent in organisations representing shipping interests. Six such organisations (including the Chamber of Shipping, London General Shipowners' Society, Shipping Federation, Imperial Shipping Committee), were represented. This is not, perhaps, very surprising since 'shipping' is one of the key income-generating sources for the City of London.

The West End clubs featured strongly once again, with 37 memberships reported. The most popular were the Reform (with seven members), Brooks's (four) and the Athenaeum (three).

Conservative Party

As the oldest party of the 'establishment', the Conservative Party was bound to be thoroughly interconnected with élite institutions. Information was available on 17 of the 24 leading Conservatives during wartime, a sample that included two prime ministers – Neville Chamberlain and Winston Churchill – and two foreign secretaries Lord Halifax and Anthony Eden.

Churchill's cabinet consisted of six aristocrats and nine professionals, out of a total of 16. According to David and Gareth Butler in *British Political Facts 1900–1985*, professionals and employers constituted almost 95 per cent of Conservative MPs in 1945; only three per cent were of working-class origin.

Eton was the first choice of public schools for seven of the 17 Conservatives; with Harrow and Rugby also popular. Nine had gone to Oxbridge, and three to other universities.

Company directorships were also numerous – 63 in all, with Sir Oliver Lyttleton (President of the Board of Trade, 1940) alone holding 22. Again, this is hardly surprising since the Conservative Party and big business have always been closely connected. Reported club memberships numbered 33, with nine at the Carlton.

Royal Institute of International Affairs

Since the RIIA was the only special interest which claimed to be impartial and objective, and interested only in scientific research rather than 'ideology' or 'politics', a detailed analysis is offered below of data that might be considered to undermine such claims. In addition, therefore, to consideration of the social and other credentials of its leading members, there is also a brief analysis of its financial sources.

A detailed analysis of the Presidents and Members of Council for four sample years (1920, 1930, 1940 and 1950) has been conducted. There were 135 presidents and members of the Governing Council for those years, although this decreases to 103 when individuals serving two or more terms are counted only once. Among the presidents (a largely honorary position) can be found some of the foremost actors on the political scene of that time and beyond, including Churchill, Eden, Stanley Baldwin, Lloyd George and Ernest Bevin. Present among the names of Council members are other well-known political, military, bureaucratic and academic names, such as Denis Healey, Arthur Creech Jones, Lord Hailey of the Colonial Office, Sir Orme Sargent, Marshalls of the RAF Viscount Portal and Lord Trenchard, and the historian, E.L. Woodward. Aggregate findings under the categories of educational background, political office, civil service and armed services connections, directorships, and social club memberships are summarised below.

Educational background

Sixty-three of the 75 (84 per cent) upon whom schooling data were available received a public school education, with 29 (38 per cent) having attended top Clarendon schools such as Eton, Harrow and Rugby. Fifty-six of them (74 per cent) went on to Oxford University (36) or Cambridge (20); ten attended other universities, while ten had trained at Dartmouth Naval College and Woolwich and Sandhurst military academies.

Political office

The sample of 103 leading figures in the Institute contained 31 MPs, of whom 12 were Conservatives, ten Labour, seven Liberal, and two were independents. At one time or another, 28 of the RIIA figures held ministerial positions. For example, those 28 enjoyed eight periods of Prime Ministerial power, six periods of Foreign Secretaryship, six Colonial Secretary appointments, and four periods as Chancellors of the Exchequer. In total, those 28 members held 112 governmental positions.

Civil service and military links

Sixty of the 103 leaders, Presidents and Council Members, held, at one time or another, 241 posts of this kind. Twenty held positions in the Foreign Office; 13 in the Ministry of Information; nine in the War Office; and 16 in the British Embassy in Washington.

Company directorships

Fifty-seven of the 103 leaders (55 per cent) had held at least one directorship. Altogether, the 57 directors held 174 directorships between them, in some of the biggest industrial, commercial and financial corporations in the country.

Social clubs

Of the 103 leaders, information on social club membership was available on 66 (64 per cent). Those 66 frequented at least 53 clubs. Thirty-four members belonged to just one club, while 32 belonged to two or more. Those 66 members between them held 129 memberships, with 12 major clubs accounting for 94 of the 129 memberships (72 per cent). The Athenaeum claimed 20 members; Brooks's 15, Travellers' and Reform nine each; eight belonged to the Carlton, seven to the University Club, six to the National Liberal, and five to various American-based clubs.

All of the above indicators point strongly to the conclusion that the Institute was firmly located in élite circles, rather than being socially, educationally or occupationally representative of the population as a whole. What are the likely effects on individuals of these social backgrounds? How does social background affect one's attitude and behaviour? Pluralists generally argue that social background is not the key to political actions, that other factors are more important. This position, however, has led them largely to ignore the degree to which academic research demonstrates a positive relationship between social origins and political and other behaviour. At the very least it can be argued that a privileged social background will tend to produce socially 'conservative' attitudes and behaviour that favour the maintenance of the status quo; and that any change that may be contemplated will be motivated by a desire either to strengthen or to limit the changes to the status quo.

Funding of Chatham House
The financing of the Institute has from the beginning been based on the donation of wealthy individuals and corporations. Thomas Lamont of J.P. Morgan was prominent; Lord Astor, the owner of *The Times* and *Observer* newspapers; and Sir Abe Bailey, the Transvaal mine owner, donated thousands of pounds; Cecil Power contributed £10,000 to finance the building of a meeting hall in 1923; Sir Daniel Stevenson set up a £20,000 fund to finance an annual survey of international affairs (which was edited by the eminent historian, Arnold Toynbee). British banks and corporations, and various American philanthropic foundations, also donated large sums to the Institute. The Bank of England gave £6,000 over three years; the Carnegie UK Trustees paid £3,000 to establish the Chatham House Library; John D. Rockefeller donated £3,000. By 1929, the Chairman of the Institute's Endowment Fund, Stephen King-Hall, reported that 'a number of the important banks, companies, firms, and individuals in the City of London . . . became corporate subscribers of the Institute, promising annual grants'. In

1932, the Rockefeller Foundation announced a donation of £40,000 over five years to finance new research using the study group method. By 1936, over 47 firms such as ICI, the Anglo-Iranian Oil Company, and Barclays Bank, were regularly donating funds.

In addition, therefore, to its strong social and political connections, the Institute also increasingly commanded the confidence of important sections of the industrial and financial élite. The financial position of Chatham House by the 1930s was guaranteed by the wealthiest sectors of British society. The élitist credentials of the Institute were impeccable.

Trades Union Congress

The TUC leaders analysed below formed a different kind of élite to those discussed above. In one sense, of course they were true achievers: they had won positions of power and influence against the odds. Despite humble social origins, these men had distinguished themselves in working-class and union politics, and become leaders. 'Privileges' had only come to some of these men very late in life, after years of manual labour and struggle for union organisation. If they constituted an 'aristocracy of labour', they had not attained such a status as a matter of birthright: they had had to fight for it every step of the way.

Of the 15 leaders identified as of importance (on the General Council) during the 1939–45 war, information was available on nine. The information was rather 'patchy', however, and important aspects of these TUC leaders' lives remain unknown. Educational information was available on seven leaders, who all reported (at least) an elementary level of schooling. Two, Sir Walter Citrine and Sir Mark Hodgson, had gone on to apprenticeships (in electrics and boiler-making respectively), while Hodgson had also attended technical college (as had Sir George Chester). In terms of higher education, only the Rt. Hon. George Woodcock reported attendance at Ruskin and New College, Oxford: Woodcock excelled at Oxford, graduating with first class honours in Politics, Philosophy and Economics in 1933.

The nine leaders were active in a broad range of trade unions, from boiler-making to transport to the merchant marine. Included among their number was, of course, Ernest Bevin of the Transport and Gerneral Workers' Union, who became a member of Churchill's Cabinet in 1940, and Foreign Secretary in 1945. Most of these leaders were drawn into wartime service, usually into one of the Production Councils. In the post-war period, several of them were drawn into other areas of public service too: George Gibson became a director of the Bank of England, for example, and Sir Luke Fawcett of the Building Trade Workers' Union served on the Atomic Energy Authority in the 1950s.

Four of the nine had connections with the business world: Gibson was chairman of North Western Industrial Estates Ltd; Sir Arthur Deakin was a director of the *Daily Herald*, Fawcett was director of Building and Civil Engineering Holidays Management Ltd; and Hodgson was manager of the Newcastle Savings Bank.

As has been noted already, nearly all of these nine leaders had been awarded either a CBE or a knighthood or appointed to the Privy Council. Only George Gibson had none of the above, having been made a Companion of Honour.

Finally, only one élite club membership was reported by this group of trade union leaders. Ernest Bevin was a member of the Athenaeum.

Labour Party

Of the 39 leaders of the party and their associates mentioned in the minutes of Labour meetings and of Cabinet, information was available on 24. In some ways, the social origins of Labour leaders must be viewed in the same manner as for the TUC. There were many more élite members of the party, however.

Twelve of the 24 had attended state schools (one of them a grammar) while seven had been educated at more privileged institutions. Clement Attlee, as noted in an earlier chapter, had been to Haileybury; Cripps had attended Winchester; and Dalton was an old Etonian. Sixteen had received a university education, the majority (nine) at Oxford and Cambridge.

Inevitably, there were strong links (nine) with the trade union movement, most notably Bevin. Three others had also held posts within the TUC, for example James Walker, former head of the Scottish section. Most of the 24 party leaders were MPs (22), with ten holding ministerial posts.

Only one of the leaders, the Rt. Hon. Arthur Creech Jones, held any company directorships. He held three in total, in the chemical and insurance industries. Jones was appointed Colonial Secretary, in 1946, in the post-war Labour Government. Three of the leaders reported élite club memberships – in the Athenaeum (Bevin, Attlee and Ivor Thomas) and Oxford and Cambridge (Attlee). Dalton was also a member of the Athenaeum, but failed to report the fact in his entry in 'Who's Who' of British MPs.

Communist Party of Great Britain

Of the 21 leaders of the party identified for this analysis, and in accordance with Henry Pelling's historical profile in *The British Communist Party*, information was available on 11. There is little reason to believe that these 11 are in any significant way unrepresentative of the Communist leadership as a whole. Most of the party's leaders and close associates, in this analysis, came from working-class and trade union backgounds – not dissimilar to those of the leaders of the TUC. Not surprisingly, then, criticism of the 'labour aristocracy' was most vociferously heard among these men, who denounced TUC leaders as 'traitors' to the working class because of their 'reformism'.

According to Pelling, the most notable feature of the early leaders of the Communist Party was the degree to which they were derived from non-English national groupings. There were Irishmen, Scots, and Welshmen, but few Englishmen. The analysis of 11 leaders carried out here also tends to confirm that view to some extent. The (admittedly small) sample contained two Scots (J.R. Campbell and William Gallacher), one Welshman (Arthur Horner), and Rajani Palme Dutt (who was of Indo-Scandinavian origin). There was also a Jewish cockney, Phil Piratin, who was to become the Communist MP for Mile End in 1945. While Pelling infers that *ethnicity* was the key driving force behind communist popularity, it is at least as important that the Scots and Welshmen concerned were members of the industrial working class, employed in the old 'staple' industries. Six of the leaders were, in any case, English, and mostly working class.

Educationally, six had received only an elementary education, while Tom Mann, the veteran trade unionist, had begun work at the age of nine. Three leaders, J.B.S. Haldane, D.N. Pritt, and R.P. Dutt, had received the most privileged schooling – Eton, Winchester, and then Balliol and New College, Oxford. Dutt, who graduated with a first class degree with honours in Classics, had been expelled from Oxford for 'propagating' Marxism in 1917.

Manual occupations dominated the early working lives of the Communist leaders, with the coalmining, transport and engineering sectors well represented. Of course, the privately educated leaders were engaged in 'mental labour' – Pritt as a lawyer; Dutt as editor of various communist publications, most notably *Labour Monthly*, and Haldane as a geneticist of world-wide reputation, having been a Reader at Cambridge University between 1922 and 1932 and Professor at the Royal Institution. Haldane was also chairman of the *Daily Worker* editorial board from 1940 to 1949.

Trade Union activity was common as a source of recruitment for communist politics, and six of the leaders had such organising experience. The most famous among these men was Tom Mann, who had joined the (highly élitist) Amalgamated Society of Engineers in 1881 and risen to become its leader by 1918; he had, according to *Who Was Who* become a 'Socialist' in 1885. William Gallacher rose to prominence during the uprisings and revolts in the Clyde shipyards in the First World War, being chairman of the Clyde Workers' Committee; he later became a member of Parliament and a leading member of the Third International. Bert Papworth also rose to significance through 'unofficial' activities within the trade union movement: he was a leading member of the 'Busman's Rank and File Movement' inside Bevin's Transport and General Workers' Union (TGWU); he later became one of the two TGWU representatives on the General Council of the TUC, but by 1950 he had been dismissed for his communist beliefs. Arthur Horner rose to become leader of the South Wales miners and then became head of the National Union of Miners in 1946.

While Oxford University had only expelled Dutt for his Marxist 'propaganda', the authorities in the 'real world' were much more harsh with certain rebels. William Rust and J.R. Campbell were both imprisoned in 1925 for 'incitement to mutiny' and 'seditious conspiracy'; Campbell was released after serving only six months as the case against him was considered to be baseless. In several ways, then, the leadership of the CPGB represented the 'social mix' recommended by both Marx and Lenin: the most 'advanced' elements from the proletariat and the most 'progressive' section of the intelligentsia.

In concluding this section of the chapter, it is clear that the leadership of the special interests, political parties and civil service analysed above was heavily restricted and narrow. There are definite social and economic institutions, which élites spring from or belong to, providing the major figures in British policy-making. This very high degree of social uniformity could have been, and indeed was, one basis of a 'common' world outlook, a particular way of perceiving and considering the problems of British society and its place in the world order. Clearly, the manner in which problems were approached, the guiding principles that were often not even open to challenge and the taken-for-granted assumptions that underpinned élite attitudes, orientated élites to marginalise certain ideas and values as superfluous and unworthy of consideration. The corollary of this is that there was a 'narrow' range of options that were considered 'practical' most of which, it could be argued, were orientated around élite interests.

If common social origins were vital in generating a certain world view, then institutions functioned to maintain élite cohesion on a day-to-day basis. That is, there were 'spaces' in which the élite members analysed above could meet and exchange thoughts and ideas, and thereby maintain élite solidarity. While there were numerous special interest groups and parties, giving the impression of a competitive élite system, there was also a great deal of overlapping between groups, especially through interlocking company directorships and club memberships. These were predominantly non-labour interconnections, according to the evidence already presented. Obviously, these interconnections were general in effect rather than policy-specific; their importance probably lay in their function of creating and reinforcing a certain climate of opinion, generally favouring the status quo. It could be argued that human beings are inherently divisive and that, rather than increasing their solidarity, the club and boardroom merely served, to some extent, to increase their contempt for certain people. This, of course, may be true. But one other factor must be taken into account too: that human beings – club members, company directors, politicians, bureaucrats, and citizens – often unite against external threats to their position; and the level of unity may be determined by the nature of the threat. What this may mean is that even if there is hostility on a personal level, members of groups, classes or nations usually unite when faced with the outsider – that is, other groups, classes or nations.

The members of the organisations and parties discussed above would have had strong group loyalties, but their level of interconnection tended to broaden their conception of 'interest'. The TUC's connections with the Labour Party were obviously numerous and ongoing; influence and ideas moved in both directions. Both groups' experience of wartime government had the effect of enhancing their contact with ministers and their civil servants. In conditions of external threat – the 'other' in this case being Nazi Germany – individuals united against the common enemy. Inevitably, perhaps, in this state of unity the groups lost much of their autonomy and individuality, which are qualities said to be the essence of pluralist democracy.

The most central special interest group, in terms of interconnectedness, was the Royal Institute of International Affairs. The RIIA was connected with every other organisation (except the communists), including the TUC. The RIIA had 11 interlocks with Labour, another 11 with the civil service, and ten with the Conservatives. Chatham House's centrality may be explained by its 'impartial' and 'non-political' character, while all of the others were agreed to be more specialised and 'biased' in character. While it would have been impolitic for TUC/Labour members to join the EIA/FBI/Conservatives, the RIIA provided a forum for sharing views with those from across the 'divide' in British politics. Civil servants could also join the RIIA, while being banned from party membership by law. The Royal Institute, therefore, played a key 'consensus-building' role in the discussion of British foreign affairs.

The least interlocked group was the TUC, with only six links – five with Chatham House and only one with the Labour Party. This is, of course, a major flaw in the interlocking type of analysis. While the TUC's five links with Chatham House suggest 'influence', the one with Labour makes it appear far less significant. The opposite is, in fact, the case. That one connection with Labour was of major importance – in the form of Ernest Bevin – to Britain's external relations and to the power of the unions inside the Labour Party. The connection between the TUC and Labour was continuous, as both bodies were represented on the National Council of Labour, the Central Committee on Reconstruction, the Labour Party Policy Sub-Committee, and so on. We could also add that the Royal Institute's relationship with the government and civil service was practically continuous too, especially because of the activities of the Foreign Research and Press Service. Finally, Labour and the Conservatives were working together in the Coalition Government for five years, again underlining the flaws in the interlocking method.

The connections and overlaps were quantitatively numerous; even more significantly, they were qualitative. The élite group, numbering only around 300-strong, directed 375 companies and held 222 club memberships. They belonged to a tiny network of official and unofficial, political and social institutions, and were in and out of a small set of occupations. They were more strongly connected to one another than they were to other, more popular (less élitist) associations and individuals. They constituted Britain's foreign policy élite.

One of the fundamental questions in political scientific and popular discussion is 'Who holds power?'. We must also address this question in this study: where did the power of decision lie in the making of the Anglo-American alliance?

NOTES

1. D.C.M. Platt, *Finance, Trade and Politics in British Foreign Policy 1815–1914* (Oxford: Clarendon Press, 1968), p. xiii.
2. Ibid., p. xvi.
3. G. Ingham, *Capitalism Divided? The City and Industry in British Social Development* (London: Macmillan, 1984), p. 9.

The State and the National Interest

4. Sir Herbert Llewellyn Smith, *The Board of Trade* (London and New York: G.P. Putnam's and Sons, 1928), p. 147.
5. Ibid., p. 149.
6. Ibid., p. 151.
7. Roger Prouty, *The Transformation of the Board of Trade 1830–1855* (London: Heinemann, 1957), p. 105.
8. Platt, op. cit., p. 104.
9. Ibid., pp. 112–13.
10. Ibid., p. xix.
11. Ibid., p. xxv.
12. Sir John Tilley and Stephen Gaselee, *The Foreign Office* (London and New York: G.P. Putnam's and Sons, 1933), p. 229.
13. Platt, op. cit., p. 364.
14. Ibid., p. 367.
15. John Connell, *The 'Office', A Study of British Foreign Policy and its Makers 1919–1951* (London: Allan Wingate, 1958), pp. 11–12.
16. Lord Strang, *The Diplomatic Career* (London: André Deutsch, 1962), p. 121.
17. 'Private Discussion Meeting', in Chatham House Archives, 9/20c, 6 Dec. 1943.
18. Another good example is Nathan A. Pelcovits, *Old China Hands and the Foreign Office* (New York: Octagon Books, 1969).
19. Sir J. Brenan, 'Anglo-Japanese Relations', 25 Aug. 1938, FO 371/22181.
20. Ball memorandum, 'Protection of British Overseas Investments in Industrial Securities', 18 April 1940, Treasury Files, T.160/1188/13062/02, in Public Record Office, London.
21. Ibid., letter, Waley to Sir Frederick Phillips, 20 April 1940.
22. Ibid., letter, Phillips to Sir Richard Hopkins, 6 May 1940; Ford memorandum, 'British Investments Overseas', 10 Aug. 1944, in T.160/1321/13062/03.
23. Note by Lothian, 'Financial Aid from USA 1940–41', 1940, in T.160-995/F19422, p. 10.
24. Letter, Halifax to Schuster, 24 Nov. 1939, and minute by Chamberlain, 15 Nov. 1939, in FO371/24247.
25. Sir Henry Ashley Clarke and Sir J. Brenan, 15 May 1939, in FO371/23441.
26. Keynes, 'Post-War Currency Policy', 8 Sept. 1941, in Bank of England Archives, OV38/1, location no., 1335/2, pp. 1–5.
27. Memorandum, 'Our Overseas Resources and Liabilities', 1 July 1944, War Cabinet Papers, WP(44)360.
28. Letter, G.B. Blaker (Department of Overseas Trade) to S.D. Waley (Treasury), 7 May 1941, and minutes of Export Committee, 9 May 1941, in T.160/1104/17610/1.
29. Annex A, Treasury memorandum, 'External Monetary and Economic Policy', 10 April 1942, in WP(42)159.
30. Ibid.
31. Nicholls, 2 July 1940, Whitehead, 2 July 1940, and Butler, 7 July 1940, in FO371/25206.
32. Sir R.I. Campbell to Eden, 15 Aug. 1941, 'Post-War Cooperation with the USA', in FO371/26151.
33. T.N. Whitehead, 21 Sept. 1941, ibid.
34. Sargent, 3 Aug. 1944, in FO371/40952.
35. Butler, 3 Aug. 1944, ibid.

36. 'The Effect of our External Financial Position on our Foreign Policy', Nov. 1944, ibid.
37. W.S. Churchill, WM (44) 93rd Conclusions, 18 July 1944, in FO371/40952.
38. Z. Steiner, *The Foreign Office and Foreign Policy, 1898–1914* (Cambridge: Cambridge University Press, 1969), p. 16.
39. Cited in Connell, *The 'Office'*, op. cit., p. 286.
40. Ibid., pp. 18–19.
41. Steiner, op. cit., pp. 19–20, 22, 217.
42. Tilley and Gaselee, op. cit., p. 87.
43. Anthony Giddens and Philip Stanworth, 'Elites and Privilege', in P. Abrams (ed.), *Work, Urbanism and Inequality* (London: Weidenfeld and Nicolson, 1978).
44. Tilley and Gaselee, op. cit., p. 96.

5

The Role and Influence of Special Interests, Political Parties and the State in the Formation of the Anglo-American Alliance

The study of 'influence' presents some of the most difficult methodological problems in political sociology: the key question is how is influence to be measured? There is little agreement on this point, however. The key principle is, of course, that actor A alters the behaviour of actor B in accordance with A's wishes, as opposed to B's original wishes. It is very difficult, however, to find influence of this 'pure' type in actual human relationships, especially when institutions such as the state and special interests (based on the defence of vested interests) are involved. They are notoriously secretive. Given the broad range of available historical material, however, we are in a fairly sound position to reach some conclusions as to the direction and nature of influence in the making of the Anglo-American alliance.

The impact of the activities of the special interest groups discussed in this study, it is argued, may be evaluated against the taking of the five 'key' decisions outlined earlier. To reiterate, those decisions were: the 'destroyers–bases' agreement of August 1940; the 'Atlantic Charter' of August 1941; the Mutual Aid Agreement of February 1942; the Bretton Woods negotiations of 1944–45; and the US Loan decision of 1945. Before examining the activities concerning the taking of these decisions, however, an outline of the general roles and influence (as far as the available evidence will allow) of the special interests and political parties will be provided.

FEDERATION OF BRITISH INDUSTRIES

From the archive material of the FBI and the state, it is quite clear that the FBI was seen as the vehicle of industrial interests. In this respect, state officials and ministers frequently met FBI leaders to explain official policy or to enquire as to the FBI's views; the FBI made representations to the state on matters such as the Sino-Japanese hostilities as they affected British interest; and the Foreign Office held confidential meetings and sent secret letters to FBI leaders. Influence in a situation such as this is very difficult to determine. Both agencies could be said to be influencing each other, or else there would be little point in the liaison. The key point is the direction of influence.

Government departments often asked the FBI for information, and, on occasions, the FBI could and did claim to have influenced official thinking. For example, the FBI convinced the Board of Trade that India had fared better than Britain as a result of the Ottawa Agreements.[1] In 1939, the FBI claimed to have directly caused an advance in government policy towards the export situation.[2] In 1943, their complaints to the Department of Overseas Trade about the American capture of South American markets led to a decision to advertise British goods and to organise foreign visits.[3] The FBI strongly urged the reform of the Foreign Service, because of the belief in the overwhelming importance of international commerce in maintaining national prosperity.[4]

Weighed against this was the rather greater power of the state. None of the above instances really militated against the views and interests of the state; and that is largely why they were accepted. It was the details of everyday foreign relations that the state accepted the FBI's opinions on, not the fundamental issues. The initiative on the major questions was in the hands of the state. On the question of Britain's policy in the Sino-Japanese War, for example, it seems quite clear that the close links with the Foreign Office were a channel for official influence. Four examples will suffice to demonstrate this point, showing that the FBI was mobilised by the state, used as a channel for official policy dissemination and legitimisation. In relation to Far Eastern policy, it can be seen that changes in the FBI's position reflected changes in official policy. When Sino-Japanese hostilities began in 1937, the China Liaison Committee (CLC) consisting of representatives of the FBI and China Association, and the Manchester, London and Bradford chambers of commerce, passed a resolution urging the British government to do all it could to protect trade.⁵ By early January 1938, the CLC urged HMG to consider the necessity of forcing Japan to recognise its liability in damaging British interests.⁶ The FBI then engaged in a series of meetings and communications with the Foreign Office, with the net result that the FBI China Committee broke away from the CLC because of the latter's increasingly strident demands for tough government action in the Far East. Perhaps the most interesting such consultation was the secret one in November 1938, just before the FBI split from the CLC. An unnamed member of the FBI China Committee revealed that he had held private talks with the Foreign Office who, he rightly claimed, 'were very anxious that American and British Far East policy should proceed along parallel lines' and that informal discussions along those lines were being held by the two governments.⁷ The effect of this revelation was pretty immediate: within a month the FBI had not only split from the CLC but also declared 'that it was useless to suggest the Government employing threats towards Japan which it was incapable of carrying out... The final conclusion reached by the China Committee was that co-operation or parallel action between the US and Great Britain [in the Far East] would be helpful.'⁸ The FBI acted on this governmental 'advice' very quickly by encouraging its members to cement Anglo-American industrial ties in the Far East because, as the China Committee argued, there was 'solid ground for such action, as the "open door" had always been the American policy and they had large interests, both missionary, commercial and financial in China'. FBI members began contacting their American counterparts with this in mind. Indeed, the above-cited unnamed member claimed that he had already contacted

> a very important American businessman with a view to exploring the possiblity of cooperation between British and American industrialists. As a practical step... they had agreed to explore the question of a common policy towards China with a view to stirring up public opinion in both countries and bringing pressure to bear on the respective Governments to ensure parallel action officially in the Far East, letting it be known that we [Britain] were merely concerned to follow the American lead.⁹

As if to reinforce this position among industrial circles, the Foreign Office sent the FBI an 'unofficial' letter in February 1939 which again urged 'cooperation between British and American industrialists.'[10] It seems reasonably clear from this reading of events and attitudes that the state exercised a vital influence over the FBI's position with regard to the Far East, and to the need for Anglo-American co-operation in all spheres.

A second example similarly demonstrates the degree of influence that the state exercised over the FBI. In late 1938, the policy of the FBI and its various constituent bodies tended to favour a very firm policy of supporting the Empire and, partly to that end, the maintenance of a European balance of power.[11] By the outbreak of war, however, industrialists became increasingly aware of the extent of Britain's dependence on the US, although the Empire was still considered as of great importance. The FBI's Reconstruction Report of May 1942 stressed the need to come to terms with American economic power but without alienating the Colonies and Dominions, and urged the development of machinery for inter-imperial consultation in order to produce a viable Empire policy.[12] But these hopes for a positive Empire-based policy were dashed during unofficial talks between FBI members and Sir Kenneth Lee, who represented the Industrial and Export Council of the Board of Trade in the US. Lee, who had travelled extensively in the US and met numerous businessmen, pointed out that certain governmental decisions and undertakings, such as the Atlantic Charter and the Mutual Aid Agreement, 'will profoundly affect our future'. He informed the FBI that Article VII of the Agreement, in particular, demanded that in place of repayment of Lend-Lease aid, there should be an elimination of barriers to trade and the reduction of tariffs. The American-based National Foreign Trade Council had impressed upon Lee that it wanted an end to the Ottawa Agreements, and he informed the FBI that they should prepare themselves 'to face up to an American demand for their [the Ottawa Agreements'] reconsideration'. The entire position was, he stated, changing the factors at work and not only included the inter-governmental agreements but also concerned 'the likely tendency of the Dominions to be drawn more closely to the USA after the War'. The net effect, he concluded, was that 'it may well be that our relationship with our Dominions, and also with our Colonies, will be very much changed after the War'.[13] This meeting, and to some degree the 'logic' of world events, instilled a greater respect for American power in FBI circles. A gradual understanding (officially and unofficially) developed that Britain would eventually have to abandon imperial preference but should not allow the Americans to discover that it would do this in return for a cut in the US tariff.[14]

That attitude became firmly entrenched in industry by the end of 1944, when the FBI and other British business organisations attended the International Business Conference in the US. In defending British imperial policy 'in face of US attacks on imperial preference' the British delegates 'made it plain that this country would work for freer trade but was not prepared to surrender any present advantages until the transitional period was over, and until it could be clearly seen what counter advantages could be obtained from their surrender'.[15]

The evolution of the industrialists' attitude towards the Empire very much reflected the changes in the official policy of the state, with the key link being the 1942 meeting between Lee and the FBI. That 'unofficial' meeting powerfully reinforced the existing trend towards the declining significance of the Empire and the increasing importance of the US.

A third example may also be cited to demonstrate the degree to which the FBI's agenda was state-influenced: the switch from a policy of Anglo-French union to Anglo-American co-operation in 1939–40. The feared collapse of France moved British policy-makers to make a number of promises of post-war Anglo-French union, and a committee to investigate such possibilities was established under Lord Hankey, the former Secretary to the Cabinet.[16] The FBI, during the same period, with government encouragement and support, had invited French industrialists to meet with them 'for political and industrial reasons . . . in line with the Federation's policy of seeking to lessen international competition and to increase co-operation'.[17] By March 1940, the FBI Grand Council was informed that the Anglo-French industrialists' talks had been successful, and that the French should be left in no doubt that Britain recognised their war effort 'and that we were in with them up to the hilt both now and afterwards'.[18] The government's desire to 'fortify' France with promises of future co-operation was certainly strengthened by the similar actions of the British industrial community.

With the fall of France, however, government attention turned to the United States. Lord Halifax informed Hankey that the Anglo-French union idea had now been replaced with 'the possibility of some sort of special association with the USA'.[19] It was after this governmental shift to a 'pro-American' post-war policy, therefore, that the FBI began to consider the post-war position, with the Americans playing the key role, seriously.

A final instance of the relative power of the state and the FBI is that of the appeasement policy of the Chamberlain Government. It is alleged, by Sam Aaronovitch, for example, that the FBI was the prime mover in shaping Britain's foreign policy in general and the appeasement policy in particular. While there is an extremely close alignment between FBI views and official policy, this does not necessarily imply that industry 'dominated' government. In fact, with the benefit of hindsight and the availability of the public records of the time, it is quite clear that the relationship was quite the reverse: the government heavily influenced industrialists' opinions and policies. Aaronovitch, in fact, admits as much when he recounts that the day after Hitler's troops marched into Prague (15 March 1939) the FBI signed an agreement with its German counterpart, the Reichsgruppe Industrie, on future friendship and co-operation. However, agreement was, he reports, 'prepared and concluded under government auspices', on Chamberlain's own admission.[20] The government's appeasement policy, supported by industry, was the basis of the FBI–Reichsgruppe Industrie agreement.

The state archives provide many instances of officials favourably receiving businessmen's reports on the situation in various parts of the world.[21] The praise, however, was forthcoming only when the unofficial view coincided with the official one. Lever Brothers were criticised for being narrow-minded, as was the FBI itself in 1943: Proctor of the Treasury was told that 'the attitude of the FBI on commercial questions is not as far-sighted or broad as one might wish and their handling of it in the past has not always been helpful'.[22]

When the evidence is weighed up, therefore, the scales tend to tilt decisively towards the state. The initiative seemed to lie with officialdom, and the role of the FBI appears to have been, at least in part, to act as a channel for official policy to be heard, understood and supported by industrial interests.

EMPIRE INDUSTRIES ASSOCIATION

The key question here is: why did the EIA fail to influence government policy in line with its own pro-Empire conviction? As a first step towards answering this question, it is necessary to be aware of the degree of unity between the EIA and the state. The 'unity' referred to relates to the seemingly shared view of the importance of international commerce in the British 'national interest'. On the need for Britain to export her manufactures and import her raw materials there is no disagreement. The key to the disagreement and conflict between the EIA and the state is to be found in the means by which the 'national interest' was to be furthered. The conflict was over the strategy Britain should pursue in order to achieve the objectives defined to be in the 'national interest'. The argument was not over 'what to' but 'how to'. This argument occurred over many years, and on each occasion the state refused to accept the EIA's views. For example, in March 1938, Sir Henry Page Croft of the EIA wrote a memo to the Chancellor of the Exchequer on the issue of Britain's balance of trade. Croft argued that Britain's balance of trade was deteriorating so severely that there ought to be duties placed on certain goods whose importance had increased. He further stated that Britain's balance of payments was in the red, as Britons were investing less abroad, and British overseas capital was being depleted.[23]

Each of the arguments put forward were rebutted in a fairly systematic manner by the Treasury, in the form of Sir Frederick Phillips, who tersely pointed out that British imports had not greatly increased in volume, but only in price terms. Meanwhile, UK exports had increased by 9.5 per cent between 1936 and 1938. The increase in the prices of primary commodities was welcomed by Phillips as the solution to a problem: by increasing the purchasing power of the primary producers of India and South America, for example, Britain would be better able to sell them her manufactures. In any case, UK exports and earnings from shipping and overseas investment had more than compensated for the price increases. When it came to falling British overseas investments, Phillips argued that between 1932 and 1938, the figure had decreased by £100m, which he considered 'a small matter', considering the wide margin of error involved in calculating these figures. In any case, Britons were probably repatriating capital as Britain was a stable place to invest in times of world economic crisis; in addition, the heavy rearmament programme was diverting investment. Therefore, the argument put forward by the EIA can be said to have been considered quite seriously, but found wanting, by the policy-makers. The other arguments of the EIA in favour of the Empire option were treated in a similar manner.

BANK OF ENGLAND

Even in terms of influence over general issues, it cannot be argued that the Bank was influential. The documentary evidence from the Treasury records demonstrates quite clearly that control over the Bank's actions lay with officialdom. This, in fact, was affirmed by the two wartime Bank governors, Sir Montagu Norman and Lord Catto.[24] Catto stated, for example, on the 250th anniversary of the Bank that 'From time to time the Bank is accused of having undue power. But neither the Bank nor any other body working for the Government can determine policy: the power to do that is the prerogative of the Government and Parliament alone'.[25] Of course, any 'servant' of the state, whose position is determined by Acts of Parliament, is likely to make such declarations, some would argue, which makes such statements meaningless for analytical purposes. Considered in conjunction with documentary evidence, however, the above quotation appears to be remarkably close to the facts. The Bank was under official control and followed official direction. A number of minor examples may be cited to that end. For instance, in the early months of the war, the Bank proposed modifications to its constitution in order to meet more efficiently the demands of war finance. Reviewing the Bank's reform plan, with which officialdom generally concurred, the Treasury concluded sternly that 'in any case, behind all these emergency arrangements there is the overriding power of the Treasury to take control. If as a result, for example, of reducing the Directors' quorum to three [from 13] something went seriously wrong, we should no doubt exercise our power at once.'[26]

In practice, Treasury orders to the Bank had to be followed by its Governor and officers, whether they agreed with them or not. With reference to the Bank of England's wartime relationship with the Bank of International Settlements, which still had Italian and German government representatives on its board, the Treasury declared that 'The Bank of England could not without Treasury permission legally comply with any instruction of the B.I.S. which they had reason to suppose might be of benefit to the enemy'. The Bank would also be held liable, however, for any actual advantages the enemy received whether or not the Bank knew beforehand of the likely benefits to the enemy.[27] A note from Montagu Norman, the Bank's Governor, to Sir Richard Hopkins of the Treasury, clearly showed his annoyance with officialdom. Despite pointing out that the abrogation of international agreements and commitments would give the enemy a chance to conduct 'hostile propaganda', Norman declared tersely: 'If this is the official decision we shall, of course, accept it'.[28] To that end, Norman drew up a proposal for the new 'code of practice' in relation to the Bank for International Settlements.

The Bank of England, like the EIA, had a very different strategy for achieving the national interest, when compared with the ideas within the state itself. Pro-imperial convictions, while very strong in certain official quarters, had gradually been accommodated to more pragmatic recognition of the importance of the United States and a more open international economic order. The state and the Bank/EIA groupings were essentially heading in different directions.

ROYAL INSTITUTE OF INTERNATIONAL AFFAIRS

One of the most important members of Chatham House in a position to make an impact on British foreign policy, Lord Lothian, was appointed ambassador to the United States in August 1939.[29] He wasted no time in beginning his task of creating conditions favourable for Anglo-American co-operation. He recommended that Britain accept the American offer of 'non-political staff talks about the possibilities of common defence of Singapore, Dutch East Indies, Australia'.[30] His recommendation was acted upon by the British government.

Lothian also tried to iron out the problem of keeping the Americans 'sweet' in the period before they entered the war. When Britain, in a bid to conserve her dollars, switched her purchases of apples and tobacco from the US to Greece and Turkey, and thereby upset southern US agricultural interests, it was Lothian who suggested that it would be wiser in the circumstances to buy American. Although the recommendation was accepted, many in the Foreign Office were clearly annoyed with the Americans.[31]

In mid-1940, Lothian also saw the necessity for the exchange of technical information between Britain and the United States, if defence co-operation were to be feasible. On his recommendation, a military mission was suggested to, and accepted by, the Americans. Prime Minister Churchill, however, postponed the mission because he felt that the Americans were 'misbehaving', that is, they were asking for too much secret information, but Lothian believed that Britain should meet all such American demands. He opposed postponement of the military mission, and wrote a note to Halifax, who passed it on to Churchill, urging swift action as time was running out because 'our inaction in this connection was providing another argument for the defeatists [in the US] who maintain that it is no use backing a lost cause'. Churchill backed down and on 25 July 1940, held a meeting to decide the details of the mission.[32]

As the 'destroyers–bases' deal has been designated a key decision, Lothian's influence in that outcome will be assessed later in this chapter. For now, it is enough to say that Lothian was very active in promoting Anglo-American harmony. He was in a position to practise what he had believed for many years, as a member of Chatham House. His was, of course, an influential voice in Anglo-American relations.

FOREIGN RESEARCH AND PRESS SERVICE

Chatham House played an important role at another level of the foreign policy process too, through the Foreign Research and Press Service (FRPS) set up in 1939 with a grant-in-aid from the Foreign Office. Its main aims were, first, to prepare reviews of the foreign press abroad; second, to produce as requested by the Foreign Office 'memoranda giving the historical and political background of any given situation', and finally, to produce any other information as required.[33]

Frank Ashton-Gwatkin, as a member of the Chatham House Council, was the key link between the Foreign Office and FRPS, and gave a very favourable report of its work. He commended very highly the Chatham House Director of Studies (and head of FRPS), Professor Toynbee, who was 'a historian of world reputation' and author of the 'famous annual publication, *Survey of International Affairs*'[34] Ashton-Gwatkin believed that FRPS needed easy access to official documents in order to conduct their research. He also recommended closer links between FRPS personnel and their Foreign Office counterparts, although some of them such as Professor Charles Webster and Sir Alfred Zimmern 'have their own channels of official contact'.[35] Ashton-Gwatkin also felt that FRPS should liaise closely with the Cabinet Committee on War (or Peace) Aims, because the committee's chairman, Arthur Greenwood, thought highly of FRPS work. The FRPS had a vital role to play in the coming peace settlement, wrote Ashton-Gwatkin:

> Any peace settlement . . . will involve the application of a vast range of knowledge about matters political, geographical, historical, social, economic, scientific, etc. . . . Government departments . . . intent on the prosecution of the war have no time for working out the long-term problems of a hypothetical peace. Yet peace might come suddenly; and its coming might find us unprepared.[36]

The men of Chatham House were also highly recommended by the Under-Secretary for Foreign Affairs, R.A. Butler, himself a member of the Institute since 1926:

> I cannot imagine any head of a Department here being so shortsighted as to underrate the value of such men ... and I say without hesitation that if these men are not used, it will be our fault. As it is I am glad to say that several of them have been started off on work of practical assistance to Departments.[37]

Early in 1940, the Foreign Office praised the work of Sir Frederick Whyte, RIIA Council member and the then Director of the American Division of the Ministry of Information, because he could 'get into' the American mind.[38] Another chance for the Foreign Office to become familiar with American attitudes came when the Rockefeller Foundation suggested linking an American scholar to FRPS in April 1941. John Balfour and Orme Sargent both believed the idea to be 'an excellent one', which ought to be encouraged, while Balfour also wanted Chatham House to go ahead with its idea of setting up an American Research Centre. To the delight of Ashton-Gwatkin, Whitney Shepardson of the Council on Foreign Relations (RIIA's American counterpart) agreed to come to Chatham House.[39]

By mid-1941, the Foreign Office was taking stock of the usefulness of FRPS, and the reports were generally very good. Nicholls, of the FO Southern Department, wrote that a paper by Laffan of FRPS on the Istrian frontier had 'formed the annex to a paper submitted to the Cabinet'. Professor T.N. Whitehead of the FO North American Department said that his section had

> derived benefit from a number of excellent memoranda by FRPS. Besides this the FRPS, in the person of Professor Webster, have done much good work in making contact with groups in America and exchanging views and information with them. It is to be hoped that the FRPS's activities in connection with North America may continue.

Finally, the Foreign Office was informed that 'Mr Greenwood has found the work of the Foreign Research and Press Service – both its press service and economic papers – of very substantial help in the preliminary survey of European reconstruction problems'.[40]

By the end of 1942, the work of FRPS had progressed to the extent that discussions began on incorporating the service into the

Foreign Office. H.M.G. Jebb, a member of Chatham House and the FO Economic and Reconstruction Department, referred to the FRPS people as the 'wise men' who needed more access to FO papers if they were really to become more involved in planning. Then, 'New and good brains would be more directly associated with the Foreign Office machine in the formulation of policy'. According to Ronald of the FO, however, the FRPS were concerned not with making policy or planning but with 'the preparations of materials for the use of those who do make policy'. Toynbee, Zimmern and Webster were all very much in favour of the plans for closer contact with official policy-makers.[41]

Anthony Eden, the Foreign Secretary, felt that the FRPS had to be brought under government control to convince the service chiefs and foreign governments that the FRPS 'is my sole responsibility'. But there was disquiet at this development among some Chatham House Council members, who felt that the FRPS should continue to expand its work for the government but without a change of status. They concurred, however, in the transfer of the FRPS to the Foreign Office and, in April 1943, the FRPS and the Political Intelligence Department merged to form the Foreign Office Research Department (FORD).

The papers that FRPS and other Chatham House members prepared for official use were a mixture of the kind that could be of immediate use, those which provided key background material for decision-makers, and those which contained speculative projections of future events in various parts of the world.

G.E. Hubbard, a former Chatham House Director of Information, wrote a paper while working in the FO Political Intelligence Department in which he advanced the practical argument that 'Nothing in the Far East matters so much as to keep China in the war'. He argued that propaganda by Britain could be used to keep Chinese morale high. He feared problems in the long run, however, especially if China played a major role in the defeat of Japan, because it would demand territorial rewards. Therefore, British propaganda could not be purely short term, that is, just to keep China in the war, but also must be long term in trying to create friendly Chinese sentiments towards Britain. Hubbard felt that Japanese internal unity ruled out effective propaganda in that quarter, though Britain should try to drive a wedge between Japan and her Axis allies.[42]

Geoffrey Hudson of the FRPS took up the question of propaganda to Japan, and suggested that Britain use Japanese nationalism and mistrust of foreigners to sow the idea that Germany was thinking of concluding a separate deal in Europe with Britain and the US, thereby giving the latter a free hand against an isolated Japan. This paper, prepared for the Political Warfare Executive, was not used, but it does show the practical and immediate nature of some FRPS work.

FRPS papers also took up issues concerning the post-war period, based on the assumption that Japan would be defeated by United Nations', Soviet and Chinese forces. According to a paper of August 1942, Britain would face serious problems in the Far East: decline in the prestige of Western Powers; chaos and disorder by Japanese armed bandits; increased influence of China among southeast Asian Chinese, and in the region generally; the revival of Koumintang anti-imperialism; and an anti-imperialist and pro-Chinese United States. The paper conceded, however, that US 'anti-imperialism' had to be set against 'the fears which American business circles [with their heavy investments in the region] would feel if there was a prospect of a period of disorder and civil wars'. The US, through Sumner Welles, had intimated that it would be prepared to participate in some kind of international police force to maintain order and deter aggression.[43]

In a separate paper it was pointed out that the end of hostilities would see the Far East dominated by America and Russia, with Japan under US control and the Russians dominating Manchuria; and with Chinese demands for Indo-China, which France would oppose, and which would affect Britain and the US. It was suggested that: 'The closest cooperation with the United States would be essential for bringing about a satisfactory settlement of the question of Indo-China.'

Impressed by the work of FRPS, Eden decided that they should help to prepare a series of handbooks for the use of ministers and their senior advisers 'in connection with the post-war settlement. It would be the object of these handbooks to define and analyse the various problems which will come up for discussion and describe the difficulties in the way of their solution. In content they should accordingly be as far as possible historical, factual and objective.' The handbooks were not to recommend solutions to international problems but 'aim at providing a background against which ministers and senior officials could judge the recommendations put up to them by their departments'.[44] Late in 1942, Hubbard was given the go-ahead to send a dozen copies of the FRPS handbook on 'British Far Eastern Policy' to the British Embassy in China. In recognition of such 'national service' by the Institute through the FRPS, Anthony Eden helped the RIIA to persuade the Portland Club to sell their premises so that Chatham House could expand.[45]

Undoubtedly, then, the RIIA got close to the heart of the governmental machinery for foreign policy formation, providing the kind of service that the founders had hoped for. The members contributed much energy, ideas and practical suggestions in their capacity as temporary civil servants and advisers. It can be said that, through Lord Lothian and the FRPS, Chatham House exercised both a specific and a general influence on the Foreign Office, though in a manner tightly controlled by that department of state. The point is, however, that Chatham House did not necessarily wish for anything more.

THE INSTITUTE OF PACIFIC RELATIONS

The close relations that existed between FRPS and the Foreign Office were paralleled by the work carried out by Chatham House as the British section of the unofficial Institute of Pacific Relations (IPR). As Lionel Curtis explained to a Chatham House meeting in 1932, the IPR was

> a federal body through which the problems of the Pacific regions are studied by national Councils and Institutes in Australia, Canada, China, England, Japan, New Zealand, the Philippines, and the United States . . . The governing body of the IPR consists of one member appointed by each national group and is called the Pacific Council.[46]

The IPR had held numerous conferences since the late 1920s,

and invited Chatham House to send a delegation and to prepare some papers for a conference in 1942.[47] Chatham House wrote to the Foreign Office outlining the necessity of British representation at a conference likely to be highly critical of British imperial policy. Britain should send a strong and authoritative group, Chatham House recommended, that could present 'the facts of the situation' on India and the Dominions. In addition, the conference would discuss the Far Eastern situation 'in regard to immediate and post-war cooperation and understanding between the United Nations'.[48] The problems were, however, that Chatham House would need, among other things, the Foreign Office and other departments to inform conference delegates on the topics to discuss and also official funding.

The Foreign Office agreed that as the conference was to go ahead, British representation should be strong and well-prepared.[49] The officials and ministers in the Foreign Office saw the conference as a chance to defend Britain's position in the Far East, and to 'carry on the process of education of American opinions' on colonial questions.[50] Ashton-Gwatkin also revealed that the Far Eastern Department of the Foreign Office had provided 'very considerable assistance . . . in the preparation of documents etc., for the United Kingdom groups to these Conferences in the past'.[51] Chatham House requested that the FRPS produce a document to act as 'a brief for the guidance of the delegation'.[52]

The seriousness with which this conference was treated is indicated in a minute of 16 June 1942, in which it was stated that Britain needed to keep American support in the region. Therefore, Britain should not suggest that she expected to resume her imperial role after the war because that 'might provoke an opposition that would have a serious repercussion on the whole American attitude towards collaboration with ourselves for post-war reconstruction'. The Chatham House delegates should be given 'some indication of the lines on which Cabinet were thinking . . . In any case, if our delegation . . . are to represent this country's interests in an effective manner, they must be able to say something authoritative about our future policy in the Far East.'[53] As Ashley Clarke of the Foreign Office pointed out on 25 June, Britain had three goals in the Far East: stability; the retention of vital interests; and Anglo-American co-operation for security. 'One of the functions of the Delegation will certainly be to expound our attitude and defend our past achievements',[54] he argued.

On the financial question, Chatham House had originally envisaged that it could finance a small number of delegates; but by the beginning of July 1942, they declared themselves totally unable to provide any funds at all.[55] Richard Law, the Foreign Office Minister of State, questioned the wisdom of asking Parliament to fund the delegation since 'we have been at great pains to dress up [the expedition] as completely unofficial'.[56] It was eventually decided that Chatham House be exempted from paying its annual FRPS subscription, and should pay for the delegation from that saving.[57]

On the question of the personnel of the delegation, Lord Hailey of the Colonial Office was appointed delegation leader, while a Labour leader, Arthur Creech-Jones, was also to attend, as this would assist in making the group 'not appear too well rehearsed from a particular brief'[58] and, in any case, 'Lord Hailey believes that he can keep him within bounds'.[59]

Once the conference actually got under way, the British delegates believed they had stated their case effectively.[60] Lord Halifax noted that the number of officials from various nations present at the conference made it 'essentially desirable that Chatham House should be more closely associated both with the various committees which carry on the work of the Institute between conferences and with the Secretariat'.[61] He continued by commenting that the 'general feeling is that the inclusion of official delegates in the British delegation was on the whole valuable . . . In our opinion the conference produced a more realistic understanding of the problems of the Far East'. In a later report on the conference, however, Halifax noted that some Americans and Canadians had 'insinuated . . . that the United Kingdom delegation was "packed", that it "played with its cards close to its chest", and that generally it had come prepared to take an unprogressive imperialistc stand'.[62]

Foreign Office advice, help and funding was also made available for the 1945 conference of IPR, and officials also attended,[63] because the Chatham House role in the IPR conferences was considered vital by the policy-makers. Chatham House was well-funded and supported. Its line at conferences was based on informal official guidance. The delegations contained officials whose role was to defend British policies and interests, and to encourage the United States to accept more responsibility in world affairs, especially in the Far East. Chatham House became almost an organ of official foreign policy. Consequently, its independent stance was compromised. It cannot be otherwise when outside funding, guidance and delegates are supplied to any organisation.

Overall, Chatham House proved successful in achieving the aims and objectives of its founders: to provide the material from which policy-makers could make 'sound' policy. Necessarily, its views became sought after and taken into account; its personnel were considered authorities on foreign affairs, and were called into government service for the war period; many of them were trusted enough to be shown secret documents and memoranda, as well as to represent British foreign policy interests.

It is also quite clear, however, that the official policy-making machinery was always in control. It was their 'guiding hand' that drew the boundaries of 'British interests' and, consequently, the general topics for study and discussion in Chatham House. No 'clash' was involved in the assumptions of Chatham House and those of British officialdom concerning British national interest. If the officials guided Chatham House studies and so on, then the Institute was willing to accept this guidance. It was recognition of their worth and stature. In terms of the influence of Chatham House over the five key decisions, analysis will be conducted after the other main groups have been analysed in general.

TRADES UNION CONGRESS

The TUC, as noted earlier in this study, played a minor role as far as the making of British foreign policy was concerned. In other respects, of course, the TUC's ability to mobilise and organise labour for the war effort played a vital role in national survival and the state's ability to develop any foreign policy at all. Directly, however, the TUC had always been mobilised by elements within the state for the achievements of certain official ends. Some of these moments have been noted: the Colonial Office's use of British union leaders to assist in developing 'responsible' unionism in the colonies; the semi-official sponsorship of Citrine's visit to the United States in 1940; and the establishment of employer–union representation on the Reconstruction Joint Advisory Council, which favoured Anglo-American co-operation. In short, the TUC exercised little general or specific influence on British foreign policy.

LABOUR PARTY

When we consider the influence of the Labour Party on the formation of the Anglo-American alliance, it is necessary to separate the leaders of the party from the rank and file members because the real power did appear to lie with the leadership. This fact is recognised by Roy Jenkins who believes that the leaders always felt that they could carry the party whatever the issue. According to Gordon, the Labour leaders failed to explain the changes of opinion they had undergone as a result of their experience of the 'realities' of power, and decided to let the force of events 'educate' the members into a new way of thinking. The major clashes, he suggests, in Labour's foreign policy in the 1945–51 period were basically caused by the 'realism' of the leadership as opposed to the socialist expectations of the mass of the party. However, the power of the leaders ensured that the new course they were taking became gradually accepted by most of the party.[64] Of course, the Labour Party was influential in the formation of the alliance with the US. It was involved, as we shall see, on the winning side in four of the five major decisions.

CONSERVATIVE PARTY

As the dominant force in the Coalition Government, the Conservatives obviously played a decisive role during the formation of the Anglo-American alliance. They, along with their Labour colleagues in government, constituted the leadership (politically at least) of the British state, and their influence will become clearer by the end of the chapter. It is to the issue of direct influence over decision-making that attention must now be turned, examining first the 'destroyers–bases' agreement of August 1940.

'DESTROYERS–BASES' AGREEMENT, AUGUST 1940

In the analysis of the activities surrounding the decision taken to conclude the 'destroyers–bases' agreement, it quickly emerges that the representatives of several of the groups and parties under analysis were involved. Lord Lothian, British ambassador to the United States, was the key to the deal. He requested Churchill, in return for American destroyers, to 'give the assurance [to the US] about the future of the [British] fleet . . . and to agree to the air and naval facilities in question'.[65] This refers to the ploy used by Britain to draw the US closer to themselves and closer to anti-German hostilities: that if Hitler defeated Britain, British leaders would not necessarily scuttle the Royal Navy or transfer it to the Americans. The defence of Britain was the defence of the United States – that was the message to Roosevelt. Roosevelt agreed with this, and asked for leases to a number of Caribbean Islands, without the transfer of sovereignty. While the agreement was clearly supported by the Foreign Office, there was some dissension in the Cabinet. Balfour of the FO summed up the majority view when he justified the agreement as in the interests of Britain:

> the future of our widely scattered Empire is likely to depend on the evolution of an effective and enduring collaboration between ourselves and the US for which we cannot reasonably hope unless we share with America the strategic facilities enabling her to discharge her part of the responsibility of guarding the English-speaking peoples.[66]

Dissension came from the representative of the Empire Industries Association, Lord Lloyd, the Colonial Secretary. He was totally opposed to the move because: 'Leases on a large scale in the oil fields of Trinidad, if once given to the Americans would amount to a virtual cession of sovereignty. Much American plant and capital would be put into the island', he argued, 'and the Americans would obtain a controlling interest.'[67] Beyond the Cabinet, the Communists also declared their opposition to the agreement. The *Daily Worker* argued that the 'deal' gave 'the dollar capitalists . . . command [of] the Western Atlantic and secure[d] the release of their fleet for work in the Pacific, if necessary against Japan'. The party's newspaper stated that the 'destroyers–bases' agreement 'means that the capitalist world has sunk deeper into war. The U.S.A., the strongest imperialist country in the world, is now wading into the carve-up and switching over to a war economy.' The party even urged British seamen not to serve on the American destroyers.[68]

However, the War Cabinet – made up of both Conservatives and Labour and other political interests – decided that there was more to be gained than lost through the Agreement. For Winston Churchill 'the survival of Britain . . . [was] bound up with the survival of the United States'. The transfer of American destroyers to Britain 'was a decidedly unneutral act by the United States. It would . . . have justified the German Government declaring war upon them'.[69] The Agreement could be said to have both short- and long-term benefits: it pulled the US militarily closer to Britain for the purposes of the war, and the future peace.

THE ATLANTIC CHARTER, 9–12 AUGUST 1941

The decision to issue a joint British–American declaration of war aims was taken on behalf of the government by Winston Churchill, in consultation with the Permanent Under-Secretary of the Foreign Office, Sir Alexander Cadogan. Even they, however, had been taken by surprise because President Roosevelt had suggested the idea 'out of the blue', on the first evening of the talks in Newfoundland. The Cabinet only knew of the decision after the joint statement had been agreed. According to Dobson, 'The Atlantic Conference was an organisational shambles'. Nothing, not even an agenda, had been prepared; neither Churchill nor Roosevelt 'had specified what the purpose of the meeting was to be'.[70] In essence of course, the United States aimed to obtain from Churchill a commitment to abolish imperial preference, free trade and non-discrimination, with the underlying threat that the US would not aid Britain militarily if it did not make such a commitment. Cadogan, who generally favoured a long-term alliance with the Americans, was later to describe such an attitude as 'impertinent blackmail'.[71]

Another indicator of the line of advice Churchill had been receiving, and was to continue to do so, was his friendship with Frederick Lindemann (Lord Cherwell), an Oxford don. According to Randall Woods, Cherwell was an ultra-conservative who favoured Anglo-American co-operation to the point of obsession.[72] Leopold Amery, however, who believed that the British Empire was 'something like the Kingdom of Heaven within ourselves', was always critical of Churchill. About the Atlantic Charter, Amery later wrote that 'I only wish I were in a free position to say what I think about the Atlantic Charter and all the other tripe which is being talked now, exactly like the tripe talked to please President Wilson'. Such was Amery's opposition to Anglo-American co-operation that he even claimed to prefer a Europe united under Hitler than US domination, even if Europe's 'advantages have to be paid for by a measure of economic as well as political servitude to Germany'.[73]

The Atlantic Charter was important not only because of the role it played at the time it was agreed, that is, that it brought the US a small step nearer to Britain in the war effort, but also because of its implications for the post-war period. The fourth of the eight main clauses of the Atlantic Charter concerned 'access, on equal terms, to the trade and to the raw materials of the world' to all nations. The fifth clause stated their common desire for world economic collaboration, while the eighth mentioned the desirability of a world system of military security.[74] These three clauses signalled a major departure for US policy – the recognition that America would and should play a greater role in world economic, commercial and military life. It signalled the second major step towards an enduring collaboration between Britain and the US that has lasted to this day.

THE MUTUAL AID AGREEMENT, 1942

This agreement, better known as 'Lend-Lease', was also of major and long-term importance. As a result of it, Britain received $27 billion of military and other supplies during the war, as well as the initiation of talks with the United States that brought about Anglo-American economic and commercial co-operation in the post-war period. As Dobson states, 'Lend-Lease was the linchpin of the Anglo-American economic relationship during the war'.[75] He goes on to suggest that Lend-Lease increased British–American 'familial ties', in the vein of conventional analyses of the 'special relationship'.

The supplies that Britain needed from the US were not to be paid for directly in cash terms, as Greenwood told the War Cabinet, but in terms of British concurrence with a general principle advocating 'agreed action to promote advantageous economic relations between the two countries and for the betterment of world-wide economic relations'. The Minister without Portfolio continued by stating that the US government wanted Britain to oppose discrimination in international trade 'and had made it clear that by that phrase they intended that we should commit ourselves to the eventual abolition of Imperial Preference.'[76] Later, however, the Americans informed Britain that the controversial Article VII of the Mutual Aid Agreement contained 'no commitment in advance to abolish Empire Preference'.[77] On that basis, the Cabinet agreed to sign the agreement in February 1942.

Once again, there had been opposition to this decision from those supporting a pro-Empire policy for the post-war years. This time Leopold Amery, the Secretary of State for India and for Burma, and leader of the Empire Industries Association, attacked the free trade principles of the Americans. The days of free trade, he argued, were over, because of economic nationalism. The US was an unstable nation, liable to economic and political isolation, and consequently could not form the basis of any long-term British strategy. Even if the US did prove reliable, the lowering of the American tariff might not be so advantageous to Britain as Empire Preference. Amery pointed out in his Cabinet paper that the percentage of British exports going to the Empire had increased from 32 per cent in 1900 to nearly 50 per cent in 1938. That was where Britain's future would lie, especially in the difficult situation after the war. Article VII threatened the future of the Empire and must be opposed.[78]

The preference of the majority of the War Cabinet and policy-makers however, was for Anglo-American co-operation, and that position won the day. It was known by policy-makers that Article VII 'impinged on the whole system of Imperial Preference', wrote FO Minister Richard Law in 1944, but it was decided by the Cabinet 'that the advantages outweighed the disadvantages'.[79]

The pro-Empire forces, however, were incensed by the perceived hypocrisy of the American position on imperial preference and their 'price-fixing' demands during the international wheat negotiations. Not only did the American administration want to fix wheat prices (at a new and higher level), but they also wanted Britain to place an embargo on wheat from any nation that was not a party to the wheat agreement. Such a stance only exacerbated divisions within Britain's political élite, many of whom felt that '[Cordell] Hull's pursuit of free trade was simply a guise for pursuing American national interests'. Keynes wrote that the Americans were proposing the most extreme form of discrimination, which would not only exacerbate Britain's balance of payments problem but also cause conflict with other nations.[80]

Pro-Americans, however, such as Cherwell and Harcourt Johnstone, the right-wing Tory and friend of Churchill, believed that Anglo-American co-operation was the key to Britain's future, especially in strengthening the international capitalist order. To Johnstone, Anglo-American co-operation would halt socialism; it was, 'broadly speaking, an attempt to make the Capitalist system work'.[81] To Cherwell, Article VII was the means by which Britain and America would 'tie the knot' between them. He wrote to Churchill in 1942 that the Article VII conversations 'concern the best way of building up Anglo-American economic co-operation within a capitalist framework after the war'.[82]

BRETTON WOODS AGREEMENT 1944–45

The negotiations between the US and Britain which led to this agreement were initiated by Article VII of the Mutual Aid Agreement of 1942. The official reasons for engaging in the negotiations were primarily cast in terms of the national interest – employment in particular. It was thought that Britain, as an international trading power, needed to accept the idea of multilateral exchange and trade as the Americans desired. At the same time, Britain had, according to the Treasury, to 'explain [to the USA] the very serious practical difficulties which confront not only the United Kingdom but other countries' in making serious progress towards multilateralism. The Treasury believed that Britain's balance of payments deficit would be very serious after the war, and that the only solution was some form of international banking system that would provide 'for participating States the functions performed for individuals by the ordinary banking system, i.e., the clearance of accounts, debit and credit, between different customers and the provision of overdrafts for those who need them'. Such an organisation would be based on Anglo-American lines. The Americans would have to be persuaded to acknowledge Britain's immediate difficulties and allow it to restrict trade in order to recover. If the US disagreed, then Britain should not commit itself to anything until the exact nature of the arrangements was known.[83]

The debates in the Cabinet on whether or not to continue the Bretton Woods (or Washington Financial) talks are illuminating as to the major factors taken into account by policy-makers. The debate between the forces supporting an Anglo-American agreement and those favouring a pro-Empire policy reached a critical point in early 1944, when a major decision had to be made.

Richard Law issued two very important memoranda in February 1944, in which he answered some of the criticisms made by those who wanted to pursue the 'Empire option'. He pointed out for Amery's benefit that, although the abolition of imperial preference would close off some markets, it would open many others, and also establish 'the whole apparatus for the adjustment of balances of payments contained in the Washington proposals'. As most nations would join this international organisation, there would be enormous benefits to British export industries.[84] Law rebutted the suggestion from the pro-Empire group that the Anglo-American financial plans represented a return to the Gold Standard, at a time when Britain had no gold: 'Anything less like a Gold Standard can scarcely be conceived', he argued.

When Britain committed itself to Article VII, Law wrote, we knew that the days of imperial preference were numbered, and that this was not to our disadvantage. Therefore: 'it is not open to us . . . to adopt now a policy which is based upon discriminatory protectionism and the unrestricted quantitative limitation of imports'. The main aim for everyone, he argued, was to provide work, homes and food for Britain, which had to be paid for by export revenues. The problem was, however, that British manufactured exports were less vital to the receiving nations than their exports of food and raw materials were to Britain. As Britain did not sell to the same markets as it bought from, a multilateral clearing system was essential. The consequence of all these factors was that it was more important for Britain to prevent its customers from imposing restrictions than to have the freedom to impose restrictions itself.

Empire bloc trading arrangements would not solve the problem because that encouraged others to impose barriers which offset the advantages. The Washington option was the best alternative, while the other options 'are so bad . . . that we would be unwise to embrace them until we are left without any other choice'. Choosing the path of Empire bloc 'will be regarded by the Americans as a Declaration of War . . . And indeed it will be nothing else, for we shall be deliberately organising the world into rival economic groupings . . . I cannot see what kind of a political structure we shall be able to erect on a foundation of this kind.' 'There would not be much left of the Empire, in any event, when the gloves are off.' Canada, South Africa and Australia were becoming closer to the United States economically and militarily. The Empire option would lead to a situation where 'the United States will certainly make economic war upon us. So much has been made clear to us. And the armoury of the United States is a very powerful one.' 'The USA have the financial power to provide subsidies to our customers, win our export markets and so on.' 'Of course, we should have to fight it out', Law argued, but 'in this field, if anywhere, the longest purse – and it is not ours – would win.' A British Empire bloc policy would 'invite the sharpest conflict . . . one in which we would find ourselves without allies'.[85]

Outside government, there were those who entertained many misgivings and doubts about the new Anglo-American financial institutions proposed at Bretton Woods. The Federation of British Industries, for example, established a Monetary Policy Panel in

September 1944 in order to advise government of the views of 'industry'. Although the panel, which included Arthur Guinness of Guinness, Mahon & Co., merchant bankers and Dr W.H. Coates of Imperial Chemical Industries (ICI), welcomed the Bretton Woods proposals, there was full realisation of the damaging effects on Britain. The negative effect of the International Monetary Fund (IMF) on the Sterling Area would be to shift 'the centre of the [world's] financial system from London to the United States'.[86]

The panel went on to express certain 'misgivings regarding the preponderant position of the USA in relation to the Fund', and warned of the problems of 'carrying on the sterling area arrangements in the face of any opposition from the USA, if the Bretton Woods Agreement were rejected'.[87] The fears of the FBI were, in many respects, a reflection of those held by nearly all of the 'pro-American' policy-makers in the Cabinet, even if the FBI played no role in the taking of this particular decision.

The Bank of England, which many have regarded as the voice of financial capital or the 'city', had an even greater vested interest than 'industry' in the preservation of the Sterling Area. If, as Marxists argue, the financial fraction of capital was predominant in British policy formation, Bretton Woods constitutes a key test case, and it must be said that there is no evidence of the Bank's influence. Before examining the historical record, however, the role of Lord Keynes needs to be clarified. Although Keynes was a director of the Bank and was highly influential in the Bretton Woods negotiations, he was never very close to the Bank's thinking and policy-making. John Giuseppe, in his history of the Bank of England, states that Keynes was the key figure at Bretton Woods not in his capacity as a director 'but . . . as the Treasury's nominee . . . [which enabled him to] put forward his plan for an international clearing union'.[88] Even the fact that Keynes was asked to be a Director by Norman was an attempt to silence or tame the outspoken economist. As Andrew Boyle cites in his biography of Norman, Keynes was accepted for directorship 'On the principle that "an enemy's teeth are more easily drawn if he sits at the same table as yourself"'.[89] This ploy obviously did not have the desired effect, as an interesting anecdote cited by Sayers in his history of the Bank demonstrates. As Keynes and a fellow director were leaving a Bank meeting, Keynes stated to his companion: 'I do enjoy these lunches at the Bank: Montagu Norman, always absolutely charming, always absolutely wrong!'[90]

As Giuseppe argues, the Bank did not engage in long-term planning for the post-war period and quotes Keynes' biographer R.F. Harrod, as stating that the Bank was 'far more concerned with immediate post-war problems than with far-reaching schemes'.[91] This point was also most tactfully made by Catto of the Treasury in 1942, when he labelled the Bank's post-war ideas as rather short-term and based on 'trial and error' methods, whereas Keynes' ideas were 'more interesting and challenging for they attempted to outline something new'.[92] This did not mean, however, that the Bank did not have ideas about the new international institutions planned in the Treasury and in Washington – especially the International Monetary Fund (IMF), the aim of which was to try and re-establish international trade, finance and production after the dislocations of the war, mainly by allowing for the convertibility of currencies. While Keynes, the Chancellor and the majority of the Cabinet and officials supported the move to multilateral trading arrangements based on Anglo-American accord,[93] the Bank of England was decidedly cool if not, at times, hostile. The Bank's role in these proceedings was rather marginal. For example, the Bank's role in response to an influential memorandum by Keynes on the 'Financial Problems in the Transition from War to Peace' was merely to check the statistics used; and despite the importance of the issue, the Bank's 'considered response' to the memo had not even been received by the Treasury a month later.[94] In fact, it was not until a full seven weeks had passed that the Bank's views were made known in a note entitled 'Sterling Balances and Transitional Arrangements'. The note was received with considerable hostility from Keynes, starting a dispute in which state officials sided with the latter.[95] The Bank expressed its scepticism about the IMF, while affirming 'sympathy' with its aims. L.S. Pressnell shows that the Bank was extremely sensitive to the IMF's likely impact on the Sterling Area, as it would tend 'to by-pass and to weaken London as a financial centre, and hence to complicate the Bank's already demanding task of the management of sterling'.[96] The IMF was also seen by the Bank as potentially encroaching on its traditional territory. As R.F. Harrod states, the Bank 'would not be human if its approach to such schemes was not influenced, even if unconsciously, by some degree of jealousy of a rival central banking institution, which might, in certain circumstances, poach on its domain'.[97] More importantly, however, Pressnell stresses the central issue as far as the Bank was concerned: 'Above all, by diminishing the attractiveness of sterling as an international currency it [the IMF] would harm invisible earnings, and much else besides: the sterling area comprised business, personal and imperial relationships of proven value, transcending banking matters.'[98] The Bank declared that the 'proponents of the [international] monetary fund, including Keynes, [failed] . . . to understand the sterling area', and had exaggerated the scale of the financial problems Britain would face after the war; and the Bank denied the necessity of an emergency loan from the US. Instead, the Bank proposed that each country be free to set its own exchange rate, that any international financial body be purely consultative, and that instead of a loan from the United States, Britain should develop an export policy and control 'domestic demand and . . . imports'.[99]

Despite the obvious importance of the Bank of England, its 'imperial' orientation had begun to render it a liability in policy formation. Keynes was the toughest and most acerbic of all on the Bank's ideas and proposals. He argued that the Bank was self-centred and tended to sacrifice 'both the country's solvency and the country's trade to the supposed interests and the prestige of sterling'.[100] An earlier draft of Keynes' response to the Bank's ideas argued that the Bank's 'plan' was merely a repetition of its plans of six months earlier, which Keynes believed he had refuted at the time. 'They now come back, however, without any reference to those arguments, or any attempts to meet them. Alas, one might as well speak to stone walls', he lamented.[101] According to Keynes, the Bank's plan would 'damage Anglo-American relations, not just by the abandonment of discussions on post-war monetary policy but particularly by giving the impression of being an organised attempt to discriminate against American trade'.[102]

Although debate over the Bretton Woods proposals was heated at this time, the actual taking of the decision was tied into the fifth key decision, the US loan to Britain.

THE AMERICAN LOAN TO BRITAIN

One week after the victory over Japan in the Far East in mid-1945, US President Truman unilaterally declared the end of Lend-Lease. This caused much disquiet in British policy-making and other circles because of the grave problems that Britain faced as a result of her war effort. In the interim period, before all lend-lease supplies had been used, Britain needed a massive injection of dollars. It was for that reason that Lord Keynes was sent to the US to negotiate a financial agreement.

In 1945, Britain's trade deficit ran to over £1.6 billion, and it was estimated that even if she borrowed around £2 billion she would still only remedy the deficit by 1949 (and even then only by cutting imports, reducing her foreign commitments, and rationing).[103] In the light of British sacrifices during hostilities, it was hoped that the Americans would advance the finance as a gift, or at least as an interest-free loan. But it was not seen in those terms by the Americans. Will Clayton, the Vice-Chairman of the US negotiating team, and many others, saw the opportunity 'to force the British to give up the sterling area, abandon imperial preference and eliminate quotas and exchange controls, all of which were seen as obstacles to American trade'. The chairman of Sears, Roebuck wrote to Clayton: 'If you succeed in doing away with the Empire Preference and opening up the Empire to United States commerce, it may well be that we can afford to pay a couple of billion dollars for the privilege.'[104]

A committee of three within the Labour Cabinet – Bevin, Dalton and Cripps – steered the Loan Agreement through, and on 29 November 1945, the government agreed to a loan on the following American-imposed conditions: (a) 2 per cent interest over 50 years; (b) liberalisation of the Sterling Area and British commercial policy; (c) to recommend the ratification of Bretton Woods to Parliament; (d) to allow sterling to become convertible into dollars one year after the loan had been advanced.

Both the loan and the Bretton Woods Agreement were ratified by Parliament in December 1945, even though 100 MPs voted against[105] and another 169 abstained.[106] The Labour government's case for ratification was founded upon the scale of the problems faced, the public interest and the wartime consensus on Bretton

Woods.[107] But there was grave disquiet inside the Labour Party, and even in the Cabinet. Aneurin Bevan and Emanuel Shinwell, both junior ministers, recorded that 'they were most unhappy and apprehensive about the future'.[108] The left-wing Tribune group declared that the US loan conditions were 'preposterous' and urged Britain to dispense with the loan completely rather than risk becoming 'enslaved to the interests of American big business'.[109] By December 1945, *Tribune* declared the Loan Agreement to be 'A Savage Bargain', and a return to the past, when 'the Money Power ... [insisted] in the name of Justice and Morality, on free competition and non-discrimination to ensure its own supremacy.'[110]

On the right of the Conservative Party, Robert Boothby flayed the loan in Parliament as designed to serve American interests alone in its attempts to 'prise open the markets of the world for the USA'.[111] A few years later, Leopold Amery argued that the Loan conditions amounted

> to an attempt to force the whole life of our country and the British Commonwealth into a pattern dictated by the out-of-date theories of the present American Administration and by shortsighted American exporting and financial interests, and to compel our Government to join, as satellites, in the task of persuading other nations to fall into line.[112]

He continued in the same vein that 'the British Empire is the oyster which this loan is to prise open. Each part of it, deprived of the mutual support of Empire Preference, is to be swallowed separately, to become a field for American industrial exploitation, a tributary of American finance, and, in the end, an American dependency.'[113] He urged Britain to issue a 'Declaration of Independence', much as the Americans had in 1776. Curiously, such a declaration of independence echoed the demand of some communists, such as R.P. Dutt of *Labour Monthly*.

The American loan was ratified in Parliament by a majority of 247, while the Bretton Woods Agreement was passed by 314 votes for and 50 against. The wartime coalition which had created the conditions for Bretton Woods and the loan was largely responsible for the outcome.

CONCLUSIONS

The most striking point that emerges is the great concentration of power and influence over the final decisions that the state wielded. Although several interest groups were active in the foreign policy area and could speak with knowledge and authority, in the final analysis it was the state that held and controlled the reins of British foreign policy. The state was the centre and focus of all policy-making activity, and was seen as the legitimate vehicle and promoter of the 'national' interest.

The activities of the RIIA were concerned with the 'national' interest and 'public' welfare, in much the same way as the British state. Chatham House demonstrated by its years of activity in foreign relations issues that it was an important group. When war looked inevitable, the state 'brought Chatham House in' allowing them a rare privilege by permitting some of its members to become a part of the official policy-making machinery (in the case of FRPS) and even a part of the policy-implementation machinery (in the case of IPR work). It must be noted, however, that Chatham House only became a part of the whole, always under the direction of the officials of the state. Its influence over the key decisions, even if we consider the activities of Lothian as entirely motivated by his Chatham House affiliations, was minimal.

The activities of the Federation of British Industries could also be said to have been characterised as rather uninfluential. It was not involved in a single one of the key decisions that constituted the post-war alliance. The issue in the analysis of FBI influence should rather be discussed in terms of how much it was influenced by the state. The policies of the FBI on many occasions, especially in matters concerning the Empire and the Far East, so closely resembled official policy that the FBI appears as a relatively weak organisation, in foreign policy matters, and the state as very powerful.

There are similarities in the relations between the state and the RIIA, and the state's relations with the FBI. The FBI was never in a position to dictate terms to the state. It was, however, used by the state – for example, the Foreign Office urged Anglo-American industrialists to co-operate in the Far East in 1938 as part of its attempt to enlist American military action in that region.

The Formation of the Anglo-American Alliance

The main challenges to the Anglo-American alliance option came from the Empire Industries Association, the Bank of England and the Communist Party. The first two organisations advanced the 'Empire option' to policy-makers in the heart of the British state itself. The Communists advanced their own ideas but largely outside the 'legitimate' politics of Westminster and Whitehall. Despite being involved in most of the key decisions, at one level or another, the EIA faced decisive defeat at the hands of a pro-American majority.

Perhaps least surprising is the relative insignificance of the TUC. Its activities on the Reconstruction Joint Advisory Council, along with the FBI and other employers, appears to have had no impact whatever. The TUC had no ideas or suggestions, no detailed plan or policy of its own, and consequently little hope of influence. From the state's point of view, however, it could be said that the TUC and FBI constituted vital 'private' organisations that could be mobilised for state ends, especially in developing Anglo-American trade unionists' and industrialists' co-operation. Again, then, we see evidence of a 'strong state' directing and leading the major interests in British political life.

The voice of the trade unions in Parliament, the Labour Party, was more influential, and shared and exercised the power of the state. Its Cabinet representatives were involved in four of the five key decisions, and were on the winning side throughout. Arguably, they were more powerful than the Conservatives because the final two decsions were made under a Labour government, while the other three were made under the Coalition.

The fact that the wartime Coalition of Labour and the Conservatives completely agreed on all foreign affairs issues is interesting when we consider that Labour claimed to be the party of radical change in the principles and methods of foreign policy. Why did the Labour leaders become traditional power-politics practitioners once they had an opportunity to implement their socialist principles? How could Ernest Bevin, who had criticised foreign policy-makers as concerned only with the interests of financiers and exporters, support, arguably, a policy based on the welfare of those groups?

One could, of course, defend Labour politicians as suffering from the dissonance between theoretical or utopian ideals and 'hard' political realities – their ideas just could not work in practice, in the real world. Yet, we have seen the extent to which the ideas of the leading Labour Cabinet Ministers could be described as being based on *realpolitik*. Men such as Bevin and Attlee had already been schooled in working-class organisations in the realities of power and power struggles. They were hardly idealistic dilettantes, ripe for an absolute conversion when things got 'tough'. It may well be that the power of the state, and the 'consensus' that it had generated within and around itself, had attracted the Labour leaders and assimilated them to its own way of thinking. As leaders of the Opposition, and as a 'government-in-waiting', Attlee and Bevin began over several years to see the world, and Britain's position within it, in a manner befitting those who would some day have to face its problems in a practical way. In short, there was a kind of reality about state power which forced itself onto the consciousness of the Labour leaders and which drew them into what has been called the 'state consensus'. Of course, the rhetoric of the Labour leaders – of socialism in world affairs – remained for the purposes of retaining mass appeal. The effect of the rhetoric was to mobilise millions of voters and members of the working-class movement behind British foreign policy, thereby further strengthening the power and influence of the state itself.

In several respects, the Conservative leaders were also part of the 'state consensus', as well as being among its primary authors and beneficiaries. What is most distinctive in the historical evidence cited in this chapter about the key decisions that made the Anglo-American alliance is the degree to which the state managed to mobilise certain groups, neutralise or defeat others, and completely marginalise or harass and intimidate those considered 'beyond the pale'. The state described in the pages of this and previous chapters was hardly a vehicle used by other forces for their own ends. It was a great power in its own right.

NOTES

1. Minutes, Grand Council (GC), 14 July 1937, in MSS 200/F/1/1/4, p. 22 (FBI Archives, Modern Records Centre, Warwick University).
2. Minutes, Executive Committee (EC), 8 Nov. 1939, in MSS 200/F/1/1/18, p. 72.

3. Minutes, EC, 8 Sept. 1943, MSS 200/F/1/1/16, p. 120.
4. Minutes, EC, 13 Aug. 1941, MSS 200/F/1/1/17, pp. 130–1; Minutes, EC, 12 Nov. 1941, MSS 200/F/1/1/16, p. 145.
5. Minutes, EC, 13 Oct. 1937, MSS 200/F/1/1/16.
6. Minutes, EC, 12 Jan. 1938, MSS 200/F/1/1/16.
7. Minutes, China Committee (CC), 17 Nov. 1938, MSS 200/F/1/1/81.
8. Minutes, EC, 14 Jan. 1938, MSS 200/F/1/1/16.
9. Minutes, CC, 17 Nov. 1938, MSS 200/F/1/1/81.
10. Minutes, CC, 1 March 1939, MSS 200/F/1/1/81.
11. Memorandum by W.A. Lee, Director of the Mining Association of Great Britain, 'The Crisis in Retrospect: Industry and Foreign Policy', in a letter to Locock, 1 Nov. 1938, MSS 200/F/3/S1/23/18.
12. Reconstruction Report, May 1942, MSS 200/F/4/57/2.
13. Report of an informal discussion, 8 Oct. 1942, MSS 200/F/3/S1/23/35.
14. WM (42) 24 Conclusions, 23 Feb. 1944, Public Records Office.
15. Minutes, EC, 13 Dec. 1944, MSS 200/F/1/1/18.
16. FO 371/25206.
17. Minutes, GC, 10 Jan. 1940, MSS 200/F/1/1/4.
18. Minutes, GC, 10 March 1940, MSS 200/F/1/1/4.
19. Halifax to Hankey, 15 July 1940, FO 371/25206.
20. Sam Aaronovitch, *Monopoly* (London: Lawrence & Wishart, 1955), pp. 90–1.
21. See report by Clive Hargreaves of the Calico Printers' Association, 1944, in FO 371/415579; papers by F.W. Gray in 1942, FO 371/31802, and by Victor Farmer, FO 371/31802.
22. Letter to P.D. Proctor of the Treasury, 26 March 1943, in T.160/1258/180003/016.
23. Croft's argument in note by Sir F. Phillips, 27 April 1938, in T.172/1892.
24. Sir Montagu Norman was a Bank Director, 1907–18; Deputy Governor, 1918–20; Governor, 1920–44; and member of the Treasury Committee, 1916–44. Lord Catto was Director in 1940; Governor, 1944–49; and on the Treasury Committee, 1944–49.
25. John Giuseppe, *The Bank of England* (London: Evans, 1966), p. 183.
26. Treasury files, 'Modification of the Constitution of the Bank of England', 1940, T.160/992/F/17064.
27. Treasury files, 'The Bank of England and the Bank for International Settlements': memorandum by S.D. Waley to Sir T. Barnes of the Treasury Solicitor's Department, 18 July 1939, T.160/1176/11282/023.
28. Ibid., 4 Sept. 1939.
29. David Butler and Jennie Freeman, *British Political Facts 1900–1960* (London: Macmillan, 1964), p. 156.
30. Telegram, 30 Sept. 1940, FO 371/24736.
31. Minutes by Lothian and Butler, FO 371/25138.
32. FO 371/24241.
33. Report on FRPS by Ashton-Gwatkin, 31 Jan. 1941, FO 371/29145.
34. Ibid.
35. Ibid.
36. Ibid.
37. Ibid.
38. FO 371/24252.

39. FO 371/29145.
40. Ibid.
41. FO 371/31499.
42. 'The Importance of Propaganda to China', FO 371/31760, 1 April 1942; and 'Notes on Principles of Propaganda to Japan', ibid.
43. 'Britain's Post-War Prospects in the Far East', FO 371/31774.
44. FO 371/32481, 6 Jan. 1942.
45. Letter, Eden to Portland Club, 21 April 1943.
46. Curtis' speech to Chatham House, 26 Jan. 1932, CHA 8/180.
47. See communiqué from Chatham House IPR Committee to the Foreign Office, FO 371/31801.
48. Ibid.
49. Ibid., minutes by Ashton-Gwatkin, 11 May 1942, Brenan, 12 May 1942, Broad, 13 March 1942, and Eden, 17 May 1942.
50. Ibid., minute by Richard Law, Minister of State in the Foreign Office.
51. Ibid., minute, 22 May 1942.
52. Ibid., minute, 3 June 1942.
53. Ibid., minute by official (name illegible), 16 June 1942.
54. Ibid., minute, 25 June 1942.
55. Ibid., minute, 1 July 1942.
56. Ibid., minute by Law, 3 July 1942.
57. Ibid., Ashley Clarke, 22 July 1942.
58. Ibid., Ashley Clarke, 19 July 1942.
59. Ibid., Ashley Clarke, 30 Sept. 1942.
60. Ashey Clarke, 8 Dec. 1942, FO 371/35905.
61. Ibid., Halifax, note on the conference, 9 Jan. 1943.
62. Ibid., Halifax, Report on the IPR Conference, 3 Feb. 1943.
63. Foreign Office letter to the Secretary of the Treasury, 9 Dec. 1944, FO 371/41769.
64. Michael R. Gordon, *Conflict and Consensus in Labour's Foreign Policy 1914–1965* (Stanford: Stanford University Press, 1969), p. 94.
65. Lothian, in FO 371/24241.
66. Ibid., Balfour, 14 Aug. 1940.
67. WM (40) 146th Conclusions, 19 May 1940.
68. *Daily Worker*, 5 Sept. 1940.
69. Winston Churchill, *The Second World War* (London: Cassell, 1949), pp. 357–8.
70. Alan Dobson, *US Wartime Aid to Britain* (London: Croom Helm, 1986), p. 63.
71. Ibid., p. 64.
72. Woods, *A Changing of the Guard: Anglo-American Relations, 1941–46* (Chapel Hill and London: University of North Carolina Press, 1990), p. 47.
73. W.R. Louis, *In the Name of God, Go! Leo Amery and the British Empire in the Age of Churchill* (New York and London: W.W. Norton, 1992), p. 146.
74. Ian S. McDonald, *Anglo-American Relations since the Second World War* (Vancouver: David & Charles, 1974), pp. 18–19.
75. Dobson, op. cit., p. 1.
76. WM (42) 1st meeting, 1 Jan. 1942.
77. WM (42) 20th meeting, 12 Feb. 1942.

78. WM (42) 23rd meeting, 12 Jan. 1942.
79. WM (44) 81st meeting, memorandum.
80. Dobson, op. cit., pp. 80–1.
81. Woods, op. cit., p. 43.
82. Ibid., p. 48.
83. Memorandum by the Treasury on 'Preliminary discussions with the United States', in Annex A, WP (42) 159, 10 April 1942.
84. Note by the Minister of State, 'Anglo-American Discussions under Article VII', in WP (44) 75, 5 Feb. 1944.
85. Memorandum by the Minister of State, 'The Washington Conversations on Article VII', WP (44) 81, 7 Feb. 1944.
86. Monetary Policy Panel minutes, 14 Sept. 1944, MSS 200/F/1/1/156.
87. Grand Council minutes, 13 June 1945, MSS 200/F/1/1/188.
88. J. Giuseppe, *The Bank of England* (London: Evans, 1966), p. 190. John Maynard Keynes (1883–1946) was created a baron in 1942; he was a Member of the Chancellor of the Exchequer's Consultative Council, 1940–46, a Director of the Bank of England, 1941–46, and Chairman of the UK Delegation at the UN Monetary and Financial Conference, Bretton Woods, 1944.
89. Andrew Boyle, *Montagu Norman: A Biography* (London: Cassells, 1967), p. 310.
90. R.S. Sayers, *The Bank of England 1891–1944* (Cambridge: Cambridge University Press, 1976), p. 602.
91. Giuseppe, op. cit., pp. 190–1.
92. Memo by Catto to Norman, 2 Feb. 1941, p. 1, Bank of England Archives, OV 38/1, location no. 1335/3.
93. For example see Keynes' memo and the official responses to it in T.160/1270/F18373; T.160/1270/F18373/01; and T.160/1270/F18373/Annexe 1.
94. Memo by S.D. Waley on Keynes' memo, 10 June 1944, noting that he agreed with Keynes and looked forward to the Bank's response; this, however, as Sir W. Eady has jotted in the margin, had not been received by 15 June 1944.
95. Letter, S.D. Waley to Sir Richard Hopkins, 31 Aug. 1944, T.160/1270/F18373/Annexe 1.
96. L.S. Pressnell, *External Economic Policy since the War: Vol. II, The Post-War Financial Settlement* (London: HMSO, 1986), p. 141.
97. Cited in Giuseppe, op. cit., p. 191.
98. Pressnell, op. cit., p. 141.
99. Ibid., pp. 141–2.
100. Note by Keynes, 13 Aug. 1944, in T.160/1270/F18373/Annexe 1, p. 1.
101. Ibid.
102. Summarised by Pressnell, op. cit., p. 143.
103. Alan Bullock, *The Life and Times of Ernest Bevin* (London: Heinemann, 1983), Vol. III.
104. Ibid., p. 122.
105. David Reynolds and David Dimbleby, *An Ocean Apart* (London: BBC Books/Hodder & Stoughton, 1988).
106. H.G. Nicholas, *Britain and the United States* (London: Chatto & Windus, 1963).

107. *The Times*, 19 Dec. 1945.
108. Randall Woods, op. cit., p. 352.
109. *Tribune*, 26 Oct. 1945.
110. *Tribune*, 14 and 21 Dec. 1945.
111. Woods, op. cit., p. 366.
112. Leopold Amery, *The Washington Loan Agreements: A Critical Study of American Foreign Economic Policy* (London: Macdonald, 1950), pp. v–vi.
113. Ibid., p. xi.

6

Conclusion

The aim of this chapter is to discuss some of the key issues raised in the foregoing analysis, draw conclusions as to the validity of competing explanations of the formation of the Anglo-American alliance, and to examine the extent to which the growth of state power undermined the principles of a democratic society.

This study has considered the impact of the state on three categories of interest groups – pro-US alliance, pro-Empire and pro-Soviet – and has indicated three types of state action: mobilisation of the pro-American groups; defeat of the pro-Empire groups; and complete exclusion of the pro-Soviet group. Given such pro-active state behaviour, the main concern here must be to consider the evidence presented and to draw some conclusions about the nature of the relations between the state and interest groups, and the theories of the state that are under consideration.

The most obvious conclusion is that the state was immensely more powerful than any interest group – whether the group in question represented a few thousand communists, or well-placed 'respectable individuals', or the nation's leading industrialists. It was the state that 'set the agenda' concerning the key issues and problems in British foreign policy to which the organised interests responded. It was also the state that determined which of the groups should be integrated into the state machine, mobilised to perform policy-related functions, or excluded from the process entirely. The role that the state played, therefore, does not rest easily beside conventional Marxist and pluralist explanations: indeed, the state demonstrated its independence of the key organised interests in British society. It could be argued, on the evidence presented above, that it was the groups representing 'civil society' that became vehicles of state power rather than the reverse.

Some neo-Marxists, such as Fred Block and Ralph Miliband, have abandoned several of their former ideas about the state being an 'instrument' of the 'ruling class' and suggest that the state is far more autonomous than even the 'relative autonomy' Marxists claim.[1] Theirs is still, to be sure, a class analysis of the state, but tempered by the onslaught of statism. Block argues, for example, that even if the state is 'relatively autonomous' of the ruling class, it (the state) must still act in such a manner as to maintain the sources of its revenues, that is taxes, which derive from capitalist economic activity. The state, therefore, is 'tied' to the business community, must maintain 'business confidence' in the country, so that big business will continue to invest and produce, generating tax revenues and helping to maintain domestic political order through job-creation, et cetera. These are the structural facts of life for the state, whatever business lobbies say at any particular time. While this argument is an undoubtedly strong one, it does imply the idea of some form of equal 'partnership' or 'division of labour'[2] between the state and the economically dominant class, which the evidence in this study shows to be inapplicable in this case. The data cited above indicate a powerful state, a dominating and mobilising state, which listened to the FBI, the Bank of England and the other groups, and asked their opinions on occasion, but acted exactly as it wished, often determining or overriding business opinion. This is not, therefore, a 'relatively autonomous' state — that concept is insufficient to deal with the reality. Rather, it is a superior state, an 'autonomous' state. This does not necessarily mean that it is always superior or autonomous, but that it has the capacity to be so, and in this case actualised that potential.

What are the sources of this autonomy? There are many sources, one of the most important being the war, which permitted the state a great deal of room for manoeuvre because of the high degree of social and political unity that prevailed. During the war, the powers of the state were drastically increased to meet the needs of total conflict. In such a situation, the 'legitimate' increase in the powers of the executive ensured that civil society would wield less influence, so that all social groups experienced a decline in their fortunes. Of course, the increase in the state's powers were only sanctioned for the duration of the war, but many of them were carried over into peacetime. At such a period of crisis, it is relatively easy to portray any opposition to the state's policies as unpatriotic or likely to play into enemy hands, thereby allowing the state to act as the sole legitimate defender of national security. The post-war period has shown,

Conclusion

however, that state power did not decline with the onset of peace, especially because of the need to restructure and regulate the economy, to reconstruct social and economic life, to provide the services associated with the welfare state. The state emerged from the war more powerful and more autonomous, and it did not yield all of those powers in peacetime.

As mentioned in the preceding paragraph, however, the war itself only heightened the powers of the state; it had not created them anew. The increases in state power over the twentieth century, as Crouch and Dore argue in *Corporatism and Accountability*, are not only wartime based phenomena, but also relate to periods of peace, economic crisis, et cetera.[3] State autonomy and power over the FBI, the Bank and other groups, therefore, cannot be seen in isolation as an aspect peculiar to wartime. In fact, some of the evidence considered in this study, especially in relation to state relations with the FBI, RIIA and the EIA, is drawn from the pre-war era and the period of the 'phoney war', showing state leadership of 'industry'. Secondary analyses of the FBI by R.F. Holland and by Ann Trotter demonstrate the same point for the 1930s: that the FBI either waited for governmental initiatives on important areas of policy, or acted as a 'front' for state diplomacy.[4] The same can be argued for the post-war period, on the issues of British defence policy, Marshall Aid and so on.[5]

Obviously, the FBI was primarily an industrialists' body, so that its major concerns would be the well-being of business in the fields of taxation, the law, production, supplies, efficiency, manpower, skills training and education, and so on. That is, to justify the annual subscription, the FBI had to provide services to its members on a regular basis that actually benefited them directly. While, therefore, some FBI committees discussed foreign affairs (which, of course, did directly affect the export trades), large sections of its members had little interest in that area. The FBI did not develop as much expertise in foreign affairs, therefore, as it did in other spheres, which meant that the state was much less likely to pay attention to its foreign policy views. Yet, the FBI was considered important enough to disseminate official views among industrialists and even to implement those views directly.

The Bank of England, while obviously having international

interests and concerns, financial and economic, was also a sectional body representing a sectional interest – finance. It also, therefore, was restricted in its outlook, its daily activities, its organisational requirements and, of course, its legal and constitutional position. Each of the other groups considered above were also narrowly focused or small in size, both important limiting factors.

The state, on the other hand, has a more global vision: it is the general organising, administrative and coercive power both within and outside the national boundaries. It is legally responsible for the maintenance of the 'national interest', especially in international affairs. It is the body that tries to come to grips with the place of the country in the world order. Its concerns, therefore, are never as narrow as that of industry, because it must plan for the short and long term, for the welfare of industry, and for commerce, finance, et cetera. Its connection to individual or group interests within a society, therefore, is distant. Yet the state personnel are British nationals – their notions of 'national interest', with which they will have been socialised from their earliest years to their formal civil service and political training, motivate state strategy. They have to think about, develop and adapt to the international frameworks within which the 'national interests' will be best served, whether they be political, economic, military or other.

The state's vision is, therefore, of necessity far broader than that of industry and finance, however well organised the latter interests may be. The state's administrative machinery for the gathering of information for the discussion, formulation, creation and implementation of policy, especially foreign policy, is far superior, its knowledge more complete, than that of any domestic social group.

The second factor follows from the previous one: the state cannot be seen in isolation; it is part of an international order of states, in which rivalry, conflict and tension are ever-present realities. The state's structure and policies are highly influenced by the international situation: if the situation is 'dangerous' then a more militaristic posture might be adopted, higher military expenditure will result, spending in other areas will be reduced. In fact, sociologists such as Giddens, Skocpol, Mann, and Shaw[6] argue persuasively that European interstate rivalry actually defined the mode of state structure, the development of citizenship rights, et cetera, rather than

Conclusion

these being developments purely internal to society. The exigencies of war, and potential war, between states created the need to consolidate and centralise internal power, to mobilise the population to develop citizen armies, in return for which the franchise was extended and state citizenship rights and benefits developed. This line of argument suggests that the states-system generates an objective set of constraints leading to state policies that are motivated by concepts like 'the balance of power' rather than class interests. This position is similar to that of the 'realists' in international relations, except that the sociologists accept the importance of internal social factors in state structure and policy-making. Again, however, we have a 'structuralist' argument, in which the state is ultimately constrained by external forces. Of course, to deny this completely is absurd; the argument here is that the structuralist argument denies state power, which is real and determining.

That Marxists have generally neglected the international, inter-state, dimension is well-known, but that is also true of most other sociological traditions too. The key question, however, is: does this mean that there can be no analysis of the state/s that allows room for a class analysis? That is not the line of argument favoured here. Ultimately, we are dealing with the behaviour of individuals and groups. Sociological explanations of behaviour have tended to divide into two types, as expressed by the action/structure debate. Crudely put, some argue that structures determine action – we are constrained by our environment, our material conditions, the organisation of the economic system, et cetera. From the structuralist perspective, the state is an actor in a particular socio-economic environment – a capitalist one. The actions perspective considers behaviour as more internally/individually motivated – no major structural constraints are recognised. In trying to explain the British state's international behaviour, however, the action/structure dichotomy is itself constraining. Instead of being two fundamentally opposed perspectives, structure and action are in fact in *continuous and mutually influencing interaction*. There is no easily drawn boundary between them. Structures can be changed by action, and vice versa.

Any explanation of the British state's foreign policy behaviour in creating the Anglo-American alliance must also begin with the recognition of the validity of Skocpol's view that the state is 'janus-faced' – looking outward and inward at the same time, balancing internal and external factors, trying to retain internal solidarity at the same time as maintaining its international position.[7] Internally, there are class forces in conflict, as well as intra-élite divisions, and externally there are various threats and opportunities. Both aspects of the equation focus pressure on the state – 'constrain' the state. The British state was both influenced by and in turn influenced the structure of world power. Where does one end and the other begin? Structure and intentionality are not opposed to each other so crudely; they are part of the same complex reality.

The British state's position has to be seen in that light. It is British-based and therefore must act to maintain the national interest – try to keep social peace and unity. It must retain its revenues and power, one source of which is industrial and financial activity. The 'fractions' of capital are therefore important – they perform, and must continue to perform, certain vital functions. The interest of the key wealth-producing groups/classes, then, will become 'national interests' as far as the state is concerned, and part of the state's activity will be to ensure their continuation and development. But this does not make the state 'a capitalist state' – it merely identifies with a key economic group or groups, and as long as those groups continue in their predominant economic position, the state will favour and encourage them. So if the state concludes international deals or provides export subsidies that benefit capital, this does not mean that the capitalists are permanently ensconced in the state. It just means that the state recognises their utility in maintaining its own power nationally and internationally. Given different circumstances, for example new powerful economic groups with other bases, the state is likely to shift its allegiance from the old to the new élites. Its own power, state interest, is the key to its behaviour, and all other groups must adapt to that.

This helps to explain the relative weakness of the FBI and the Bank of England, and the autonomy of the state in foreign policy-making. It was not the capitalist class that actually held state power – it was the state itself, although it identified the capitalists as the key class to foster and harness at the time. This does mean, of course, that the owners and controllers of finance and industry would enter the state in various capacities, and that a similar movement occurred in the opposite direction. But even this 'personal union' is important only insofar as the state's interest allows it, because ultimately the state is concerned with system survival which is a pre-condition of its own existence.

The importance of transnational factors in British state policy-making is often neglected, despite the contributions cited above. At a time such as the Second World War, however, such neglect leads to severe problems in explaining British foreign policy, because it was a period of genuinely profound change in the structure and distribution of world power. Such change, whether it occurred during war or peace, could only realistically be 'dealt' with by a set of institutions specifically charged with the purpose of maintaining the 'national interest' in global terms: that is, by the state. It was the state that had to deal with the relative decline of Britain from its world-leader status from a position when the Empire spanned 13 million square miles containing 550 million people on a quarter of the globe, to the realisation that those assets faced military, political, commercial and financial threats. Indeed twentieth-century wars and British state decline have proceeded hand in hand: from the Boer War, when American loans were needed, through to the 'Great War' when British overseas investments were devalued by 15 per cent, and again war debts accumulated.[8] Conversely, the United States had, partly, established its position of relative pre-dominance in world affairs through wars, which provided major boosts to its industrial, financial and military systems. Of course, to any power that is used to near complete domination of world power as Britain was, the emergence of the United States was seen as a threat, and the diplomacy of the 1920s and 1930s demonstrates this in many ways. Yet the rise of other, more militaristic powers – Germany and Japan – 'pushed' Britain into an alliance with the United States because the British state could no longer defend its world-wide possessions and its power single-handedly. In short, the British state suffered from the same problem as all world powers have encountered at a certain point in their history: that its commitments exceeded its capabilities.[9] The increased reliance on the United States, especially in military terms, was fully understood by British state leaders such as Eden and the Chiefs of Staff. They

Special Interests, the State and the Anglo-American Alliance, 1939-45

knew that the British state must have as its 'constant aim in peace time to increase as far as possible the likelihood of the US giving us armed support in case of war'.[10]

In addition to the menace of militarist Germany and Japan, the British state also had to reckon with the decline and disintegration of the Empire – of both colonies and dominions. That is, the most important bases of the British state's world position were crumbling under the weight of increased naionalism, anti-colonialism, the attraction of the United States as a market and, later, as a military protector. Even in terms of Imperial Preference, the British state found it unduly restrictive to British economic and financial interests, and therefore policy shifted at this conjuncture to seek a new way to resolve an old problem: the maintenance of the state's position in the interstate system.

The external position of the British state was considerably weakened by the Second World War, despite military triumph: the war cost Britain £7,300 million; she sold 50 per cent of her overseas investments; and accumulated a foreign debt of over £3,000 million.[11] This position provided further incentives to the British state to find a suitable ally in order to assist it to try to retain, develop and maximise its world position in a precarious situation. The debates in the Foreign Office and the Cabinet demonstrate this very clearly. The Anglo-American alliance was seen as best for the 'nation', that is, the state, hence the appeals to British industry to co-operate with US industry, for the city to abandon Empire preference, and to look to Bretton Woods to provide the framework for Britain's international economic future.

If this study does not wholly reject society-centred Marxist analysis (on which more will be said later), it is more thoroughly critical of the pluralist perspective. Indeed, the reasons for rejecting key tenets of pluralism constitute some of the important reasons for retaining certain of the insights of Marxism. Fundamental among these is the pluralist assumption of some level of equality between organised interest groups in capitalist societies. The historical record, however, reveals that some groups were 'more equal than others'. The FBI, Chatham House, the Bank of England, et cetera, were far more privileged in their discussions and liaisons with the official makers of foreign policy, than were, for example, the

Conclusion

'reformist' TUC and the 'revolutionary' Communist Party. These groups were differentiated not only in terms of resources and the social origins of their leadership, but also in terms of the distance between them and the state. They were not embraced by policy-makers despite their size and/or political influence. The FBI and the like, on the other hand, seemed to be the groups which were consulted most 'naturally' or as a matter of established custom and practice. Ultimately, it was their leaders who were appointed to positions closest to the heart of the foreign policy-making apparatus.

Big business, as Prime Minister Neville Chamberlain has been cited as saying, had to constitute the central force in planning for post-war economic and foreign policies. Despite the later entry of the Labour Party into a coalition government, the central force of Chamberlain's argument remained essentially unaltered. Immediately, this signals the existence of a hierarchy of groups in civil society that the state relates to and interacts with; it signals the type, nature and extent of state–interest group relations; it signals the likely political 'distance' that may prevail between 'state' and 'group'; and the likelihood of mobilisation, co-operation, consultation, incorporation, marginalisation, or exclusion, of the 'group' by the state. It never went as far as business group domination of the state, as the evidence clearly reveals; but, the 'business interest' (broadly conceived) was a powerful factor in policy-makers' definition of the national interest. Certainly, it outweighed most other factors.

The pluralist assumption of independent interest groups has also been challenged by the evidence of overlapping group membership. The interconnections between the leaders of industry and finance, between Chatham House and the main political parties, are highly important: they suggest the existence of a fairly cohesive, well connected social, economic and political élite in British society, with strong links to the means of political influence. The notion that the British political system is characterised by competition between independent groups is severely undermined by such evidence. Given the intimacy between certain groups and the policy process, it is surprising that some observers of this 'corporatist' trend have remained wedded to the idea that Britain remained pluralist. Keith Middlemas, for example, in his excellent *Power, Competition and the State*, in which he convincingly demonstrates the growth of state power and the incorporation of key interest groups, clings to the view that pluralism remains the best description of the British political system. At one point, Middlemas argues that the British state helped create 'private' organisations (such as the FBI), helped isolate 'responsible' from 'revolutionary' labour, and 'manipulated' public opinion to such an extent as to cause 'the more or less successful ostracism of political movements designed to overthrow the system'.[12] Yet, he concludes that this is merely a form of pluralism, a conclusion that appears to be at variance with the evidence cited in this study and, indeed, in Middlemas' own work.

Pluralism has also been associated with the notion of policy choice: that the state selects a policy option from among several in a competitive environment. But, despite the debate between the pro-US and pro-Empire options, no other genuine options were held to be worthy of consideration. While the 'policy shift' from Empire to an alliance with the United States represented no small change, the debate referred largely to the means of achieving a 'national interest', the principal tenets of which were shared by the 'competing' parties. The struggle in the Cabinet was not over the fundamental principles of British foreign policy: it was over the best institutional means of realising them. The debate, therefore, was very narrow in terms of ideas and even institutional choices; it was also narrow because of the extremely circumscribed élite that had the opportunity to engage legitimately in it.

The final nail in the pluralists' coffin, according to the evidence cited above, is the overwhelming superiority of the state in not only making the 'key decisions', but also in determining the agenda, the actors, and their prospects for inclusion, neutralisation or exclusion concerning the policy process.

In relation to many of the criticisms of the pluralist view noted above, Marxist ideas on the class system and social and political inequality have greater credence: they better explain the proximity of business and other élite associations to centres of political power and their similarities of outlook, if not institutional interest. It is the Marxists' lack of belief in the enormity of independent state power that constitutes the largest problem as far as this case study is concerned. Yet, it is only a synthesis of notions of class influence

Conclusion

and state power that provides an adequate basis on which to understand the creation of the Anglo-American alliance. It is, therefore, a 'modified statism' that is considered to be the most adequate explanation of the making of British foreign policy, with particular reference to the United States. Such a position allows for state power which derives from its special position with reference to the domestic and international systems, and for the insights as to political and social inequality in capitalist society championed by Marxists. The essential conclusion is that the state was independent. It was more powerful than the interest groups examined above. It made the Anglo-American alliance. But the fact remains that state power could only be realised if it could successfully mobilise key domestic forces in its favour, neutralise its 'internal' foes (that is, forces within the state opposed to the dominant trend) and 'ostracise' its radical enemies. At all times, however, the evidence suggests that the greatest actual power of decision lay in official hands, despite reliance on certain domestic forces.

The conclusions drawn above must be considered in the light of the limitations of a case study. Being thus limited in scope, its conclusions must also be limited. This must be so even if the Anglo-American alliance has constituted the fundamental basis of Britain's post-1945 foreign policy. This study does highlight, however, certain features of the British political system that may be seen as enduring and relatively stable. One such enduring and evolving tendency already discussed is that of 'corporatism', which we usually associate with, say, Italy in the 1920s. Another is the continuing importance of élites in the political order.

It is worth discussing 'political élites' at this stage, because many 'structuralists' reject their importance in the political order. Because of 'systemic imperatives' they argue, the personnel of the state are irrelevant: they are the bearers of roles that are determined by the 'needs of the system' rather than individuals engaging in purposive action or whose ideas are formed in some other way. It does not matter about the social origins of leaders because the 'structure of their situation' determines their behaviour. As was argued earlier, this view cannot be rejected out of hand: it has legitimate claim to validity. Yet, élites are important as this study has tried to demonstrate. Why else would recruitment to the state élite be almost completely restricted to the most artistocratic/privileged sections of the population? If the personnel make no difference, why bother being exclusive? A related point emerges from the evidence concerning the distance maintained between sections of the 'left' and the state machine. If 'structure' wholly determines 'action' then why did communists need to be excluded from the policy process and intimidated and disrupted in such a systematic way; why were even members of the TUC kept at arm's length and excluded from the British delegation to the United Nations conferences?

The point may be illustrated further by a counter factual: how would policy be affected if a previously excluded group were to constitute a sudden new majority within the state?; if African-Americans were to form the majority of the appointees of a new President of the USA?; or women were to be so represented?; or, for that matter, the working class of Britain were to predominate numerically at the British Foreign Office, Treasury, Board of Trade, et cetera? Would the racial, gender and social class orders remain unchanged and intact? Would the wielding of state power by these forces leave the domestic and international policies of the state unaltered? Of course, the changes might not be 'revolutionary' or permanent but such sudden changes of personnel would be unlikely to leave the status quo unchanged. Elites, and therefore élite studies, are important: they tell us a great deal about the nature and loci of power in society; they also tell us much about the extent and distribution of opportunities; and the formal and informal means by which power and position are perpetuated in formally democratic systems. 'Structures', in fact, are constituted, perpetuated and altered by 'actors'.

Power in British society, as a huge number of studies – and as this case study confirms, is heavily concentrated in a few hands. Great decisions are made affecting the lives of millions by a few men drawn from a restricted range of strata. Really great power resides in the state executive. The state élite has fashioned for itself an almost unrivalled position; even the largest organisations of 'big business' would find it difficult to pursue effectively a course of action fundamentally opposed by the state. As the twentieth century has progressed, the British state has increased its strength

Conclusion

through war, peace and economic crises. It was, by 1939–45, the centre of a political order that resembled the solar system: the state was like the sun, with its huge gravitational pull, attracting those who sought influence and confining them to a particular orbit. But, unlike the sun, the state élite exercised their considerable power also in the opposite direction: they also repelled forces whose ideas, customs and aspirations conflicted too greatly with their own. In such ways did the state attract and bring close the forces that were élitist in membership and aspiration, and malleable enough to be fashioned into state-dependent 'private' actors (FBI, RIIA and, occasionally, the TUC); retain at hand forces that were oppositional but within an ideological and political spectrum recognised as 'legitimate' (EIA, Bank of England); and exclude altogether those whose aims, theories, assumptions and aspirations violated their notions of the 'acceptable' and 'legitimate' (CPGB).

Given such concentration of power and its exercise by such means, the notion of a 'democratic' state is severely undermined. Rather than equality of opportunity for all (or even the majority) to enter the political fray, politics remained the province of the few. And the few allowed new entrants only occasionally, and on certain terms: they had to play by the 'rules of the game'. Anthony Eden was surely right when he argued in 1928 that 'We have not got democratic government today. We have never had it and I venture to suggest to Honourable members opposite that we shall never have it. What we have done in all progress of reform and evolution is to broaden the basis of oligarchy.'[13] The British state élite has only slowly opened its doors to 'outsiders', provided they learnt the 'rules of the game'.

The 'few', the narrowly recruited political élite, made British foreign policy; certainly, it was they who made the Anglo-American alliance. If they exercised *realpolitik* in domestic politics, then they undoubtedly transferred that approach to interstate relations. Considerations of power and interest lay at the heart of Britain's approach to foreign relations. Yet, the post-1945 period, as noted in Chapter 1, has witnessed the popular and academic acceptance of the 'special relationship' explanation of Britain's relations with the United States. According to this view, considerations other than those of power politics are at the heart of the Anglo-American alliance – such as ties of blood, common language, and the like. This study has demonstrated that the underlying definition of national (that is, state) interest centred upon strategic and economic concerns, and that a similar set of considerations account for the international, political, economic and financial institutions which the state worked to build for the post-war era. Certainly that is the only conclusion that can be drawn from the documentary evidence itself. When state policy-makers discussed and debated the necessity of an alliance with the US, they rarely mentioned 'blood ties'. They *did* mention their fears of growing British dependence on the United States and the problems that that could cause with reference to national sovereignty, but they decided that the 'advantages outweighed the disadvantages', in true *realpolitik* fashion.

We are back, then, to the question asked at the beginning of this study – how did British dependence on the United States come about? According to the interpretation favoured here, it came about because of the conception of British state policy-makers that they should maintain a global role – a so-called 'forward projection of British power'. If it meant dependence on the greatest military and industrial power on earth, so be it. If it meant massive military expenditures to remain faithful to US policy, that was what state interest required. If it meant staying aloof from things 'European', and thereby undermining Britain's economic position, that was also in order. It also meant, in practice, that Britain became America's 'unsinkable aircraft carrier', with 100 military and air force bases which could be put on nuclear alert *without consultation.*[14]

The analysis of the making of the Anglo-American alliance has provided a useful focus for studying questions big and small. It has also (hopefully) provided a number of answers about the factors that underpin the policy-making process and the overwhelming power of the modern British state. While Britain remained a democratic 'state' in the 1940s, the boundaries of public discussion and debate were narrowly drawn: the politically 'legitimate' agenda allowed a circumscribed debate between policy options that, in several respects, were founded on identical considerations. The state rarely told Britons what to think; but it did, through its differential treatment of special interests promoting differing policy options, tell them 'what to think about'.[15] As Alexis de Tocqueville

Conclusion

said about the modern state: it organises social, economic and intellectual life to such an extent that it almost relieves citizens 'from the trouble of thinking'. The state, he suggested, embraces the whole society yet

> it does not break men's will, but softens, bends, and guides it; it seldom enjoins, but often inhibits action; it does not destroy anything, but prevents much being born; it is not at all tyrannical, but it hinders, restrains, enervates, stifles, and stultifies so much that in the end each nation is no more than a flock of timid and hard-working animals with the government as its shepherd.[16]

NOTES

1. F. Block, 'Beyond Relative Autonomy: State Managers as Historical Subjects' (Socialist Register, 1980); Miliband, 'State Power and Capitalist Democracy', in Krishna Bharadawaj and Sudipta Kaviraj (eds), *Perspective on Capitalism* (New Delhi: Sage Publications, 1989); and Miliband, *Divided Societies* (Oxford and New York: Oxford University Press, 1991).
2. F. Block, 'Marxist Theories of the State in World Systems Analysis', in Barbara H. Kaplan (ed.), *Social Change in the Capitalist World Economy* (Beverly Hills: Sage Publications, 1978).
3. Colin Crouch and Ronald Dore (eds), *Corporatism and Accountability* (Oxford: Clarendon Press, 1990).
4. R.F. Holland, 'The Federation of British Industries and the International Economy, 1929–39', *Economic History Review*, Second Series, Vol. 34, No. 2 (1981), p. 295; Ann Trotter, *Britain and East Asia* (London: Cambridge University Press, 1975), pp. 115–32.
5. See Minutes of the FBI Grand Council (GC), 12 May and 29 July 1948, in MSS 200/F/1/1/188; and 23 Aug. 1950, in MSS 200/F/1/1/190.
6. Anthony Giddens, *The Nation-State and Violence* (Cambridge: Polity Press, 1985); Theda Skocpol, *States and Social Revolutions* (Cambridge: Cambridge University Press, 1979); Michael Mann, *States, War and Capitalism* (Oxford: Blackwell, 1988); Martin Shaw, *Dialectics of War* (London: Pluto Press, 1988).
7. Skocpol, op. cit., p. 32.
8. W. Ashworth, *A Short History of the International Economy Since 1850* (London: Longman, 1987), p. 229.
9. Paul Kennedy, *The Rise and Fall of the Great Powers* (London: Fontana Press, 1989).
10. Eden cited by David Reynolds, *The Creation of the Anglo-American Alliance, 1937–41* (London: Europa Publications, 1981), p. 22.
11. F.S. Northedge, *Descent from Power: British Foreign Policy 1945–73* (London: Allen & Unwin, 1974), p. 22.
12. Middlemas, pp. 3–7.

13. Cited by W.L. Guttsman, *The British Political Elite* (London: Macgibbon & Kee, 1965), p. 368.
14. David Reynolds, *Britannia Overruled* (London and New York: Longman, 1991), p. 244.
15. This is an adaptation of Bernard C. Cohen's assessment of the power of the American press in his *The Press and Foreign Policy* (Princeton: Princeton University Press, 1963), p. 13.
16. A. de Tocqueville, *Democracy in America* (New York: Fontana, 1968), Vol. II, pp. 898–9.

Index

Aaronovitch, Sam, 146
Advisory Committee on Colonial Development (1929–30), 88
Advisory Committee on International Questions (1939), 84
Aldrich, Winthrop, 34
Amalgamated Society of Engineers, 135
American Civil War (1861–85), 23
American Federation of Labour (AFL), 78
Amery, Leopold, 46, 47–50, 55, 64, 125, 127, 162, 163, 171
Anderson, Sir John, 115
Anglo-American relations, post-war, 1–8, 15, 18
Anglo-American Trade Agreement (1937–38), 34, 47
Anglo-Iranian Oil, 132
Anglo-Soviet Trade Union Committee, 80
anti-colonialism, US, 43, 44–5, 154, 186
appeasement policy, 41, 99n, 146
Ashton-Gwatkin, Frank, 70–1, 111, 151, 152, 156
Asquith, Herbert, 124
Astor, Lord, 131
Association of British Chambers of Commerce, 35
Athenaeum, 121, 124, 127, 128, 131, 133, 134
Atlantic Charter (1941), 16, 38, 44, 141, 144, 161–2
Attlee, Clement, 81, 83, 85, 89–90, 91, 92–3, 103n, 133, 134, 174
Australia, 23, 38, 39, 70, 87, 125, 150, 155, 166

Bachrach, P., and Baratz, Morton S., 14
Bailey, Sir Abe, 131
Baillieu, Sir Clive, 30, 36, 38, 123
Baldwin, Stanley, 27, 79, 129
Balfour, A.J., 65
Balfour, John, 152, 160
Ball, Sir Joseph, 112
Bank of England, 17, 22, 47, 51–6, 86, 108, 115, 121, 131, 133, 167–9; Court of Directors, 53; role and influence of state and, 148–9, 173, 180, 181–2, 184, 186, 191; social background of directors, 127–8; Treasury Committee, 53; 'War Book', 53

Bank of International Settlements, 149
Barclays Bank, 132
Barnby, Lord, 34
Beaverbrook, Lord, 86, 94
Bentley, A.F., 11
Bevan, Aneurin, 171
Bevin, Ernest, 73, 76, 82, 83–4, 85, 88–9, 90–1, 92, 103n, 129, 133, 134, 135, 138, 170, 173, 174
Block, Fred, 179, 180
Board of Trade, 13, 31, 32, 34, 79, 86, 106, 107, 108–9, 115, 116, 120, 129, 142, 144, 190
Boer War (1899–1902), 23, 89, 185
Bolton, G.L.F., 54
Boothby, Robert, 171
Brady, Robert A., 30
Bremner, D.A., 37
Brenan, Sir J., 112, 114
Bretton Woods Agreement (1944–45), 16, 33, 39, 81, 89, 141, 164–9, 170–1, 186
Bridge, Colonel Robert, 5
British Commonwealth Union, 124, 126
British Empire, 16, 23, 24–5, 38–9, 41–2, 54, 55–6, 57, 64, 65, 68, 74, 75–6, 83, 87, 88, 89, 90, 91, 94, 110, 117, 124, 144–5, 160, 162, 163–4, 165, 166, 171, 172, 179, 186, 188; *see also* Empire Industries Association; Imperial Preference; Sterling Area
British Empire League, 127
British Empire Producers' Association, 126
British Employers Confederation, 77, 78
Brook's Club, 121, 128, 131
Bullock, Alan, 88
Bülow, Chancellor Bernhard von, 25
Burnham, Peter, 12
Bush, US President George, 5
Butler, David and Gareth, 128–9
Butler, N., 117
Butler, R.A., 116, 151–2
Byrnes, James, 90

Cabinet, 13, 73, 85, 86, 92, 115, 117, 161, 163–4, 165, 170, 171, 173, 186, 188
Cabinet Committee on War (or Peace) Aims, 151
Cadogan, Sir Alexander, 120, 121, 161, 162

195

Campbell, Duncan, 6
Campbell, Sir Edward, 127
Campbell, J.R., 134, 136
Campbell, Sir R.I., 116–17
Canada, 16, 23, 37–8, 39, 70, 86, 125, 155, 166
Canning, George, 110
capitalism, 11–12, 31, 42–3, 76, 77, 83, 84, 93–4, 96, 107, 184, 186
Carlton Club, 124, 127, 131
Carnegie, Andrew, 24
Carnegie UK Trustees, 131
Catterns, B.G., 55
Catto, Lord, 121, 128, 148, 168
Central Committee on Reconstruction, 138
Chamberlain, Joseph, 107–8
Chamberlain, Neville, 27, 46, 73, 114, 128, 146, 187
Chatfield, Admiral, 25
Chatham, Lord, 110
Chatham House see RIIA
Cherwell, Frederick Lindemann, Lord, 162, 164
Chester, Sir George, 132
China, 4, 23, 26, 31–2, 43, 112, 114, 142–4, 153–4, 155
China Association, 142
China Liaison Committee, 142, 143
Churchill, Sir Winston, 2–3, 25, 43, 56, 57, 63, 77, 78, 80, 85, 88, 89, 90, 92, 95, 103n, 117, 128, 129, 133, 150, 160, 161, 162, 164
Citrine, Sir Walter, 73, 75–8, 80, 81, 132
City of London, 51–2, 53, 55, 128, 131
civil servants, 130, 136, 137, 138; social background of, 106, 118–22
Clark, Alan, 3
Clarke, Ashley, 114, 156–7
class system, 12, 28, 29, 51, 57, 83, 93, 94, 118–20, 183, 184, 188
Clay, Sir Henry, 128
Clayton, Will, 170
Cliveden Set, 62, 99n
club membership, West End, 136, 137; Bank of England, 128; civil servants, 121; Conservative leaders, 129; EIA, 127; FBI, 124; Labour leaders, 134; RIIA, 130–1
Clyde Workers' Committee, 135
Coalition Government, wartime, 138, 159, 171, 173–4, 187
Coates, Dr W.H., 33, 39, 167
Cole, G.D.H. and M.I., 29
Colonial Labour Advisory Committee, 75
Colonial Office, 44, 67, 75, 129, 157
Commonwealth, 8, 64, 92, 171
Communist Party of Great Britain (CPGB), 18, 22, 74, 93–9, 122, 134–6, 161, 173, 187, 191

company directorships, 136, 137; Bank of England, 128; civil servants, 120–1; Conservative leaders, 129; EIA, 125–6; FBI, 123; Labour leaders, 134; RIIA, 130
Conference of Institutions for the Scientific Study of International Relations (1932), 67
Connell, John, 110, 119, 122
Conservative Party, 8, 17–18, 56–7, 123, 127, 128–9, 130, 137, 138, 159–60, 171, 173, 174
Constitutional Club, 127
corporations, 28, 30, 76, 187, 189
Council of Action, TUC–Labour, 83
Council of Foreign Bondholders, 112
Council of Foreign Relations, US, 152
Creech-Jones, Arthur, 129, 134, 157
Crick, W.F., 39, 40
Cripps, Sir Stafford, 15, 70, 87–8, 133, 170
Croft, Sir Henry Page, 46, 147
Crouch, Colin, and Dore, Ronald, 181
Crowe, Eyre, 62, 63, 110–11
Cruise Missiles based in Britain, 1–2
Curtis, Lionel, 63–6, 155

Dahl, Robert, 11
Daily Worker, 94, 97–8, 135, 161
Dalton, Hugh, 79, 81, 85–7, 89, 91, 92, 134, 170
Davidson, Lord, 79
Dawson, Geoffrey, 64
defence policy, British, 1–3, 6, 8, 181, 192
decision-making, key decisions, 13, 14–16, 18, 106, 141, 150, 188
Denny, Ludwell, 24
Destroyers-for-Bases Agreement (1940), 15–16, 141, 150, 160–1
Dobson, Alan, 161, 163
Docker, Frank Dudley, 29–30, 32–3, 123
Dockrill, M.L., 62
Dominions, 42, 43–4, 54, 55, 64, 70, 86, 91, 144–5, 156, 186
Dulles, J.F., 19n
Dunning, John, 7
Durbin, Evan, 87, 103n
Dutt, Rajani Palme, 95, 134, 135, 171

Eady, Sir Wilfred, 55
Eden, Sir Anthony, 27, 63, 80, 81, 90, 119, 128, 129, 153, 154, 155, 185, 191
education, 29; Bank of England, 127–8; civil servants, 119, 120; Conservative leaders, 129; CP leaders, 135; EIA, 124–5; FBI, 122–3; Labour leaders, 133; RIIA, 130; TUC leaders, 132
Empire Industries Association (EIA), 17, 22, 43–51, 56, 124–7, 137, 149, 160,

Index

163, 173; origins and aims, 46; Parliamentary Committee, 47; role and influence of state and, 147–8, 181, 191; social background of members, 124–7; world outlook, 46–51
Engels, Friedrich, 74
Eton, 94, 119, 120, 122, 124, 128, 130, 135
European Community (EC), 8
Export Credits Guarantee Department, 32

F-111 jet fighters, US, 1, 3
Fawcett, Sir Luke, 133
Federation of British Industries (FBI), 17, 22, 29–43, 50–1, 55–6, 78, 79, 80, 85–6, 89, 114, 137, 173, 180, 181; China Committee, 31–2, 143; and declining significance of Empire, 41–2; Empire Executive Committee, 37, 42; Grand Council, 31, 34, 37, 39, 43, 145; International Trade Policy Committee, 33, 38, 42; Monetary Policy Panel, 39–40, 166–7; and national interest, 31–7, 42–3; Reconstruction Report (1942), 33, 35, 36, 38, 40, 41, 50, 144; role and influence of state and, 141–7, 172, 180, 181, 184, 186–7, 188, 191; social origins of membership, 122–4; and US economic aggression, 37–41
Finer, S.E., 30–1, 43
Foreign and Diplomatic Service, 119, 142
Foreign Office, British, viii, 13, 15, 17, 30, 31, 33, 62, 67, 69, 70, 87, 92, 106, 107, 109–11, 112, 114, 116, 117, 118–19, 120, 121, 142, 143, 144, 150, 156–7, 160, 161, 186, 190; Commercial Section, 30–1; and FRPS, 151–5; Political Intelligence Department, 153; Research Department, 113
Foreign Office Research Department (FORD), 153
Foreign Research and Press Service (FRPS), 138, 151–5, 172
France, 15, 27, 45, 94, 110, 161, 145–6, 154
Francis, Ben, 94
Fraser, Carey, 44
Fussell, Paul, vii

Gallacher, William, 134, 135
Gamble, Andrew, 57
Gamage, Leslie C., 37
General Electric Company, 123
General Strike (1926), 76
Germany, 25–6, 27, 41, 47, 71, 80, 90, 96, 98, 110, 114, 185, 186; Nazi, 15, 95, 137, 146, 154, 161
Gibson, George, 79, 133
Giddens, Anthony, 119–20, 182

Giuseppe, John, 167–8
Glyn, A., and Sutcliffe, B., 7
Godson, Dean, 6
Gordon, Lord Dudley, 34–5, 37
Gordon, Michael R., 82, 84, 159
Great War (1914–18), 23, 25–6, 135, 185
Greenham Common, US Cruise Missiles based at, 1–2
Greenwood, Arthur, 79, 81, 85, 91–2, 151, 152, 163
Grenada, US invasion of, 6
Grey, Lord, 65
Guinness, Sir Arthur, 30, 39, 167
Gulf War, 'friendly fire incident' (1992), 4–6

Hailey, Lord, 129, 157
Haldane, J.B.S., 135
Halifax, Lord, 15, 114, 128, 146, 150, 157
Hambro, Sir Charles Joseph, 128
Hankey, Lord, 145, 146
Hannington, Wal, 98
Hannon, Sir Patrick, 37
Hansard, J., 114
Hardinge, Charles, 62
Harris, Kenneth, 90
Harrod, R.F., 168, 169
Harrow school, 94, 122, 124, 129, 130
Healey, Denis, 8, 129
Heath, Edward, 3
Henderson, Sir Hubert, 86
Hirst, Lord, 30, 123, 124
Hitler, Adolf, 26, 146, 160, 162
Hodges, M.R., 7
Hodgson, Sir Mark, 132
Hoffman, Paul, 4
Hogg, Quintin, 57
Holland, R.F., 181
Hopkins, Sir Richard, 85, 149
Horner, Arthur, 134, 135
Howell, David, 92
Hubbard, G.E., 153–4, 155
Hudson, Geoffrey, 154
Hull, Cordell, 48, 50, 164
Huskisson, William, 108

IBM (International Business Machines), 4
ICI (Imperial Chemical Industries), 30, 120, 123, 125, 132, 167
IMF (International Monetary Fund), 16, 39–40, 85, 167, 168–9
Imperial Institute, 126
Imperial Preference, 16, 17, 38, 41, 42, 43, 49, 51, 85, 86, 145, 163, 170, 171, 186
India, 23, 42, 142, 147, 156
Industrial and Export Council, 115
Ingham, Geoffrey, 52, 108

197

Institute of Pacific Relations (IPR), 155–8, 172
International Business Conference, US, 35–6, 42, 145
International Clearing Union, 115, 116
International Federation of Trade Unions, 80
International Relationships Sub-Committee, Economic Section, 84
Iran hostage crisis, 6

Japan, Japanese, 23, 25, 26, 27, 47, 70, 95, 114, 142–4, 153–4, 155, 170, 185, 186
Jebb, H.M.G., 153
Jenkins, Roy, 159
Johnson, US President Lyndon B., 2
Johnstone, Harcourt, 164
Jones, Clement, 65
Jones, Sir Edgar, 79
Jordan, Virgil, 24–5
Joseph, Sir Francis, 43, 123
Jowitt, Sir William, 78–9, 81

Kaufman and Jones, 13–14
Kautsky, Karl, 74
Kelso, William, 11
Kennedy, US President John F., 2
Kerr, Phillip *see* Lothian, Lord
Keynes, J.M., Lord, 36, 85, 164, 167–8, 169, 170, 177n
Keynes, J.R.M., 114–15, 120, 121
Kilner, A.H., 40
King-Hall, Stephen, 67–8, 131
Kinnock, Neil, 8
Kipling, Rudyard, 89
Kirkpatrick, W.M., 32
Knapp, Wilfrid, 68
Kolko, Gabriel, 45
Koszul, J.P., 7
Krasner, Stephen, 13

Labour Monthly, 95, 96–7, 135, 171
Labour Party, 8, 17–18, 22, 57, 74, 77, 80, 81–93, 98, 130, 137, 138, 159, 170–1, 173–4, 187; Clause IV, 82; communists within, 93, 96; conferences, 89, 90, 91; foreign policy, 82–92; NEC, 84, 91, 92; social origins of leaders, 133–4
Labour Representation Committee, 73, 81
Laffan (of FRPS), 152
Lamont, Thomas W., 63, 131
Langley, Kathleen, 28
Laski, Harold, 89, 103n
Lavin, Deborah, 65–6
Law, Richard, 157, 164, 165–6
League of Nations, 49, 83
Lee, Sir Kenneth, 33–4, 38, 41–2, 144–5
Lee, W.A., 41

Leith-Ross, Sir Frederick, 121
Lend-Lease (Mutual Aid Agreement, 1942), 16, 34, 37, 38, 81, 86, 96, 141, 144, 162–4, 170
Lenin, V.I., 74, 94, 107, 136
Lever Brothers, 30, 114, 146
Liberal Party, 8, 73, 74, 81, 123, 130
Libya, US bombing of (1986), 1, 3, 6
Lloyd, Lord, 160–1
Lloyd George, David, 83, 129
Lockerbie air disaster, 3
Locock, Sir Guy, 30, 32–3, 34
Longstreth, Frank, 51–2
Looker, H.W., 123
Lothian, Phillip Kerr, Lord, 64, 69, 70, 113, 149–50, 155, 160, 172
Louis, William Roger, 44, 45
Lovell, John, and Robert, B.C., 72
Lukes, Stephen, 14
Lyttleton, Sir Oliver, 129

Macadam, Ivison, 67, 71
Macdonogh, George, 31–2
McGowan, H.D., 123,
MacKenzie, John, 88
McKinstry, A., 35
McLaine, Ian, 66
Macmillan, Harold, 2–3
McNamara, Robert, 2
McNaugher, Tom, 19n
Mahan, Admiral Alfred T., 45
Major, John, 3, 5
Manchuria, Japanese invasion of (1931), 26
Mann, Michael, 52, 182
Mann, Tom, 135
Marlborough Club, 127
Marshall Aid to Europe, 4, 181
Martin, R.M.I., 72, 73–4
Marxism, 10, 11–13, 14, 27, 74, 106, 135, 136, 167, 179–80, 183, 186, 188–9
Mason, John, 98
Mass-Observation project, 96
Meacher, Michael, 8
Middlemas, Keith, 187–8
Middleton, J.S., 84
Miliband, Ralph, 179
Milner, Alfred, Lord, 46, 63, 64
Ministry of Information (MoI), 80, 120, 130, 152
Monroe Doctrine, US, 23
Monthly Bulletin, EIA's, 47, 50–1
Morgan, J.P., 131
Morgan, Kevin, 98
Morgan Grenfell, 121
Most-Favoured Nation (MFN) clause, US, 38, 42, 47, 49
Mutual Aid Agreement *see* Lend-Lease

Index

National Association of Wholesale Newsagents (NAWN), 97
National Council of Labour, 138
National Federation of Building Trade Operatives, 77
National Foreign Trade Council, US, 35, 42, 144
national interest, 11, 13, 18, 31–7, 42–3, 57, 90, 106, 111–18, 147, 172, 182, 184, 185, 187, 188, 192
National Liberal Club, 131
National Provincial Bank, 120, 121
National Union of Miners (NUM), 135
NATO (North Atlantic Treaty Organisation), 1, 3
Nelson, George, 30
New Zealand, 39, 70, 155
Nicholls, J., 116, 152
Nicolson, Harold, 64
Norman, Sir Montagu, 47–8, 54, 55, 148, 149, 167, 168
North Atlantic Relations Conference, 71
North Sea oil, 7
nuclear defence/weapons, 2, 6, 8
Nugent, Roland, 30

Ormsby-Gore, William, 75
Ottawa Agreements, 38, 42, 50, 142, 144
Oxbridge, 94, 119, 120, 123, 124, 127, 128, 129, 130, 132, 133, 135
Oxford and Cambridge Club, 134

Pankhurst, Sylvia, 93
Papworth, Bert, 135
Paris Peace Conference (1919), 62, 63, 64
Pease, J.A., Lord Gainford of Headlam, 124
Pelling, Henry, 134
Pentagon, US, 5
People's Convention, Communist, 97
People's Press Fighting Fund, 98
Philippines, 155
Phillips, Sir Frederick, 113, 147–8
Pijl, Kees van der, 12
Piratin, Phil, 134
Pitt the Younger, William, 107
Platt, D.C.M., 106–7, 110
pluralism, 10, 11, 12, 14, 106, 179, 186–8
political parties, 16, 17–18, 22, 106;
  see also Communist Party; Conservative Party; Labour Party; Liberal Party
Political Warfare Executive, 154
Pollitt, Harry, 95–6
polls/surveys, 6
Polsby, Nelson, 11, 14
Portal, Viscount, 129
Pouty, Roger, 109
Power, Cecil, 131

power, concept of, 9, 10, 13–14, 15, 190
Prais, S.J., 28
Pressnell, L.S., 47, 168, 169
primary producing countries, 33–4, 50
Pritt, D.N., 135
public/private schools, 94, 119, 120, 122, 124, 127–8, 129, 130, 133, 135
Pugh, Arthur, 73

Reagan, US President Ronald, 6
Reconstruction Joint Advisory Council (RJAC), 78–9, 173
Reform Club, 121, 124, 128, 131
Rifkind, Malcolm, 5
Riverdale of Sheffield, Lord, 37–8
Robertson, Sir Malcolm, 33
Rockefeller, John D., 131
Rockefeller Foundation, 132, 152
Ronald (of Foreign Office), 153
Roosevelt, US President Franklin D., 27, 43, 44, 45, 78, 113, 160, 161
Roosevelt, President Theodore, 45
Rose, Archibald, 69–70
Ross, John, 56
Round Table movement, 63
Royal Colonial Institute, 124
Royal Empire Society, 126
Royal Institute of International Affairs (RIIA: Chatham House), 16–17, 22, 62–72, 79, 80, 129–32; Economic Group, 70–1; Executive Committee, 66; and FRPS, 151–5, 172; funding of, 131–2; influence and role of state and, 149–51, 172, 181, 186, 187, 191; interconnections, 137, 138; and IPR, 155–8, 172; origins and aims, 63–7; policy or 'line', 67–72; social and political background of leaders, 129–31; Special Group on Anglo-American relations (1928–29), 69
Rugby school, 120, 124, 128, 129, 130
Rust, William, 136
Rylands, Sir Peter, 33

St James's Club, 121
Salisbury, Lord, 110
Sargent, Sir Orme, 117, 129, 152
Sbrega, J.J., 45
Schlesinger, Arthur, 45
Shaw, Martin, 182
Shephardson, Whitney, 65, 152
Smith, Hubert, 108
Shepherd, J., 39–40
Shinwell, Emanuel, 171
Sino-Japanese hostilities, 26, 114, 142–3
Skocpol, Theda, 13, 182, 184
Social Darwinism, 25
South Africa, 23, 39, 64, 112, 125, 166

199

South and Central America, 23, 37, 142, 147
Soviet Union (Russia), 4, 7, 22, 26, 47, 54, 80, 83, 87, 90, 92, 93, 95, 96, 98, 154, 179
Spanish–American War (1898), 23
Spanish Civil War, 73
special interest groups, 9, 11, 14, 16–17, 18, 22, 29–81, 118, 136, 141, 179, 186–7; interconnections, 136–8; social origins, 106, 122–33; *see also* Bank of England; EIA; FBI; FRPS; IPR; RIIA; TUC
special relationship, Anglo-American, 6, 8, 10, 146, 191–2
Stammers, Neil, 9–10
Stamp, Josiah, 121, 128
Stanworth, Philip, 119–20
state, vii, 9, 10–11, 53, 57, 106–72, 179–93; autonomy and power of, 12–13, 179–91; and national interest, 106–38; personnel of, 106, 118–22; role and influence of special interests, political parties and, 141–74, 179
statism, 10, 12–13, 106, 180, 189
Steiner, Zara, 118, 119
Sterling Area, 16, 39–40, 47, 54, 55, 115, 167, 168, 170
Stevenson, Sir Daniel, 131
Strang, Lord, 111
Suez Canal Company, 121

Tariff Reform League, 17, 46, 126
Tawney, R.H., 89, 103n
Tebbitt, Norman, 4
Thatcher, Margaret, 3
Third International, 135
Thomas, Ivor, 134
Thorne, Christopher, 62
Tilley, Sir John, 110, 120
Titmuss, Richard, 29
Tocqueville, Alexis de, 192–3
Toulmin, G.E., 34
Toynbee, Arnold, J., 70, 131, 151, 153
Trade Agreement, Anglo-American, 34, 47
Transport and General Workers' Union (TGWU), 135
Travellers' Club, 121, 127, 131
Treasury, 13, 17, 31, 52, 55, 85, 86, 112, 115, 116, 120, 121, 147, 148–9, 165, 167, 168, 190
Trenchard, Lord, 129
Tribune, Tribune group, 95, 97, 103n, 171
Trident nuclear deterrent, 8
Trotter, Ann, 181

Truman, David, 11
Truman, President Harry S., 2, 3, 170
TUC (Trades Union Congress), 17, 22, 72–81, 83, 92, 93, 132–3, 134, 137, 138, 158–9, 173, 187, 190, 191; Economic Committee, 79; General Council, 73, 88, 134, 135; and post-war reconstruction, 77, 78–81; social and educational background of leaders, 132–3

United Empire Club, 124
United Nations, 87, 95, 96, 156, 190
United University Club, 121
US Loan to Britain (1945), 16, 141, 169, 170–1
US military and air bases in Britain, 1–3, 8, 192
USAF, 'friendly fire' incident (1992), 4–6

Varga, E., and Mendelsohn, L., 28
Versailles, Treaty of, 25
Vickers, 30
Visiting Forces Act (1952), 6

Waley, S.D., 112–13, 121
Walker, James, 134
Wall Street crash and Great Depression (1930s), 24
Warnke, Paul, 19n
Watergate scandal, 6
wealth and income, inequalities of, 28–9
Weber, Max, 14, 52, 121
Webster, Charles, 151, 152, 153
Wedgwood, Josiah, 128
Weiler, Peter, 88
Welles, Sumner, 154
West Indies, Royal Commission on (1938–39), 75
Westergaard, J., and Resler, H., 14
Westland affair (1985–86), 1, 3, 6, 7
Whitehead, T.N., 116, 117, 152
Whyte, Sir Frederick, 152
Williams, Francis, 92
Wilson, President Woodrow, 24, 45, 162
Winchester school, 120, 122, 133, 135
Woodcock, George, 132
Woods, Randall, 162
Woodward, E.L., 129
Woolton, Lord, 121
World Bank, 85
World Trade Alliance Association, 79

Zilliachus, Konni, 92
Zimmern, Sir Alfred, 151, 153

For Product Safety Concerns and Information please contact our EU representative GPSR@taylorandfrancis.com
Taylor & Francis Verlag GmbH, Kaufingerstraße 24, 80331 München, Germany

www.ingramcontent.com/pod-product-compliance
Lightning Source LLC
Chambersburg PA
CBHW070608300426
44113CB00010B/1455